SONGWRITING

SONG

STEPHEN CITRON

WRITING

A Complete Guide to the Craft

Limelight Editions · New York

Limelight Editions
An Imprint of Hal Leonard Corporation
19 West 21st Street, New York, NY 10010

Second edition published in 2008 by Limelight Editions

First edition published in 1985 by William Morrow
Reprinted in 1990 by Limelight Editions

Printed in the United States of America

Book design by Kristina Rolander

Grateful acknowledgment is made for permission to quote song lyrics and music as detailed in the Permissions section, which begins on page 313.

Library of Congress Cataloging-in-Publication Data is available upon request.

ISBN: 978-0-87910-357-6

www.limelighteditions.com

CONTENTS

PART II: MUSIC

PREFACE TO THE NEW EDITION

A GENERATION HAS PASSED since I wrote the first edition of *Songwriting: A Complete Guide to the Craft*, but the principles that make a well-crafted song memorable, as outlined in that book are still valid.

With the coming of the computer age, today's composers and lyricists have much more help at their disposal. They can avail themselves of the assistance of computer-based music scoring and notation software, including Finale and Sibelius. Gone is the laborious process of writing out the melody on manuscript paper, having it reproduced by the diazo process, performing it live at an audition and eventually recording a demo. Today's composer can play the song on a digital keyboard, which will immediately provide him or her a printed copy of the song. All that has to be done is to type in the lyric, and out comes a printed lead sheet that formerly took hours of laborious work. Further, the software allows a songwriter to add instant instrumentation, including sampled sounds, drum beats, and other elements that take a song beyond the lead sheet and right into a recorded version on disk.

Still, I feel it is advisable to learn the principles of perfect rhyme. After all, rhyme is only present for the ear and the senses to enjoy. When it is imperfect, it offends the ear and most listeners' sensibilities. Because so many fledgling songwriters sing their own songs and habitually slur the words, bad rhyming is hardly noticed. But to me it feels as though the lyricist didn't try hard enough to get the message across artfully. Notation, another facet of the pages ahead, is also important, because it will allow you to spot your melody and see whether it is static or fluid; notation alone will show you how your harmony is dull (if you persist in using the same chords) or exciting (if you use the whole palette of chords available to you), and to some extent, the same goes for voicings/harmonies you choose when writing for back-up singers or duet. All these will help you to control your material, *not allowing the material to control you*. Each of these facets will make you a better songwriter.

Our present computer age not only gives us easier access to a completed song but also allows contemporary composer/lyricists great leeway. In some cases, melody or even lyrics are dispensable. For example, many "rap" songs use strings of rhythmic syllables against a steady beat. "Hip-hop" often employs a minimal melody, while some "heavy metal" groups have abandoned the strong soaring melodies of Broadway or pop, and substituted instead the rhythmic deep sound of the bass guitar.

But no matter which style you choose for your song, you should try to polish it to a gleam. Remember, people—hopefully thousands and millions—will memorize your words and music, and you want to give them your very best.

PREFACE

How is a song written? Which comes first, melody or lyrics? How does one find a collaborator? What's a demo? When does the publisher come in? Who is the A & R man? Is a lead sheet necessary? What's a verse, a burthen, a release, a channel, a bridge?

If you are the kind of person who, while walking to the corner drugstore, suddenly hums a tune that sounds original or if you are the one chosen by the office committee to write a rhymed birthday greeting for a coworker, then maybe you are an amateur, untrained songwriter and as such may be intrigued by some of the terms in the paragraph above. You could be one of the thousands of people who from time to time have an idea for a melody or who have been obsessed with a title or fragment of a lyric. This book is for you.

If you are a knowledgeable amateur or a professional songwriter who understands all the terms at the top of this page, this book is for you, too. Each of us, amateur and professional, needs frequently to review our product, to examine a song that may be going nowhere and to discover the reasons why it remains in our trunks. Perhaps the hook isn't strong enough, or maybe the range is too wide. Could the phrases be too skimpy or, worse, too long? This book will provide a checklist of things to watch for, which will improve your songwriting technique.

"Technique, yes," you may be saying. "But what about inspiration?" No book can inspire you to write a soaring melody or a brilliant lyric (although in later chapters I discuss where to *look* for inspiration). Inspiration has to come from within you, but once you have it, you must know what to do with it. And again, this book is for you, for it will show you your options.

And what are the options? Take the opening of "Three Blind Mice," for example. Hum the notes to yourself and you'll discover they go down. And after that little downward fragment, what happens? The composer-lyricist repeats the same three notes with the same three words in exactly the same way. Did the anonymous creator who invented that song so many centuries ago have other options? Could he or she have gone to different notes (pitches) or chosen different words? Of course! Could the pitches be mixed up? Certainly! The words? Perhaps. "Blind Mice Three" isn't bad, "Blind Three Mice" is cruel, for it treats the adjective *blind* as a verb, and "Three Mice Blind" is senseless. The professional is usually aware of the options and can find the direction that will make the best song, but the amateur often becomes so enmired in the choices of where his melody and lyric can go that the song is abandoned.

When composer/lyricist Jerry Herman wrote the line "And then he walked away," he might have followed it with "And I never saw him again," which is prosaic, or "And now I'm lonely," which is trite. But he followed his line with "And took my smile with him," which is sheer and memorable poetry (and eminently singable). So you see, the songwriter, being constantly faced with choices, must opt for the most memorable. Simply stated, my advice is to dig down into your musical imagination and come up with the best you are capable of.

This book will show you how to hone your melodic ideas for best impact and how to select a rhythm that is appropriate to your melody. It will also help you choose an appropriate title that embodies your concept and give you ideas about writing a lyric that is wedded to the melody. The final section will show you how to get your creation on a recording or paper and copyright it.

Everyone dreams of writing and selling a hit song that will reach the top of the charts and make mountains of money for the composer and lyricist. In truth, of the literally millions of songs that are written every year, only about five hundred ever end up making money, and these are almost entirely the products of songwriters who have been writing for some time.

This is not said to discourage you, but to encourage you to write, write, and write some more *before* you aim to sell. Jimmy Webb ("Up, Up, and Away," "Didn't We," "MacArthur Park") has said he became a songwriter by writing a song a day for two solid years. Richard Rodgers, one of America's greatest composer-lyricists (yes, he often wrote lyrics, too), told me that, when possible, he wrote several songs for every situation in his shows and selected the best for the final production.

In my years of teaching songwriting at the New School for Social Research and Carnegie Hall, I have seen too many gifted composers and lyricists write one or a few compositions, receive rejection slips, and turn away forever from an art that might have enriched their pockets and their lives. All of us who have had song successes know that a really good song will always sell; we are also aware we have had to write many, many bad songs before we were able to write a good one.

So let's plow ahead into writing songs, not caring whether they are good or bad just as long as they are completed. and with only one condition — that each one be better than the one before.

ACKNOWLEDGMENTS

ALTHOUGH I HAVE BEEN involved in the writing of this book for the last two years, I have to own that this volume began forming in my head decades ago.

As a young musician and lyricist eager to become a songwriter, I pored over hundreds of songs from Schubert to Romberg to Gershwin to Ellington and books of harmony and counterpoint searching for some clue to writing a memorable lyric or the secret to a popular melody. Years later, after I had cast all these theory books aside and had written many songs and taught hundreds of songwriters, I realized that no how-to books on the subject existed. Self-aggrandizing as it sounds, I felt that if others were to learn the art of songwriting, I had better write a book. Instinct told me that if my reader-students were to learn, they would have to be taught the way I had been — by absorbing a great number of examples.

And so, my thanks first to the lyricists and composers of the examples in this book, for their output is its essence. Then I must thank the publishers and copyright holders who so generously allowed me to print from their catalogs. Several of them, Joseph Weiss of Frank Music Co., Arlene Mullen of MCA Music, and those who control the rights to the works of Oscar Hammerstein, Neil Diamond, and Bruce Springsteen, gave me valuable advice as well.

My thanks to Lizanne Feller for her parody, Polly Brown Edwards for her research, Barry Downes for his succinct suggestions and especially to Mitch Douglas, who wears the several hats of lyricist, marketing expert, agent, dramatist, and friend.

Although editors are generally known for their scimitar "blue pencil," Alison Brown Cerier's green one organized this unwieldy manuscript with stepwise clarity. Songwriters are miniaturists and I am no exception, but ABC put all my pieces together into a logical progression. For her enormous help, a deep bow.

The headliner always comes last and to headline the bill in personal acknowledgment, I thank my wife, Anne Edwards, whose masterful books attest to her writing skill. For her apt suggestions and her patience with my irascibility in the two years this manuscript took to complete, all my gratitude. She got my love long ago.

But I cannot leave this page of acknowledgments without recalling Oscar Hammerstein's wise lyric that so appropriately sums up the source of whatever knowledge there is between these covers. For this book formed itself from the hundreds who wanted to write songs, all those whose urge to create forced me to formulate a complete method.

It's a very ancient saying
But a true and noble thought

That if you become a teacher
By your pupils you'll be taught.

To my students, my ultimate thanks for sharing their creations and intimate thoughts with me, showing me their confusions and their understandings so I could put the words and music together for other future songwriters.

FIRST CONSIDERATIONS

CONCEPT

THERE IS ALWAYS one major decision to be made *before* putting a section of lyric on a yellow pad or dreaming up a melody: *concept*. Without it, your song will wander and lack cohesion.

Concept is the distillation of what the song will say. The clearer your concept, the more professional your song.

Let's say you want to write a love song. Before you write it, you must know what kind of love it will describe. Will it be parental ("Watching Scotty Grow") or paternal ("My Dad"); about love of country or city ("America the Beautiful"; "New York, New York") or love of God ("I Believe"); or will it be, as the great majority of songs written today are, about the love of two people for each other?

Assuming you have chosen the idea of two adults in love, you still have a great deal of narrowing down to do. Will it be about love continuing or love past? Will you write about lovers who have just found each other or ones who have known each other for a while. If you have narrowed it to a long-established relationship, will it be a growing one ("Things Are Getting Better") or one that's on the way down ("You've Let Yourself Go"; "You've Changed")? Will you talk about what happened when they met ("The First Time Ever I Saw Your Face") or how they met ("I Found a Million-Dollar Baby in a Five-and-Ten-Cent Store")? How long their love will last ("Always")? How strong their love is ("So in Love"; "Hopelessly Devoted to You") or how precarious ("You Were Only Foolin' While I Was Fallin' in Love")?

Once you have decided the main aspects of the relationship, you should spend some time zeroing in on the kind of people you are going to write about. Will they be the kind who want to shout their love ("I'll Tell the Man in the Street") or hide it ("People Will Say We're in Love")? Will the protagonists be young lovers rejoined after a spat ("Reunited and It Feels So Good") or mature lovers reminiscing ("I Remember It Well")?

If you are writing the kind of song that describes the loved one, it is best to narrow down further to one trait or feature ("Them There Eyes"; "I've Grown Accustomed to Her Face"; "The Shadow of Your Smile"). In "Michelle," Paul McCartney and John Lennon tell us why the name Michelle suits the girl of the title. We are left at the end of thirty-two bars with a lasting image of a girl, sweet, perhaps French, who has a gentle manner. That's the concept, one that is original and fresh. The melody has a gentleness that complements the lyric — but we'll talk about that later.

The best songs narrow a big subject down to a specific aspect. This need not take endless hours — indeed, your mind can race through the process in only a few minutes, but be sure you spend these valuable few minutes before you write.

You should never forget that a song is only a moment in time and does not have the giant canvas on which you can paint a novel or even the smaller dimension of a short story. Unless your song is a narrative one, its characters are frozen from the time we find them until we leave them. They don't grow. So narrowing your subject will give a photographic impression that can make the people you write about indelible, and your song memorable.

Here are the concepts of some well-known songs.

"My Heart Will Go On" (1997)
  Music by James Horner
  Lyric by Will Jennings

Although you are gone, I remember you and I will always love you.

"A Foggy Day" (1937)
  Music by George Gershwin
  Lyric by Ira Gershwin

A visitor to London, bored with the city and its museums, suddenly spies the "love object" whose presence erases the fog and makes the sun come shining through.

"Cabaret" (1965)
  Music by John Kander
  Lyric by Fred Ebb

The singer exhorts us to go out and have a good time; enjoy life, for it is all too brief.

"Do It Again" (1938)
  Music by George Gershwin
  Lyric by Ira Gershwin

I ought to be a proper girl and not let you kiss me again, but I can't resist you.

"Do That to Me One More Time" (1979)
    Music and lyric by
    Toni Tenille

Once is never enough with a man like you, so kiss me again. (The theme is the same as in "Do It Again," but the concept, because of the prevailing freer morality in 1979, approaches the kiss from joy rather than from guilt.)

"Ain't No Mountain High Enough" (1966)
    Music and lyric by
    Nickolas Ashford and Valerie Simpson

Crossing mountains, valleys, and rivers will not keep me and my love from you.

"People" (1963)
    Music by Jule Styne
    Lyric by Bob Merrill

Those of us who need others are (contrary to what used to be thought about self-sufficiency) fortunate indeed.

"Killing Me Softly with His Song" (1972)
    Music by Charles Fox
    Lyric by Norman Gimbel

Attending a rock concert and identifying with the songs of the artist who exposes all the troubles and pain of the listener.

"Superstar" (1970)
    Music and lyric by Leon Russell and
    Bonnie Bramlett

A rock artist promised to return and see his fan again, but never did. This fan has had a relationship with the idol, while the fan in "Killing Me Softly with His Song" would not have the courage to approach the star.

"Send In the Clowns" (1972)
    Music and lyric by Stephen Sondheim

An ironic, farcical situation—when one lover is unattached, the other is temporarily in love and vice versa. The parallels to circus and theater are apparent in the title, and the lyric ends on the ray of hope that the lovers may meet on common ground next year.

WHICH COMES FIRST, MELODY OR LYRICS?

If your interests lie in writing both music and lyrics, you might be puzzled by this common question. There is no blanket answer, but I have found that most songwriters who create both music and lyrics have similar working patterns.

Once you have written down the concept, your first goal is to get the essence of the song. Call it the hook, grabber, germ, nut, or what you will, it must sum up the concept in a few words. Usually, this will become the title of your song. Once that essential phrase is created, you should go about inventing music to suit it.

A simple example is "People," whose title was created first (always after the concept) and whose two adjoining pitches came after. Notice how the ascending pitches sound optimistic. Or take Leonard Bernstein's setting of Stephen Sondheim's title "Maria." Sing the three pitches that make up the title and notice how they follow the contour of the name, how they almost caress it. They were carefully chosen for originality as well as emotional tone.

If you listen to Irving Berlin's "Puttin' On the Ritz," the words will tell you that the song is about someone who's down at the heels but happy. The jagged, bouncy melody that Berlin found *after* he had created the title gives us the feeling that this person, though broke, doesn't care much. When Joan Baez created "Until It's Time for You to Go," she knew she had to precede that line with a heartbreaking melody full of short gasped phrases suggesting goodbye. *Then* she began to create this kind of tune. In "After You," Cole Porter began with the title words "After you, who?" forcing the melodic line to rise up on the word *who*, as it would in a normal question. He has said he was intrigued with the then popular greeting "yoo-hoo" and that this forced the lyric and melodic fragment to come into his head *at the same time.*

Lacking Porter's inspiration and as a blanket rule, I'd say invent your title, and if it pops into your head along with its music, consider yourself lucky, but if not (as most often is the case), go about setting that title to music.

Once they have arrived at that lyric germ and have set that phrase to music, many songwriters like to carry the music to its conclusion, but I always advise beginning songwriters to go away from their instruments at this point and try to complete a part of the lyric. Then I suggest they return to their instruments to complete the melody of the first part.

Since musical form dictates that whole sections of a song be repeated for unity, most songwriters would then go on to write a further section of the lyric, being careful that the words carry the concept along and that the rhythm of the words fits as closely as possible the music already composed. The second section of Jim Webb's "By the Time I Get to Phoenix" is a good example of a repeat that conforms closely but not rigidly. "By the time I get to Phoenix" has eight notes, while the second line, "By the time I make Albuquerque," has nine.

Once you have roughly completed (don't stop to polish now) a total section and its repeat, you may decide the song needs contrast at this point. Perhaps the melody is static, or you feel you have repeated the title too many times and the song bores you. This might be a good time to insert a release or bridge, which is a contrasting section that will eventually lead back to the first part. Again, I would write the lyric first, then set it to music.

When songwriters are unable to think of a line that satisfies them in the moment of musical creation, they improvise anything fitting the concept that comes quickly to mind. To ease their consciences, they call these dummy lyrics. They know that those words will later be polished or totally abandoned, but they sing them to maintain the flow of the melody. Don't be afraid to use dummy lyrics at this point — otherwise, your melody will be stop and go, and your tune may sound crafted rather than flowing. Conversely, if your natural proclivity is to write the lyric first, don't be afraid to sing a dummy tune that fits your words; it can help the later creation of a real melody.

And so the answer to the question which comes first, music or lyrics? must be a bit of each. But for the beginning songwriter, the best process is:

1. Create the title idea.
2. Set the title to music.
3. Complete the lyric of the first section.
4. Repeat the section with different lyrics (use dummy lyrics if you wish).
5. Examine what you've written to see if you need a bridge or release at this point; if you do, then write the lyrics for this section and later set them to music.
6. Work back and forth this way until you complete the song.

COLLABORATION

When songwriters are working together, who writes first, the musician or the lyricist? Each team finds its own way.

When Richard Rodgers was working with Larry Hart, he always wrote the melody first, then handed it to Hart, who would deliver the completed lyric, usually the next day. Sometimes the facile Hart came up with two or three sets of lyrics and asked Rodgers to take his choice. After Hart's death, when Rodgers began working with Oscar Hammerstein, Rodgers worked the other way around. He found Hammerstein's lyrics to be like poetry and would set the total poem to music. Hammerstein, who had formerly worked with Jerome Kern until his death, was accustomed to putting words to Kern's music, and yet the Rodgers-Hammerstein partnership produced some memorable songs even though each man worked in a manner to which he was not previously accustomed.

George Gershwin wrote the music first, and then his brother, Ira, added the words. Often, George created the title along with the melody. Hal David writes the words first, and Burt Bacharach adds the music. Each team finds the manner of working that suits them and that turns out better songs.

Collaborators meet often, usually daily, to discuss new ideas and the direction their work is taking. Some prefer a short meeting to listen to what the other has produced, after which each will retreat to work in private; others prefer to work side by side, on call as it were, so a lyricist can read the composer an especially apt line and the composer can get the lyricist's opinion of a melodic snatch hot off the keyboard.

Professional collaborators know a great deal about each other's art. A lyricist must understand musical composition to feel where beats, sequences, and repeats will be coming. A composer should understand lyric writing and poetry so he can use melodic pitches that will enable the lyric to sing. Should the musician select high pitches on closed vowel sounds (try singing the word *glove* on a high note—impossible) or very speedy notes on long syllables, the words, and the message of the song, will be unintelligible. *Craft, splice, through* are examples of long syllables that should be avoided on rapid notes.

FINDING AND WORKING WITH A COLLABORATOR

Sometimes it is more difficult to locate a sympathetic songwriting partner than to find a suitable marriage partner. But, like love, you'll know a good match when you've found it. In teams of Rodgers and Hart, George and Ira Gershwin, David and Bacharach, Lennon and McCartney, Kander and Ebb, each has tailored his work to the other's style and thus enhanced the partner's creation.

You may have to try many partners before you come up with someone with whom you can work comfortably. Personality, work habits, proximity, dedication to work, similarity of point of view, and equality of technical advancement are all considerations. Most songwriters have to go through several collaborators to find the partner with whom they can eventually turn out worthwhile songs. Here are some ways you might contact a kindred spirit.

1. If you live near a major city, contact the American Society of Composers, Authors, and Publishers (ASCAP) or Broadcast Music Incorporated (BMI). ASCAP has offices in New York, Los Angeles, Nashville, San Francisco, North Miami, Atlanta, Chicago, New Orleans, Boston, Minneapolis, Cleveland, Detroit, Philadelphia, and Houston. BMI has offices in many of these cities. Both organizations sponsor songwriting workshops in many of the cities in which they have offices.
2. Visit your local music store. Placing a notice on the bulletin board there may put you in contact with a collaborator. Be specific about what kind of songs you are capable of and interested in writing, how much training you have had, and what you expect of your partner.
3. Telephone local music teachers and music schools to see if some of the teachers know of possible collaborators.

4. Advertise in your local paper, especially if there is an alternative paper. For example, *The Village Voice* has many listings of composers seeking lyricists and vice versa.
5. Contact the musicians' union in your local area. This should be listed in your local telephone directory under AFL (American Federation of Labor). It can put you in contact with other working lyricists and composers.
6. Advertise in national magazines that are concerned with music: *Keyboard*, *American Songwriter*, *Rolling Stone*, etc.

Although it is not the purpose of this book to probe the psychology of a smooth working relationship, I should like to let you know one method that has always helped me have harmonious relationships with my collaborators. We have always decided beforehand that both artists must approve of both music and lyrics. That means if anything does not appeal to one, the other will change it—and no questions asked!

There has to be something you both agree upon, that you both like still lurking there in your imaginations, or why are you collaborating? I have seen too many beginning collaborators waste an awful lot of time arguing about the merits of what they have each turned out: one defending, the other attacking, when they could have dropped the phrase in question and used the time to find a new phrase that would have satisfied them both. But don't accept from your collaborator material you know to be trite or second-rate, just to ensure a smooth relationship.

HOW MUCH TECHNICAL TRAINING DO YOU NEED?

As much as you can get. Unfortunately, there is no school that offers a degree in songwriting. Many colleges offer courses in theory of music, harmony, sight singing, keyboard harmony, counterpoint, and fugue, and these are a far cry from the simple melodic style necessary for a songwriter. Yet even though they are not exactly down your alley, they help you become a better composer. Likewise, most colleges offer courses in poetry, drama, short story, and literature. I would suggest to all budding lyricists that they take such courses, for they can only help you understand lyrics better. And then there are courses available in singing that I suggest all songwriters take, for truly, unless you sing all the time, you can hardly expect to create a singable melody.

A knowledge of harmony enables a songwriter to create a release that modulates to a new key or to write an especially inventive chord line against a worn melody. Understanding poetry gives a lyricist access to simile, metaphor, and onomatopoeia, fancy words for word imagery. Understanding trochees and iambs might not seem important, but they lead the lyricist down interesting rhythmic paths. Singing, and listening to yourself and others, lets you know what works for the voice and what does not.

SUPPLIES

You will need nothing but your imagination, but most songwriters have some way of creating a hard copy of their work for polishing or a recording that they can play back and clean up. They can digitally record their song on their computer, make changes, and then burn it to a CD or create an mp3. If you understand notation, you will want to invest in most of the supplies listed in this section. If you have either the Finale or Sibelius music-notation software (see the Appendix page 284), the system will do most of the notation work for you.

1. Paper
   - Several yellow legal-size pads (the kind with the left margin already printed in). These are for writing lyrics.
   - Some spiral-bound music manuscript books
        Standard ruling (I like paper with a 6-stave layout)
        Professional ruling (I like paper with a 12-stave layout)
   - A pocket manuscript notebook (to carry with you for sketching)
   - A package of 8-stave music paper; loose sheets with title drop
   - A package of 8-stave music paper; loose sheets without drop (Although there are a good number of different manuscript papers available, many are of poor quality. Do your best to find one that has a heavy, good-quality stock that will stand up to erasing and be quiet when turning. Also, you can now buy every size manuscript paper on a CD-ROM and simply print out the stave size you want. Just make sure you load your laser printer with paper of a quality better than copy paper so it holds up.)
2. Pencils
   - #2 lead pencils. Have several sharpened ones handy. Make sure they have good erasers. Composers and lyricists do more erasing than anyone.
3. Recording device
   There are a variety of recording devices available at difference price levels. Visit your local retail music outlet and consult with an experienced sales representative to see what will work best for your particular situation.
   - For recording your song at creation, or just to have idly recording while you improvise or hum. In playback you may discover some really good ideas that would otherwise have been lost. Buy the kind that can be plugged into normal household current, and keep it plugged in most of the time. Nothing is more maddening than to be in the process of

songwriting and to have your batteries go dead, so I keep my recorder always plugged into an outlet.

4. Portable file and folders
   - This is a good way to organize what you write, especially songs that are partially completed. Wherever you may be, if you are suddenly visited with an idea for a lyric or a snatch of melody, jot it down. When you get home, toss it into a file kept for that particular song, taking it out later, when you have a chance to sit down and work on the song.

5. Reference books
   - Rhyming Dictionary

     Cole Porter had thirty-one of them, in all languages. Get the most complete and latest one you can afford. I prefer Lee's, Wood's, or Johnson's. (For others, see page 129.)
   - Dictionary

     Any good standard one will do. Often when I am stuck for a rhyme, I refer to the dictionary for a synonym that rhymes more easily than the word that sticks me.
   - Thesaurus

     Use it the same way you would a dictionary. The thesaurus can help you create better word imagery, and it allows you to be more specific about the meaning of your words.

6. Instrument
   - Most composers play some instrument. It is usually the piano, organ, or guitar, for these instruments can create harmony. If you play none of these and are interested in songwriting, it would be wise to study one, but remember—many excellent songs have been written by people who cannot play anything more complicated than a kazoo or harmonica. Songs written by non-instrumentalists are sometimes purer, simpler, and more direct.

7. Pitch pipe
   - This will not be necessary if you are working at an instrument but is essential to a composer working without one. Also, when you perform your material without accompaniment (a cappella), it enables you to start on a note that comfortably accommodates both your vocal range and the range of the song.

8. Time and privacy
   - These are things you cannot buy, but nevertheless, they are essentials. No songwriter can create his or her best effort under pressure of time or give it the complete concentration necessary with a television set blaring in the background. Try to set aside a certain amount of time each day in which you can go to a quiet place and give your best efforts to your song.

PART I
LYRICS

1 CONSTRUCTION AND FORM

ONCE A LISTENER gets beyond being aware of concept, his or her strongest satisfaction will come from form and balance. A lopsided song, one that uses only choruses, will maintain its "highs" and ultimately bore its auditors. Conversely, a song built only of verses will put everybody to sleep because of its dullness.

Although the public is not aware of how much sectional balance affects what they hear, every professional songwriter is, and spends much creative effort deciding which sections must follow each other to build unity.

The form of popular music has changed greatly in this century, and every songwriter must be aware of what forms are currently used. A musical-comedy song set in punk or bubblegum form is doomed from the outset, and a rock song that uses operetta or show form is equally headed for disaster.

What follows, then, is a chronological rundown of the forms popular song has taken throughout this century.

You should become familiar with all the forms available to you even though the largest part of songs performed and recorded are in verse-chorus form or ABACA form. You cannot consider yourself a songwriter unless you know all the ways of constructing a song. If you try to create a show tune (whose form is generally AABA or ABAC) and cast it in the form of punk rock (often AAAA), the show tune will come out sounding like punk rock.

On the other hand, "By the Time I Get to Phoenix," "Changing Partners," "Folsom Prison Blues," "The Coward of the County," and "Don't It Make My Brown Eyes Blue?" are all considered country songs, and yet each has a different form.

Don't neglect understanding any of the forms—even though some may be considered old hat. Even the forms that do not interest you should be in your bag of tricks waiting for a suitable melody to come to you. That way, you will be able to cast your song into the form most suitable to your melody, one that allows the lyric to sing naturally and sound professional.

This discussion is placed in the section on lyrics even though both music *and* lyrics are affected by formal considerations because we generally think of form as instigated by the lyric and as an outgrowth of concept, a literary idea.

HOW AND WHY WE LABEL FORM

Form is another word for construction. Everything about us has form. A tree has form: roots, trunk, branches, leaves. A play has form: often, boy meets girl, boy loses girl, boy gets girl. This is sometimes referred to in more technical language as rising action, climax, denouement. So a song has form, and that form also can be referred to in technical language. Every work of art has form, without which the creator's effort would be sprawling and non-cohesive.

A simple and satisfying song form can be achieved by creating a main, strong melody; repeating that melody with different lyrics to intensify and imprint the melody on our consciousness; then departing from that melody into a totally different idea; and at last returning to that main melody once more. Now that the tune is familiar, we feel complete when we hear it again. The public is rarely aware of this manipulation, but every songwriter must be conscious of the construction of the song. And the form should be apparent to a professional on first hearing.

If you listen to Kern and Hammerstein's "Can't Help Lovin' Dat Man" followed by Billy Joel's "Just the Way You Are," you'll notice that although six decades separate the songs, they both use the familiar form outlined above. It almost goes without saying that the principles of good balance and design in art never change.

Concert music (I don't like the term *classical*, for it refers to one particular era; nor do I like the term *serious music*, for it implies that all popular music is frivolous) may or may not come back to repeat sections within its first statement. The opening theme of Rachmaninoff's well-known Second Piano Concerto is a long flowing melody that never once turns on its heels to repeat. This is called through-composed, and the melody takes 67 measures to make its statement. Popular composers and lyricists don't have that much latitude. The song has to impress us in the first 15 seconds, and whereas a section of a concerto may run half an hour, a total song usually lasts no longer than 2 minutes. (A single side of a 45 rpm record averages 4 minutes, but much of this is repetition.)

Most popular songs run no more than 32 measures (as contrasted to Rachmaninoff's 67) and are divided into 4 sections, each of which is 8 measures long. Musicians generally label these alphabetically for convenience. The substitution of alphabetical letters for identical sections makes the form apparent. These days, most of our music is written down and read from standard arrangements, but formerly, when musicians got together to jam, they would generally improvise and the leader would say, "Let's play AAABAC," instead of the longwinded "Now we'll play the first section three times and then go to the second tune, then we'll go back to the first section and close the piece with that new final section."

But sometimes composers don't use the *exact same* melody in their repetition, and to be more specific, we'll say, "Let's play A¹, A², A³, B, A⁴, C." That's the way I prefer to identify sections whether or not they're exactly the same, for I believe it makes the form even clearer.

HOW AND WHY WE LABEL RHYMES

In a way, the lyricist has a more demanding job than the composer, for while following the form, he must also add rhyme. Whereas the composer may decide to write an 8-measure section, repeat it, depart from it with a release or bridge (a total of 16 measures of creative effort to come out with a product 32 measures long), the lyricist must set up a rhyme scheme in the first section and, using different words and different rhymes, must carry the concept ahead.

Unfortunately in labeling rhyme, most lyricists use the same alphabetic letters they do for form. This can only be confusing, and so throughout this book, except when indicating rhyme construction, I have chosen to use the same *numbers* to indicate words that rhyme and *letters* to indicate the form. The example below will make it clear.

"That's My Dream" (Music and lyric by Marc Stephens)

A¹	A house in the valley, two bedrooms and bath,	(1)
	With red rambling roses that border a path	(1)
	To a doorway that splits into two:	(2)
	THAT'S MY DREAM	(3)
A²	The car in the driveway has hardly a dent,	(4)
	There's money enough in the bank for the rent,	(4)
	And the Hoover is practic'ly new:	(2)
	THAT'S MY DREAM	(3)

B	A husband who comes from the office each day	(5)
	And needs me to ease away * (5) his cares.	(6)
	Then, after our supper there's records to play,	(5)
	And sometimes we dance our way upstairs.	(6)
A³	The ring on my finger his grandmother wore.	(7)
	There's nothing so fine in the jewelry store.	(7)
	Where's the man (8) who will make it come true?	(2)
	'Cause that's my plan,	(8)
	That's my scheme—	(3)
	THAT'S MY DREAM	(3)

VERSES AND CHORUSES

If I were asked to name the most confusing concept in lyric writing, I'd have to say it was the word *verse*, because it had a totally different meaning before the mid-sixties. Formerly, a verse was a section of the song that set the stage, and preceded the melodic or catchy tune. In contemporary songs, the story is told in the verse.

Referring to page 31, "Kiss Me Again" has an enormous verse that begins "If I were asked ..." and ends 25 lines later with "a dreamy, sensuous waltz I'd sing," leading to the chorus or refrain, which begins "Sweet summer breeze."

"I'm Falling in Love with Someone" (page 33) employs the typical operetta verse of 8 lines, as does "After the Ball" (page 35), in each of its three verses. Notice that in the latter case, the story is told in the *verses*, like a *contemporary* song. Here we find out that the old man is alone, that his sweetheart, whom he suspected of infidelity, was merely giving her brother a friendly embrace, and in typical melodrama fashion, we learn that it was the hero's refusal to see her that caused his fiancée to languish and die eventually of a broken heart. On page 36, in "Meet Me in St. Louis, Louis" we get the reasons why Flossie left and Louis's reactions in two verses, and the refrain or chorus, beginning "Meet Me in St. Louis, Louis," gives us the strong melody and memorable hook with the doubling of *Louis*.

Sometimes the verse merely sets the story going. In "Don't Bring Lulu," the first verse tells about an invitation to a party. The second verse is totally unnecessary, but it was included because the convention of the twenties demanded more than one verse.

---

* "Away," rhyming with "day" and "play," departs from the general rhyming design of the song. It is an attractive dividend, known as an inner rhyme (see page 113).

In the thirties, we come back to the expendable verse. Because our popular songs were now recorded, American music started to become more commercial, and the long expansive verses that could set the scene began to disappear. To be successful, a song had to make its point in the first few seconds (this is still true) with title and hook. Always published, but often omitted in performance, the verse became more cumbersome than helpful.

Everyone knows Richard Rodgers's "My Funny Valentine," one of his most beautiful melodies, set to the memorable lyric by Larry Hart, in which he used the hook of unexpected word juxtaposition: (*funny* and *valentine* are unforgettable because they don't seem to belong next to each other). The chorus or refrain begins

MY FUNNY VALENTINE
SWEET COMIC VALENTINE
YOU MAKE ME SMILE WITH MY HEART.

But how many of us know the archaic verse that precedes the chorus? Coming right up front, and usually omitted, it sets the scene with:

Behold the way our fine feathered friend
His virtue doth parade,
Thou knowest not, my dim-witted friend,
The picture thou hast made.
Thy vacant brow and thy tousled hair
Conceal thy good intent.
Thou noble, upright, truthful, sincere,
And slightly dopey gent, you're
MY FUNNY VALENTINE ...

Similarly, George and Ira Gershwin's "The Man I Love," gives us an indelible opening chorus line with

SOMEDAY HE'LL COME ALONG,
THE MAN I LOVE.

but only specialists in esoterica know the opening verse, which tells us what occurs before that man comes along.

When the mellow moon begins to beam
Ev'ry night I have a little dream,
And, of course, Prince Charming is the theme:

The he, for me.
Though I realize as well as you
It is seldom that a dream comes true,
To me it's clear
That he'll appear.

The music of most verses was usually so weak, and the lyric so superfluous, that all but the most sophisticated aficionados of pop song skipped right over them. Sometimes at cocktail parties in New York penthouses you can overhear the tuxedoed pianist playing the "verse game" with the guests. He plays the first line of a verse by Kern or Rodgers or Porter or even Arlen and the assembled guests try to sing the first line of the chorus. That shows how recherché these verses have become.

The verse of pre-rock songs was generally an 8-line section. Usually, the music was divided into 4 lines and 4 lines of repetition. Of course this was because the verse had its origins in operetta, and the resultant predictability would be expected. Typical of the 8-liners are the two below; each sets the mood and improves the total concept of the song.

> "Bewitched, Bothered and Bewildered" (Music by Richard Rodgers,
> Lyric by Lorenz Hart)

> He's a fool and don't I know it
> But a fool can have his charms;
> I'm in love and don't I show it
> Like a babe in arms.
> Love's the same old sad sensation
> Lately I've not slept a wink,
> Since this half-pint imitation
> Put me on the blink.

CHORUS   I'M WILD AGAIN, BEGUILED AGAIN,

A WHIMPERING, SIMPERING CHILD AGAIN,

BEWITCHED, BOTHERED AND BEWILDERED AM I

> "Night and Day" (Music and lyric by Cole Porter)

> Like the beat, beat, beat of the tom-tom,
> When the jungle shadows fall,
> Like the tick, tick, tock of the stately clock
> As it stands against the wall

> Like the drip, drip, drip of the raindrops,
> When the summer show'r is through;
> So a voice within me keeps repeating, you —— you —— you ——

CHORUS　　NIGHT AND DAY

　　　　　　YOU ARE THE ONE

　　　　　　ONLY YOU BENEATH THE MOON

　　　　　　AND UNDER THE SUN

All through the pre-rock era occasional songs were written without verses ("Smoke Gets in Your Eyes," "Blue Moon," "Dancing in the Dark"), and while most songs had the 8-line verse, many had even longer verses containing 10 lines (divided thus: 4-line stanza, 4-line stanza, 2-line couplet). The 10-line verse was very popular with Ira Gershwin and Lorenz Hart.

"Someone to Watch Over Me" (Lyric by Ira Gershwin, Music by George Gershwin)

4-LINE　　There's a saying old says that love is blind

STANZA　　Still, we're often told, "seek and you will find,"

　　　　　　So I'm going to seek a certain lad

　　　　　　I've had in mind.

4-LINE　　Looking ev'rywhere, haven't found him yet

STANZA　　He's the big affair I cannot forget

　　　　　　Only man I

　　　　　　Ever think of with regret.

2-LINE　　I'd like to add his initials to my monogram

COUPLET　　Tell me, where is the shepherd for this lost lamb?

CHORUS　　THERE'S A SOMEBODY I'M LONGING TO SEE

　　　　　　I HOPE THAT HE TURNS OUT TO BE

　　　　　　SOMEONE TO WATCH OVER ME ...

"It Never Entered My Mind" (Music by Richard Rodgers, Lyric by Lorenz Hart)

4-LINE　　I don't care if there's powder on my nose,

STANZA　　I don't care if my hair-do is in place,

I've lost the very meaning of repose,
I never put a mudpack on my face.

4-LINE Oh, who'd have thought
STANZA That I'd walk in a daze now?
I never go to shows at night
But just to matinees now.

2-LINE I see the show
COUPLET And home I go.

CHORUS ONCE I LAUGHED WHEN
I HEARD YOU SAYING
THAT I'D BE PLAYING SOLITAIRE,
UNEASY IN MY EASY CHAIR,
IT NEVER ENTERED MY MIND.

Since the fifties and sixties there has been a great revival in folk music, and the *original* verse-chorus form is now the predominant one. One can hear this kind of form used in country songs, especially those that tell a story.

Here are examples of pop verse-chorus; folk verse-chorus; and country verse-chorus.

Pop Verse-Chorus Form

"I Got Rhythm" (Music by George Gershwin, Lyric by Ira Gershwin)

VERSE

Days can be sunny
With never a sigh
Don't need what money
Can buy.

Birds in the tree sing
Their dayfull of song
Why should we sing
Along?

I'm chipper all the day
Happy with my lot
How do I get that way
Look at what I've got.

CHORUS

I GOT RHYTHM
I GOT MUSIC
I GOT MY MAN
WHO COULD ASK FOR ANYTHING MORE?

I GOT DAISIES
IN GREEN PASTURES
I GOT MY MAN
WHO COULD ASK FOR ANYTHING MORE?

OLD MAN TROUBLE
I DON'T MIND HIM
YOU WON'T FIND HIM
'ROUND MY DOOR

I GOT STARLIGHT
I GOT SWEET DREAMS
I GOT MY MAN
WHO COULD ASK FOR ANYTHING MORE?
WHO COULD ASK FOR ANYTHING MORE!

Folk Verse-Chorus Form

"Clementine" (Traditional)

VERSE

In a canyon, in a cavern
Excavating for a mine
Lived a miner, 'Forty-niner
And his daughter, Clementine.

CHORUS

OH, MY DARLIN'
OH, MY DARLIN'
OH, MY DARLIN' CLEMENTINE
THOU ART LOST AND GONE FOREVER
DREADFUL SORRY, CLEMENTINE.

VERSE

Light she was and like a fairy
And her shoes were number nine
Herring boxes without topses
Sandals were for Clementine.

CHORUS

OH, MY DARLIN'
OH, MY DARLIN'
OH, MY DARLIN' CLEMENTINE
THOU ART LOST AND GONE FOREVER
DREADFUL SORRY, CLEMENTINE.

VERSE

Drove she ducklings
To the river
Ev'ry morning just at nine
Hit her foot against a splinter
Fell into the foaming brine

CHORUS

OH, MY DARLIN'
OH, MY DARLIN'
OH, MY DARLIN' CLEMENTINE
THOU ART LOST AND GONE FOREVER
DREADFUL SORRY, CLEMENTINE.

Country Verse-Chorus Form

"The Coward of the County" (Music by Billy Ed Wheeler, Lyric by Roger Bowling)

VERSE 1

Ev'ryone considered him the
   Coward of the County
He'd never stood one single time
   to prove the county wrong.
His momma named him Tommy
but folks all called him "yellow"
But something always told me
they were readin' Tommy wrong.

He was only ten years old when
   his daddy died in prison,
I looked after Tommy cause he
   was my brother's son.
I still recall the final words my
   brother said to Tommy,
"Son, my life is over, but yours
   has just begun."

CHORUS

PROMISE ME, SON,
NOT TO DO THE THINGS I'VE DONE
WALK AWAY FROM TROUBLE IF YOU CAN.
IT WON'T MEAN YOU'RE WEAK
IF YOU TURN THE OTHER CHEEK
I HOPE YOU'RE OLD ENOUGH TO
   UNDERSTAND,
SON, YOU DON'T NEED TO FIGHT
   TO BE A MAN!

VERSE 2

There's someone for everyone
And Tommy's love was Becky.
In her arms he didn't have to
   prove he was a man.
One day while he was workin', the
   Gatling boys came calling....

FOLK SONGS

When we think of folk songs, we think of songs that arose from the people, usually with fewer phrases than are required in today's songs. Because they had their origins in unschooled common folk rather than sophisticated lyricists, we often find them with many lines repeated, sometimes totally lacking rhyme:

SKIP, SKIP, SKIP TO MY LOU (1)
SKIP, SKIP, SKIP TO MY LOU (1)
SKIP, SKIP, SKIP TO MY LOU (1)
SKIP TO MY LOU, MY DARLIN' (2)

or

WE WISH YOU A MERRY CHRISTMAS (1)
WE WISH YOU A MERRY CHRISTMAS (1)
WE WISH YOU A MERRY CHRISTMAS (1)
AND A HAPPY NEW YEAR (2)

This simple construction is not unlike the strong repetition found in most hard rock and punk rock choruses. Compare the above with a song success of 1981, "Hit Me with Your Best Shot," which repeats the title three times in its chorus.

"Down in the Valley," "On Top of Old Smokie," and "Clementine" are good examples of folk song form. Although many folk songs are constructed with the very simple form of "Skip to My Lou," the majority have a slightly more complicated construction of 4-line verse, 4-line chorus, 4-line verse, 4-line chorus, etc. In most cases there are more verses than you'd care to sing in a single performance, but you must remember these songs were passed down from generation to generation and from family to family with each singer adding what he or she thought was happening on top of old smokie or just what was going on down in the valley. There are usually several published versions of each folk song depending on who collected it and wrote it down or in which region of the country it was discovered.

"I've Been Workin' on the Railroad" is an example of a song whose form gets tiresome simply because it just kept growing. That happened because the groups singing it were having too much fun to stop. The song originally ended after "Dinah, blow your horn."

I've been workin' on the railroad
All the livelong day,
I've been workin' on the railroad
Just to pass the time away.

Can't you hear the whistle blowin'
Rise up so early in the morn
Can't you hear the captain shoutin'
Dinah, blow your horn.

DINAH, WON'T YOU BLOW,
DINAH, WON'T YOU BLOW,
DINAH, WON'T YOU BLOW YOUR HORN, YOUR HORN
DINAH, WON'T YOU BLOW
DINAH, WON'T YOU BLOW,
DINAH, WON'T YOU BLOW YOUR HORN.

Someone's in the kitchen with Dinah
Someone's in the kitchen, I know
Someone's in the kitchen with Dinah,
Strumming on the old banjo.
Singin'
Fee, Fie, Fiddlie-I-oh
Fee, Fie, Fiddlie-I-oh, oh, oh, oh
Fee, Fie, Fiddlie, I-oh
Strummin' on the old Banjo.

In the original version, Dinah is an affectionate name for the railroad worker's engine, but as the song became lengthened by what sounds to me like singers who came in in the middle, Dinah becomes a flirtatious kitchen maid, and the visual picture of the engine sounding its horn to clear the tracks for the workers' safety is muddled.

In "I've Been Workin' on the Railroad" the melody changes as the song progresses, but many simple folk songs do not vary the melody between verse and chorus. They create interest by using in the chorus a strong, repetitious, uncomplicated line that everybody can sing along with. If you sing the tune of "Clementine" in your head as you read through the lyrics, you'll see typical folk song construction.

VERSE   In a cavern, in a canyon
Excavating for a mine, (1)
Lived a miner (2), 'Forty-niner (2)
And his daughter, Clementine. (1)

CHORUS   OH MY DARLIN', OH MY DARLIN',
OH MY DARLIN' CLEMENTINE,
THOU ART LOST BUT NOT FORGOTTEN
DREADFUL SORRY, CLEMENTINE.

The rhyme of *mine* and Clemen*tine* happens only in the verse. Note also that although there is no rhyme in the chorus, we are set up for the chorus by the *ine* sound everywhere. Later, in succeeding verses, the lyricist tells us that "her shoes were number n*ine*;" and that she "fell into the foaming "br*ine*," hitting home the *ine* sound and creating unity for the entire song.

Today's songs *avoid* the similarity of rhyme between verse and chorus, for we find the lack of contrast dull; but dull or not, its use will give your songs a certain unity.

The typical folk song construction of verse, chorus, verse, chorus, etc., is the most prevalent form today, having largely superseded the pop form of AABA or ABAC. It is used in such widely divergent songs as "The Coward of the County," "Yellow Submarine," "Put Your Hand in the Hand," and "Hit Me with Your Best Shot," and it will come up again when we discuss the form of the lyrics of country songs.

SPIRITUALS

Most spirituals were inspired by the black preoccupation with Bible stories, especially those of the Old Testament. Gospel is more concerned with the life of Jesus. The rigors of slavery were made bearable by a strong faith and the ability to sing at prayer meetings or while working in the fields. On large plantations a leader, acting as the minister, could shout, "When Israel was in Pharaoh's land," and the rest of the workers, stooped over, picking cotton, could answer as a congregation without losing a boll, "Let my people go." As the leader continued with "Oppressed so hard they could not stand," the bent-over slaves could respond again, "Let my people go."

Out of the ecclesiastical idea of responsive prayer, the spiritual was born, and the power and exaltation inherent in this pattern of questioning and identical answering has created some of the most moving and lasting folk music the world has known. This kind of responsive song is a far cry from its only predecessor, the Gregorian chant of the Middle Ages, and is much more melodic than previous religious music.

"Swing Low, Sweet Chariot," uses the responsive line "Comin' for to carry me home." Sometimes the line is rhymed as below.

Leader: I looked over Jordan and what did I see?
Group: COMIN' FOR TO CARRY ME HOME
Leader: A band of angels comin' after me,
Group: COMIN' FOR TO CARRY ME HOME.

Similarly, and happily resounding with a naïve interpretation of the tenth chapter of the Book of Ezekiel, "Ezekiel saw the wheel; WAY UP IN THE MIDDLE OF THE AIR," and later, departing from a true Bible story and substituting homespun philosophy—"I'll tell you what a hypocrite'll do; WAY UP IN THE MIDDLE OF THE AIR; He'll talk about me and he'll talk about you; WAY UP IN THE MIDDLE OF THE AIR."

One of the most moving questioning-and-answer spirituals, derived atypically from the New Testament, is:

Oh, they crucified my Lord
    AND HE NEVER SAID A MUMBALIN' WORD
Oh, they crucified my Lord
    AND HE NEVER SAID A MUMBALIN' WORD

Oh, they nailed Him to a tree
    AND HE NEVER SAID A MUMBALIN' WORD
Oh, they nailed Him to a tree
    AND HE NEVER SAID A MUMBALIN' WORD

Oh they pierced Him in the side
    AND HE NEVER SAID A MUMBALIN' WORD
Oh, they pierced Him in the side
    AND HE NEVER SAID A MUMBALIN' WORD

Oh, the blood came twinklin' down
    AND HE NEVER SAID A MUMBALIN' WORD
Oh, the blood came twinklin' down
    AND HE NEVER SAID A MUMBALIN' WORD

Oh, He bowed His head and died
    AND HE NEVER SAID A MUMBALIN' WORD
Oh, He bowed His head and died
    AND HE NEVER SAID A MUMBALIN' WORD

You will notice there is no rhyme here (except for the "side" and "died" in the third and last verses, and I feel that even this rhyme was accidental), but the constant repetition of and he never said a mumbalin' word gives the whole song unity and rhythmic design.

When you are creating the lyric for a spiritual, pick your hook, title, and concept and cast them together into one strong line. This will be the second line of your song and will constantly comment or answer all questions you may have asked in the preceding line.

BLUES, CLASSIC AND POP

If the greatest contribution America has made thus far to world theater is our Broadway musical, certainly our greatest contribution to popular music in the twentieth century was the blues. Capable of infinite variety, blues has affected worldwide music from rhythm and blues in the sixties to the hard rock of the eighties and beyond.

Classic or 12-bar blues sprang from a mostly illiterate and depressed black population in the early 1900s. It expressed their misery and soon became a cathartic way of expressing their feelings. The single outpouring, very close to a spoken complaint, was a mere one-line interjection thrice repeated; something like, "Oh, I don' know what I'm gonna do/ Oh, I don' know what I'm gonna do/ Oh, I don' know what I'm gonna do!" was able to verbalize the singer's quandary.

While the spiritual expressed the belief in the Bible and the hereafter, the blues avoided religion and was concerned with now; while the spiritual lent itself to choral or group singing, the blues was a one-person situation. Some consider the blues to be music of protest, others feel it is music of self-pity, but in any case it is a personal expression of the singer at the time.

In discussing blues form, we refer to each 12-bar section as a verse. The total song can be made up of several or as many as several dozen verses. Length can make the concept sprawling, and indeed blues has often been criticized for that, but remember — the emotional expression is paramount.

From the single line repeated,

Gwine take morphine an' die,
Gwine take morphine an' die,
Gwine take morphine an' die

it was a short step to create the rhyming third line, which is the classic blues we know today. This rhyming and resolving line is perhaps responsible for the enduring quality of the blues up to the present. If the first two lines expressed grief, the third line could express the reason for the grief. The third line could always resolve the situation.

I'm tired of Jim Crow, gonna leave this town,
I'm tired of Jim Crow, gonna leave this town,
Doggone my black soul — I'm Chicago bound

The third line often released the tension or self-pity built up in the other two; sometimes it was downright humorous, devil-may-care, or ironic.

When you see me comin, h'ist your window high
When you see me comin', h'ist your window high
When you see me goin', hang your head and cry.

Gonna lay my head right on the railroad track,
Gonna lay my head right on the railroad track,
If the train come 'long I'm gonna snatch it back.

What you gonna do when they burn the Barrelhouse down
What you gonna do when they burn the Barrelhouse down?
Gonna move out the piano and barrelhouse on the ground.

Boll-weevil, where you been so long?
Boll-weevil, where you been so long?
You stole my cotton, now you wants my corn.

The indomitable humor was always introduced in the third line, as in the kind of blues that was often sung when returning from a funeral:

Ashes to ashes an' dus' to dus'
Ashes to ashes an' dus' to dus'
If de whisky don' get ya, den de cocaine mus'.

As in most popular music, love plays an important part. In the blues it is rarely the emotion that is dwelt upon—that was for the later—white—torch song lyricists to explore. Instead, the blues express the feelings of a couple separated by a population that was migrating from the South to the North. The black classic-blues innovators rarely exposed their feelings for each other, merely the circumstances that kept them apart.

Michigan water taste like sherry wine
Michigan water taste like sherry wine
I'm goin' back to bring the one I left behind.

Oh, the Mississippi River is so deep and wide,
Oh, the Mississippi River is so deep and wide,
An' my sweet gal, she live on de odder side.

I don't mean to imply that all blues were lighthearted or ironic. By far the most frequent expression was of abject tragedy:

Oh, the graveyard sure is a nasty place,
Oh, the graveyard sure is a nasty place,
They shovel you under and throw dirt in your face.

Did you ever wake up in the middle of the night with blues all 'round your bed
Did you ever wake up in the middle of the night with the blues all 'round your bed?
An' no one near to soothe your achin' head.

It was another short step from the single line repeated with its third rhyming line to the verse with three different lines, each of which rhymed. The rhymes were often approximate.

I'm goin' up north where they say the money grows on trees,
I don't give a doggone 'bout what I leaves
Goin' where I don't need no B.V.D.'s

or

When I leave my gal, I go 'way feelin' sad
Cause that woman's mean an' she treats me awful bad
She's the wussest gal a feller ever had.

and thence to the full-blown song. I quote the first and last verse.

"Dallas Blues" (Music by Hart A. Ward, Lyric by Lloyd Garrett)

12 BARS   When your money's gone, friends have turned you down,
You wander 'round jus' like a lonesome hound
Then you stop and say, "let me go 'way from this town."

12 BARS   Sent a telegram, this is what it said:
"Baby, bring a cold towel for my head,
Got the Dallas Blues, and your lovin' man is almost dead."

The chorus conforms to the repeated first line form, and this repetition actually helps make it sound like a chorus:

12 BARS   I'VE GOT THE DALLAS BLUES AND THE MAIN STREET HEART DISEASE
(repeat)
BUZZIN ROUND MY HEAD LIKE A SWARM OF LITTLE HONEY BEES.

12 BARS   I'M GONNA PUT MYSELF ON A SANTA FE AND GO (repeat)
TO THAT TEXAS TOWN WHERE YOU NEVER SEE ICE AND SNOW.

Each of the verses in this and so many blues songs, is a complete 12-bar blues; what looks like the chorus is two 12-bar blues strung together.

"Dallas Blues" became so popular that singers were urged to go on singing encores, and rather than trust the performers to make up their own couplets, Lloyd Garrett created three more choruses. Unfortunately, these seem to have nothing to do with the city of the title, but aim for a glib humor. I quote the best of the three below:

I WONDER IF MY SWEET LOVIN' BABE STILL WAITS FOR ME (repeat)
MAYBE SOMEBODY ELSE STOLE THE JUICY PEACHES OFF MY TREE.

In his masterful "St. Louis Blues," W. C. Handy, who wrote both the music and lyrics, broke with the tradition of total 12-bar blues by inserting a 16-bar section before the chorus. The following analysis will make the form clear:

12 BARS   I hate to see de ev'nin sun go down,
Hate to see de ev'nin' sun go down,
Cause my baby, he done lef' dis town.

12 BARS   Feelin' tomorrow lak ah feel today,
Feelin' tomorrow lak ah feel today,
I'll pack my trunk and make ma gitaway.

16 BARS   St. Louis woman wid her diamond rings
Pulls my man 'round by her apron strings
'Twant for powder and for store-bought hair
De man I love would not gone nowhere

12 BARS   GOT DE ST. LOUIS BLUES JES AS BLUE AS AH CAN BE,
DAT MAN GOT A HEART LIKE A ROCK CAST IN DE SEA
OR ELSE HE WOULDN'T HAVE GONE SO FAR FROM ME.

The total song is three times longer, most of the other verses and choruses talking about how wonderful her man is. I quote from the third verse because it is irresistible.

Blacker than midnight, teeth lak flags of truce,
Blackest man in de whole St. Louis
Blacker de berry, sweeter am de juice.

A song like "St. Louis Blues" seems to fall somewhere between the classic 12-bar blues and the domain of the pop song, and it was indeed W. C. Handy's music and lyrics—written down with technical efficiency, recorded, and published — that influenced composers like Jerome Kern, Harold Arlen, Cole Porter, Arthur Schwartz, and Irving Berlin to incorporate blues effects in their music. In the mid-1920s a young Oscar Hammerstein was assigned to set lyrics to Jerome Kern's music for *Show Boat*. One of its numbers "Can't Help Lovin' Dat Man," was a pure pop torch song, but its verse had been written in 12-bar blues.

> Oh, listen sister, I love my sister man (and I can't tell you why)
> There ain't no reason why I should love that man.
> It must be something that the angels done planned.

> The chimney's smokin', the roof is leakin' in (but he don't seem to care)
> He can be happy with just a sip of gin,
> I even loves him when his kisses got gin.

Hammerstein, familiar with the repetition of the first line that the blues demands, observes convention in the first verse. Then, breaking convention, he uses the identical final syllable on the second and third lines in the second verse. The chorus, too well known for me to quote more than a snippet, uses a typical blues melodic trick, which is discussed on page 224.

> FISH GOT TO SWIM, BIRDS GOT TO FLY
> I GOT TO LOVE ONE MAN TILL I DIE
> CAN'T HELP LOVIN' DAT MAN OF MINE.

Other popular songs used blues effects, but mostly in their melody — Cole Porter's "What Is This Thing Called Love," "Too Darned Hot," "From This Moment On"; Harold Arlen's "Blues in the Night," "The Man That Got Away," "Happiness Is Just a Thing Called Joe," "Stormy Weather," "Ill Wind"; George Gershwin's songs in *Porgy and Bess* and his "How Long Has This Been Going On?" "The Man I Love," "Soon," "Somebody Loves Me," "Lady Be Good," "I'll Build a Stairway to Paradise"; Hoagy Carmichael's "Lazy Bones," "Rockin' Chair," "Washboard Blues"; Fats Waller's "Ain't Misbehavin'," "Black and Blue," "Your Feet's Too Big"; Ellington's "Mood Indigo," "I Got It Bad and That Ain't Good," "Satin Doll."

OPERETTAS

The operettas we are familiar with, some American creations and others, translations from the German, were unfortunately all modeled after the Viennese and German models prevailing at the turn of the century. Too bad they sidestepped the excellent works of Gilbert and Sullivan and went for inspiration instead to Kalman and Lehar, but New York, the center of the American music world, was taken with German culture. The choral societies had German names and the Metropolitan Opera presented most of its works in German, translating even operas that had originally been written in French and Italian. Producers eager to get the scoop on the competition hired hack translators to get all the latest Viennese works on to New York stages. These hacks turned out lines like "Black-eyed soldier on me beaming" or "When the world is all unruly." Most of the operetta works written between 1890 and 1920 abound in this kind of inverted English, often excused as "poetic license." This kind of arty lyric writing has never been good. Glen MacDonough, in *Babes in Toyland*, wrote "You must near me stay" and "Since I a certain party saw" when he would have better written "You must stay near me" and "Since I saw a certain party."

Most of the operetta songs had long, pretentious verses leading eventually to a short melodic chorus. The long AABA sections leading to the memorable chorus of "Kiss Me Again" (music by Victor Herbert, lyric by Henry Blossom) are forgotten by even the most avid operetta buff. I print it here so that you may observe the kind of language and sentiment to avoid.

A   If I were asked to play the part
Of simple maiden light of heart
A village lass in country clothes.
As to and from her work she goes:
I'd sing a merry lilting strain
And gaily dance to this refrain
Tra, la la … [inserted for vocal pyrotechnics]

A   If they should offer me some day
A primadonna role to play
A stately queen with powdered hair
Her costly gown and jewels rare
I would not act the part amiss
I'd sing a polonaise like this.
Tra, la, la …

B   "Ah, you will agree that happy I should be
Ah, I'm queen of the land Ah! Ah!
Ah, with lords and ladies great to kneel and kiss my hand
A king upon the throne, to woo me for his own
Ah, the fairest I've ever seen
Ah, Ah, Ah, Ah, Who would not be a queen!?"

A   But best of all the parts I'd play
If I could only have my way
Would be a strong romantic role,
Emotional and full of soul
And I believe for such a thing
A dreamy sensuous waltz I'd sing.

C   SWEET SUMMER BREEZE, WHISPERING TREES
STARS SHINING SOFTLY ABOVE
ROSES IN BLOOM, WAFTED PERFUME
SLEEPY BIRDS DREAMING OF LOVE
SAFE IN YOUR ARMS, FAR FROM ALARMS
DAYLIGHT SHALL COME BUT IN VAIN.
TENDERLY PRESSED CLOSE TO YOUR BREAST
KISS ME!
KISS ME AGAIN.
KISS ME AGAIN,
KISS ME, KISS ME AGAIN.

Eliminating the overlong verses AABA and examining the chorus C, it becomes clear that the true operetta chorus has a form split down the middle, a form that has remained one of the staples of show music even up to recent years. It has been used in hundreds of thousands of musical compositions because it is so satisfying musically. Of course, the lyric has to follow suit. The form of the C or chorus section can itself be subdivided into an ABAC:

A   SWEET SUMMER BREEZE, WHISPERING TREES STARS SHINING SOFTLY ABOVE   First melody, main idea, melodic hook

B   ROSES IN BLOOM, WAFTED PERFUME SLEEPY BIRDS DREAMING OF LOVE   Something like the first melody, but more emotional, reaching a climax and returning to earth, settling on a chord that will prepare us to begin again.

A	SAFE IN MY ARMS,
	    FAR FROM ALARMS
	DAYLIGHT WILL COME,
	    BUT IN VAIN.
		Exactly like the first melody, but reaching an intense climax on the word "vain."

C	TENDERLY PRESSED CLOSE TO YOUR BREAST KISS ME! KISS ME AGAIN.	A totally new melody, one that uses the most emotional skips the composer is capable of. The melody settles down to completion and could stop here.
CODA	KISS ME AGAIN, KISS ME, KISS ME AGAIN.	This section (called a coda) is merely a tag ending. In operetta, it was used so the singer could reach a high note, which elicited much applause.

Rida Johnson Young, who wrote the lyrics for several Victor Herbert operettas, used the same form (omitting the coda this time) for "I'm Falling in Love with Someone," although the verse is quite different.

VERSE	I've a very strange feeling I ne'er felt before 'Tis a kind of a grind of depression My heart's acting strangely, it feels rather sore At least it gives me that impression. My pulses leap madly without any cause Believe me, I'm telling you truly I'm gay without cause, then sad without cause, My spirits are truly unruly.

CHORUS

A	FOR I'M FALLING IN
	    LOVE
	    WITH
	    SOMEONE
	SOME YOUNG GIRL
		First melody, melodic hook

B	YES, I'M FALLING IN	Melody similar to the first theme,
	LOVE	but more emotional ending
	WITH	prepares us to begin again.
	SOMEONE	
	HEAD A-WHIRL	
A	YES, I'M GIVING MY	Like the first melody, but reaching
	HEART	a harmonic climax.
	TO	
	SOMEONE	
	PLAIN TO SEE	
C	I'M SURE I COULD	New melody, most emotional
	LOVE	melodic line (the coda is not
	SOMEONE	necessary because a high note is
	MADLY	reached on the word madly).
	IF SOMEONE COULD	
	ONLY	
	LOVE ME.	

Although this is not the section of the book where we discuss what *not* to do in lyric construction, I cannot move ahead without mentioning that operetta lyrics are generally a compendium of the worst sins in all songwriting. It was a period when artiness prevailed and good sense didn't matter so long as words rhymed.

1900–1920

In contrast to the romantic operetta lyrics — sung by "Princes of Pilsen" or "countesses from Vienna" — the songs that were being sung on theater stages and in vaudeville houses across the country and the music that tinkled out of the pianos that every parlor boasted were more natural. The public had little patience with lyrics full of contractions and inverted sentences, and although they still wanted a strong melody, lyrics became increasingly important.

Music and lyrics at this time headed in two distinct directions: the farcical comedy song and the sentimental ballad.

Not unlike the operetta song, the successes of the early 1900s relied heavily on their verses to set the mood of the song. Frequently, these verses were written *after* the strongly melodic chorus had been created, and as often as not, the patching job shows, but the public swallowed the whole package, verse and chorus.

Repeating a sad chorus three times as in "After the Ball" could only have brought the entire audience to tears. (As you read through the lyric, it would be wise to repeat the chorus each time it appears, so you can get the cumulative effect this kind of repetition had on audiences in 1900.)

"After the Ball" (Music and lyric by Charles K. Harris)

> A little maiden climbed on an old man's knee
> Begged for a story, "Do, Uncle, please,
> Why are you single, why live alone?
> Have you no babies, Have you no home?"
> "I had a sweetheart, years, years, ago.
> Where she is now, pet, you will soon know
> List to the story, I'll tell it all
> I b'lieved her faithless, after the ball!"

CHORUS   AFTER THE BALL IS OVER
AFTER THE BREAK OF MORN
AFTER THE DANCERS' LEAVING,
AFTER THE STARS ARE GONE.
MANY A HEART IS ACHING,
IF YOU COULD READ THEM ALL
MANY THE HOPES THAT HAVE VANISHED
AFTER THE BALL.

> "Bright lights were flashing in the grand ballroom
> Softly the music playing sweet tunes
> There came my sweetheart, my love, my own.
> I wish some water, leave me alone!
> When I returned, dear, there stood a man
> Kissing my sweetheart as lovers can.
> Down fell the glass, pet, broken, that's all
> Just as my heart was, after the ball.

(Repeat Chorus)

> "Long years have passed, child, I've never wed.
> True to my lost love, though she is dead.
> She tried to tell me, tried to explain
> I would not listen, pleadings were vain.
> One day a letter came from that man
> He was her brother, the letter ran
> That's why I'm lonely, no home at all
> I broke her heart, pet, after the ball.

(Repeat Chorus)

Comedy songs fared less well with these repeated verses than the "tear jerkers." Having several verses diminished the joke in the chorus. But the lighter songs served a useful purpose for the strait-laced Victorian audience. One could sing about a woman walking out on her husband ("Meet Me in St. Louis, Louis") or joke about using a forbidden word like *hell* ("If I Knock the 'L' out of Kelly") or vocalize the scandalous things that went on in France ("Now She Knows How To Parlay-Voo").

As you might have observed, the form of these overlong verses was 8 lines, a double stanza. This form would be standard until well into the twenties.

> "Meet Me in St. Louis, Louis" (Music by Kerry Mills, Lyric by
> Andrew B. Sterling)

When Louis came home to the flat,
He hung up his coat and his hat,
He gazed all around but no wifie he found
So he said, "Where can Flossie be at?"

A note on the table he spied.
He read it just once, then he cried.
It ran, "Louis dear, it's too slow for me here,
So I think I will go for a ride.

CHORUS   "MEET ME IN SAINT LOUIS, LOUIS
MEET ME AT THE FAIR.
DON'T TELL ME THE LIGHTS ARE SHINING
ANYPLACE BUT THERE.
WE WILL DANCE THE HOOCHEE KOOCHEE,
I WILL BE YOUR TOOTSIE WOOTSIE.
IF YOU WILL MEET ME IN SAINT LOUIS, LOUIS
MEET ME AT THE FAIR."

The dresses that hung in the hall
Were gone, she had taken them all.
She took all his rings and the rest of his things:
The picture he missed from the wall.

"What, moving?" the janitor said.
"Your rent is paid three months ahead!"
"What good is the flat?" said poor Louis, "Read that."
And the janitor smiled as he read.

(Repeat Chorus)

1920S

The era that began with the end of World War I and ended with the stock market crash in '29 was one of great change in American popular music. The optimism, freedom, and joy of most of the lyrics and melodies are apparent with a simple scanning of titles. Songs like "Ain't We Got Fun"; "Baby Face"; "Barney Google with the Goo Goo Googly Eyes"; "California, Here I Come"; "Hard-Hearted Hannah"; "Tea for Two"; "Here Comes Charley"; "Don't Bring Lulu"; "Sweet Georgia Brown"; "Mountain Greenery"; "Ain't She Sweet"; "Let's Do It"; "You Do Something to Me" and "Happy Days Are Here Again" spoke of the prosperity that pervaded the country.

Language, too, had changed. Songwriters were no longer able to sell maudlin slow waltzes. The public wanted snappy tunes that would accommodate the latest dance craze, the Charleston. Songs of the twenties abound in phrases from common street language, like *peaches and cream, sentimental sap, cute, phone me, hot and bothered.*

Lyricists, too, were tired of the perfect, often stilted grammar that had been used before; now they purposely used incorrect contractions and phrases like: "Ain't we got fun"; "Do, do, do what you done, done, done before"; "If he don't come back." Some words were shortened to end according to the cute way flappers talked; they were reputed to say things like, "Oh, go jump in the riv." Ira Gershwin wrote "in my humble fash" and rhymed it with "tender pash"; later in the same song, he penned "my emosh" and "my devosh." Entirely new sounds were created — "embraceable"; "s'wonderful, s'marvelous"; "boop-poop-a-doop"; "wicky-wacky-woo."

It was a time for the unexpected concept: throw your job away; the rich get richer and the poor get children, in rhyme: travel on to avalon; on your knees in your b.v.d.'s; in morality: lock the doors, call me yours; birds do it, bees do it, let's do it; two little babes in the wood (about two kept women); just a gigolo (about a kept man).

The form of the chorus (all the twenties songs still had verses) was largely what we had seen before, ABAC. But A^1, A^2, B, A^3 songs were starting to become more prevalent at the end of the decade, since they were preferred by the younger songwriters like Rodgers and Hart and the Gershwins.

1930S AND 1940S

Lyrics (and melodies) changed much during the next two decades. The most prevalent form became A^1, A^2, B, A^3, while the ABAC waned. Concept changed certainly in the Depression. Songs about hard times included "I've Got Five

Dollars"; "Brother Can You Spare a Dime?"; "I Found a Million-Dollar Baby (in a 5 and 10 Cent Store)"; "When My Dreamboat Comes Home"; "Let's Have Another Cup of Coffee"; "Ten Cents a Dance"; "We're in the Money"; and "A Shine on Your Shoes and a Melody in Your Heart."

Now folks wanted to sing about the simple things, things that didn't cost money. Fine and dandy; young and healthy were not only clichés of the times, they were song titles. Songwriters tried to assuage the Depression with titles like "You and the Night and the Music"; "I Get a Kick out of You"; "You're a Builder Upper"; "I Got Rhythm," stating that as long as one was healthy and had a good love relationship, poverty didn't matter.

As the importance of the love relationship grew, so did the emotional doldrums that were reached when love affairs fell apart. Thus was the torch song born, and it came fully in flower in the thirties and forties. Titles like "(I Don't Stand) A Ghost of a Chance"; "Glad to Be Unhappy"; "Don't Worry 'Bout Me, I'll Get Along"; "Body and Soul"; "When Your Lover Has Gone"; "Nobody's Heart Belongs to Me"; and "You Don't Know What Love Is" were rife.

The movies, which now were able to talk and sing, were an enormous morale booster to starving America during the thirties, and were able to dance wonderfully by the forties. The extravagant Hollywood musicals demanded and got daring, sprawling songs from some of the country's best lyricists and composers. Since the movies could set a scene in moments, the long lead-in verses became superfluous and were abandoned. Irving Berlin, who wrote for Astaire-Rogers, stretched form to its utmost in "Cheek to Cheek" (A^1 = 16 bars; A^2 = 16 bars; B^1 = 8 bars; B^2 = 8 bars; C = 8 bars; A^3 = 16 bars), and other composers and lyricists began extending the 32-bar chorus into other, longer forms.

"The Waltz in Swingtime"; "The Continental"; "The Lullaby of Broadway"; "I'll Remember April"; "The Gypsy in My Soul"; "Blues in the Night"; "That Old Black Magic"; and "Begin the Beguine" (which had the distinction of being the longest popular song ever written at 108 bars) all use longer formats.

But the free-form songs were the exceptions. The forms of most songs in this period were similar to the torch song Johnny Green composed in "I Cover the Waterfront," which has lyrics by Edward Heyman. Usually they were in A^1, A^2, B, A^3 form with a verse, and the title was usually the first line of the chorus.

"I Cover the Waterfront"

VERSE   Away from the city that hurts and mocks
         I'm standing alone by the desolate docks,
         In the still and the chill of the night.
         I see the horizon, the great unknown
         My heart has an ache; it's as heavy as stone,
         Will the dawn coming on make it light?

CHORUS A¹   I COVER THE WATERFRONT
I'M WATCHING THE SEA
WILL THE ONE I LOVE
BE COMING BACK TO ME?

A²   I COVER THE WATERFRONT
IN SEARCH OF MY LOVE
AND I'M COVERED BY
A STARLESS SKY ABOVE.

BRIDGE   HERE AM I PATIENTLY WAITING
HOPING AND LONGING — OH, HOW I YEARN
WHERE ARE YOU? ARE YOU FORGETTING
DO YOU REMEMBER? WILL YOU RETURN?

A³   I COVER THE WATERFRONT,
I'M WATCHING THE SEA,
FOR THE ONE I LOVE
MUST SOON COME BACK TO ME.

Having this A¹, A², B, A³ song available was a great boon to America's songwriters who were thoroughly conversant with it and ABAC. They availed themselves of each (as they still do). There was also another form which is best illustrated by Vincent Youmans' melody and Irving Caesar's lyric to the all-time classic "Tea for Two." (Incidentally, the song is reputed to have been written in fifteen minutes, music and lyrics.)

"Tea for Two"

VERSE A¹   I'm discontented with homes that are rented
So I have invented my own.
A²   Darling, this place is a lovers' oasis
Where life's weary chase is unknown.
B   Far from the cry of the city
Where flowers pretty
Caress the streams.
A³   Cozy to hide in to live side by side in
Don't let it abide in my dreams.

CHORUS A¹   PICTURE YOU UPON MY KNEE
JUST TEA FOR TWO AND TWO FOR TEA
JUST ME FOR YOU AND
YOU FOR ME, ALONE.

A² NOBODY NEAR US TO SEE US OR HEAR US,
NO FRIENDS OR RELATIONS ON WEEKEND VACATIONS,
WE WON'T HAVE IT KNOWN, DEAR, THAT WE OWN
A TELEPHONE, ——— DEAR. ———

A³ DAY WILL BREAK AND YOU'LL AWAKE
AND START TO BAKE A SUGAR CAKE
FOR ME TO TAKE FOR ALL THE BOYS
TO SEE. ———

B WE WILL RAISE A FAMILY,
A BOY FOR YOU, A GIRL FOR ME, OH
CAN'T YOU SEE HOW HAPPY WE WOULD BE?

Although the A¹ and A² appear to have different lengths, they as well as the final A³ are the same bar length. The composer and lyricist have merely added more syllables and notes within each bar. If you have a good ear, you may notice that the composer has chosen a new key for the A² and returned to the original key for the A³. Obviously, three times in a row on the same melody (even with added quick notes) would be boring. The B section, though using totally new material, does wind up with the original melody, which ties the whole song together with a ribbon.

This form (used also in "Always," "All Alone," and many other songs) works best when there is a dramatic conceptual change at the end of the song.

Below is a list of well-known songs that were cast in the forms introduced so far. Of course, this list is far from complete.

ABAC

"But Not for Me"
"The Shadow of Your Smile"
"If They Could See Me Now"
"Come Rain or Come Shine"
"Bill Bailey, Won't You Please Come Home"
"After You've Gone"
"April Showers"
"Tenderly"
"My Man"
"I'm Gonna Sit Right Down and Write Myself a Letter"
"I Love a Piano"

"Here's That Rainy Day"
"A Foggy Day in London Town"
"Love Walked In"
"Hey, Look Me Over"

A^1 A^2 *Bridge* A^3

"Old Man River"
"Lover"
"The Way We Were"
"Tomorrow"
"What I Did for Love"
"On the Sunny Side of the Street"
"Blue Moon"
"Don't It Make My Brown Eyes Blue?"
"Honesty"
"Alfie"
"Memory"
"Ob-La-Di, Ob-La-Da"
"Misty"
"Stormy Weather"
"Strike up the Band"
"I Could Have Danced All Night"
"If Ever I Would Leave You"
"I Don't Know How to Love Him"
"The Man I Love"
"Get Me to the Church on Time"
"Just the Way You Are"
"Yesterday"
"I Will Wait for You"
"The Sound of Music"
"New York, New York"

A^1 A^2 A^3 B

"All Alone by the Telephone"
"Always"
"Around the World"
"Gigi"

MUSICAL THEATER SINCE WORLD WAR II

The Late Forties

Theater music had been America's antidote to the Great Depression of the thirties. "One to one" and "You and me, kid," were not only lines from popular songs, but battle cries to the middle classes, and often were enough to talk a public existing on rice and beans into "looking for the silver lining," because he or she had "someone to love." Yes, with "love just around the corner," we were "lucky so and sos."

Yet by the next decade, with the coming and going of World War II, cynicism had begun creeping into popular music. People began to look for more honesty from their songwriters. All was not moon, June, honeymoon. There were things like war, prejudice, and oppression, and they were ready to hear about them from their balladeers or folk singers.

Postwar theater music had to be more sophisticated, for in its audiences were former soldiers who had seen much while stationed in foreign lands. Until the late forties, pop and theater music traveled parallel roads. It was not until the early fifties that their courses diverged, never to meet again. (*Hair*, a 1968 Broadway success, was perhaps Broadway and pop's only reunion.)

At this point we are confining our discussion of theater to form and construction of lyrics, not their content, but it should be noted that it is almost impossible to discuss form without infringing on concept.

In the late forties, theater composers began to take more chances. *Allegro* by Richard Rodgers and Oscar Hammerstein, tried to break the mold of the AABA song by introducing a Greek chorus to comment on the action. It failed as a musical, but its daring use of form was much admired. Nineteen forty-eight brought Broadway Benjamin Britten's *Rape of Lucretia*, an opera that tried to emulate the success of Menotti's *The Medium*. The most sophisticated work up until the dawn of the new decade was Cole Porter's *Kiss Me Kate*, based on Shakespeare's *Taming of the Shrew*, which, although it had its share of songs in ordinary commercial style ("Another Op'nin', Another Show"; "So in Love"; "Wunderbar"—all in A^1, A^2, B, A^3), is able to capture in a song like "I Hate Men!" the true Shakespearean invective. Later in the score, Cole Porter creates a pseudo-Elizabethan love sonnet with "Were Thine That Special Face," and in "Where Is the Life That Late I Led?" he is able to leave standard form and create a series of couplets that walk the ground between the antique and the contemporary.

"Where Is the Life That Late I Led?"

Where is the life that late I led?
Where is it now? Totally dead.
Where are the friends I used to find?

Where have they gone? Gone with the wind! *
A married life may all be well,
But raising an heir could never compare
With raising a bit of hell!
So I repeat what first I said,
Where is the life that late I led?

"I've Come to Wive It Wealthily in Padua," another plot song, uses a five-line limerick for its chorus:

I'VE COME TO WIVE IT WEALTHILY IN PADUA,
IF WEALTHILY THEN HAPPILY IN PADUA
IF MY WIFE HAS A BAG OF GOLD,
DO I CARE IF THE BAG BE OLD?
I'VE COME TO WIVE IT WEALTHILY IN PADUA.

Setting up a totally new form, Porter creates a long series of rhyming couplets (repeating the same melody) to explain why the hero has come to Padua...

I heard you mutter, "Zounds! A loathsome lad you ah!"
I shall not be disturbed one bit
If she be but a quarter wit,
If she only can talk of clo'es
While she powders her goddam nose!

and later...

'Twouldn't give me the slightest shock
If her knees now and then should knock,
If her eyes were a wee bit crossed,
Were she wearing the hair she'd lost,
Still the damsel I'll make my dame,
In the dark they are all the same.

With another verse the author concludes the song with a slight mercenary wink of a coda.

With a nunny, nunny, nunny and a hey, hey, hey,
Not to mention money, money for a rainy day.
I'VE COME TO WIVE IT WEALTHILY IN PADUA!

* Pronounced to rhyme with find, à la Elizabethan poetry.

The above should give the songwriter some insight into the theater lyricist's mind. A cardinal rule is that *form is not an iron bar. It can be bent in the service of the concept.*

The opening of Rodgers and Hammerstein's *South Pacific* coincided with the advent of LP records, and for the first time, the public was able to take home on a single disc virtually all of a show's songs. Selections from hit shows had formerly been recorded on acetate, but these recordings were fragile and cumbersome. Spinning at 78 rpms, they were frequently full of surface noise. The new 33s opened up a whole new world of easier listening, storage, and preservation. The development of this simpler way of recording was to change the system of marketing recordings and to influence the future creation of music and lyrics to a tremendous extent.

South Pacific, with its enormously long and successful score, did nothing to change theatrical form, but it did break new ground in the musical theater by exposing the senselessness of prejudice. (It even introduced a song that seems like an appendage to the score. "You've Got to Be Carefully Taught," although it may have disturbed the tired businessman, subtly brings across the point that prejudices are not inborn but acquired.)

The Fifties

This was perhaps the richest, most productive period the American musical theater has ever known. The names of shows that opened in this decade recall a treasure chest of musical ideas and a great freedom of form: *Guys and Dolls*; *The King and I*; *Wonderful Town*; *Kismet*; *The Golden Apple*; *The Pajama Game*; *Fanny*; *House of Flowers*; *Silk Stockings*; *Damn Yankees*; *My Fair Lady*; *The Most Happy Fella*; *Bells Are Ringing*; *Candide*; *West Side Story*; *The Music Man*; *Gypsy*; *The Sound of Music*.

The decade opened with one of the masterpieces of the musical theater, *Guys and Dolls* (book by Jo Swerling and Abe Burrows, music and lyrics by Frank Loesser, based on characters created by Damon Runyon). In the first number, called "Fugue for Tinhorns" in the score, and retitled "Three-Cornered Tune" for the commercial sheet copy, three horse players argue in canon or round style about the merits of each one's favorite horse. In spite of the musical and lyrical overlapping, we comprehend everything. Loesser has chosen an argumentative musical style and achieved it through counterpoint. One character cannot finish his say before the other butts in. Benny begins his pitch for Valentine while Nicely is still singing about Paul Revere. The lyrics ring true because they are pure racetrack jargon.

NICELY: I got the horse right here
His name is Paul Revere,
And there's a guy who says

if the weather's clear

Can do, Can do   BENNY: I'm picking Valentine

Cause on the morning line

This guy has him figured at five to nine.

Has chance, has chance.

If "Fugue for Tinhorns" gives us insight into the racetrack characters' psyche, the "Oldest Established Permanent Floating Crapgame in New York" gives us a view of the poker-playing Runyonesque protagonists — including the leading man. In the next song, "I'll Know," the title suggests we are in for a romantic ballad, and that is exactly what we get, but a non-sentimental one. "Adelaide's Lament" has become a classic comedy song-scene built on a solid psychosomatic foundation. Adelaide, stood up by her boyfriend, Nathan Detroit, is trying to ferret out the reasons for her frequent sneezing fits. The song is in slow tempo and is usually sung in halting, mispronounced "Brooklynese." There are 3 verses and 3 choruses, winding up to a coda transposed into a higher key. Contrary to the songs of Cole Porter or the lyrics of Larry Hart, where succeeding choruses offer diminishing inspiration, Loesser saves his most amusing lines for the later repetitions. He rhymes "post nasal drip" with "la grippe," and tickles us with "from a lack of community property, and a feeling she's getting too old, a person can develop a bad, bad, cold!"

An analysis of the first verse and chorus will make the daring form of "Adelaide's Lament" apparent:

VERSE   The average unmarried female, basically insecure

Due to some long frustration may react

With psychosomatic symptoms, difficult to endure

Affecting the upper respiratory tract.

CHORUS A   IN OTHER WORDS, JUST FROM WAITING AROUND

FOR THAT PLAIN LITTLE BAND OF GOLD

A PERSON ... CAN DEVELOP A COLD.

B   YOU CAN SPRAY HER WHEREVER YOU FIGURE THE STREPTOCOCCI LURK,

YOU CAN GIVE HER A SHOT FOR WHATEVER SHE'S GOT BUT IT JUST
WON'T WORK.

IF SHE'S TIRED OF GETTING THAT FISH-EYE FROM THE HOTEL CLERK

A   A PERSON CAN DEVELOP A COLD.

Notice the freedom in the verse-chorus form, the unequal line length, the reprise of "cold," which ties the whole together. These illustrate Loesser's use of form to serve the needs of the character in the play.

Guys and Dolls had other startling departures. "Sit Down, You're Rocking the Boat" is a gospel song sung, oddly enough, by a group of gamblers. There are a couple of wonderful duets in the score; one for the two female leads, each espousing that the other "Marry the Man Today," and a number that finds Adelaide ranting at Nathan for his unfair treatment while he stoically repeats the chorus lines "SUE ME, SUE ME,/ SHOOT BULLETS THROUGH ME/ I LOVE YOU!/ CALL A LAWYER AND HATE ME, HATE ME/ GO AHEAD AND HATE ME/ I LOVE YOU!"

Perhaps the most remarkable number in that score is a song that is through-composed (a term drawn from "concert" music for a type of song that is free in form, does not repeat whole sections, but keeps spinning ahead and achieves unity through use of tiny phrases). In a way, "My Time of Day" was a precurser of modern rock, which also builds its energy by repeating small fragments.

Sky Masterson talks in the song about the "dark time, a couple of deals before dawn"

AND THE STREET LAMP FILLS THE GUTTER WITH GOLD.
THAT'S MY TIME OF DAY,
MY TIME OF DAY
AND YOU'RE THE ONLY DOLL I'VE EVER WANTED TO SHARE IT WITH ME.

The King and I, Rodgers and Hammerstein's heartwarming musical about the relationship that develops between an English schoolmarm and the stubborn king of Siam, did little to advance form in the American musical, but it did give the heroine a chance to sing the kind of soliloquy that Rogers and Hammerstein wrote so well. In "Shall I Tell You What I Think of You?" form is at the service of the schoolteacher's anger. In "Hello, Young Lovers," in which she reminisces about her late husband, we are given a long verse, the kind we used to get in operetta and fortunately haven't heard since. This one, however, is truly poetic.

"Hello, Young Lovers" (Music by Richard Rodgers,
    Lyric by Oscar Hammerstein II)

When I think of Tom,
I think about a night
When the earth smelled of summer
And the sky was streaked with white,
And the soft mist of England was sleeping on a hill.
I remember this
And I always will.
There are new lovers now on the same silent hill,
Looking on the same blue sea.
And I know Tom and I are a part of them all
And they're all a part of Tom and me ...

HELLO, YOUNG LOVERS, WHOEVER YOU ARE
I HOPE YOUR TROUBLES ARE FEW,
ALL MY GOOD WISHES GO WITH YOU TONIGHT
I'VE BEEN IN LOVE LIKE YOU ...

Although the locale of this musical is exotic, the form of most of the songs couldn't be more Broadway (A^1 A^2 B A^3 and ABAC). In a later musical, *Kismet*, whose music was adapted by Wright and Forrest from melodies by Borodin, although we sense the commercial, the odd-shaped melodies of the Russian composer allow for more freedom of form.

Opera almost resurfaced with *The Golden Apple*, *The Consul*, *Candide*, *West Side Story*, *The Most Happy Fella*, and *Sandhog* (yes, an abysmal effort set under the Hudson River). Each of these mixed aria with pop song. But it remained for Lerner and Loewe's *My Fair Lady*, in 1956, to combine all the elements that the musical theater does incomparably: pop song ("On the Street Where You Live"); aria ("Just You Wait, 'Enry 'Iggins"); soliloquy ("Why Can't the English Learn to Speak?," "Let a Woman in Your Life"); trio ("The Rain in Spain"); dance tune ("Get Me to the Church on Time"); gavotte ("The Ascot Gavotte"); waltz ("The Embassy Waltz"); tap tune ("With a Little Bit of Luck").

It seemed to be one of those times when everyone concerned with the project was at his or her most inspired. Unquestionably, *My Fair Lady* represented the glorious fruition of the contemporary school of musical plays. The cohesiveness of the plot, based on George Bernard Shaw's *Pygmalion*, and the way the songs are integrated into the story set a model for all musicals to come. Because its period was turn-of-the-century London, a time of social upheaval, Alan J. Lerner took his concepts (and frequently his lyric titles) from Shaw's soap-box oratory. There are amusing, never-before-encountered situations, as when confirmed bachelor and linguistic expert Henry Higgins asks "why can't a woman be more like a man?" or when aptly named freeloader Doolittle gives the audience his recipe for avoiding work: "with a little bit of luck."

Early in the work's creation it was decided that the role of Professor Higgins would be played by an actor rather than a singer. Rex Harrison spoke-sang the lines suavely. After this, it was acceptable to cast stars in pivotal roles to ensure box-office success. Composers, and especially lyricists, had to give the stars wordy songs in rapid tempo, hoping audiences would not notice that their voices did not have timbre, power, or pitch. Jule Styne, who composed *Gypsy*; Meredith Willson, who wrote *Music Man*; Frank Loesser, who wrote *The Most Happy Fella*; and Leonard Bernstein, who wrote the music for *West Side Story* and *Candide* before the decade expired would have none of this half-singing. Their scores needed resonant singing by strong voices. In the search for soaring melodies and realistic plots, they all tried to break out of formal ABAB or AABA constructions. In those scores, they succeeded.

The Sixties

Throughout the fifties there was always the hope in the hearts of Broadway musical aficionados that the musical, which had led so much of popular music, would take back its rightful place when America had had its fill of rock and roll. But in the sixties it became clear that Broadway was now selling a recherché product to a few rich buyers.

The young talent that New York had once attracted now had a brief love affair with the stage, then deserted it for Hollywood and more lucrative concert appearances or recordings. Witness Barbra Streisand. All the big names preferred arenas or stadiums, which would hold 50,000 fans, to the confining 2,000-seat-maximum Broadway theaters.

Merely getting to the theater was becoming something of an ordeal. New York's theater district was also its sleaziest. The Times Square area was crowded with shops vending pornography, derelicts, male and female prostitutes, and muggers. Dinner and a show were costly now. Theater-ticket prices skyrocketed from $6 to $20. Inflation made the cost of other diversions more appealing, rendering the musical more elitist, depending on the expense-account trade. To compensate for costs that were going out of sight, theatrical producers began to skimp; they drastically reduced the size of their chorus, frequency of costume changes, and lavishness of their scenery. Broadway's heyday was over, and even today it continues to limp along sadly beside the movies, television, and the concert circuit.

This does not mean to imply that there was nothing to be gained by popular music from Broadway's musicals. No one can ignore some of the great musicals that opened in that decade: *Bye Bye Birdie*; *The Fantasticks*; *The Unsinkable Molly Brown*; *Camelot*; *Wildcat*; *Milk and Honey*; *How to Succeed in Business Without Really Trying*; *No Strings*; *All American*; *I Can Get It for You Wholesale*; *Stop the World—I Want to Get Off*; *Hello, Dolly*; *Funny Girl*; *Anyone Can Whistle*; *Fiddler on the Roof*; *On a Clear Day You Can See Forever*; *Sweet Charity*; *Mame*; *I Do, I Do*; *Hair*; *Promises, Promises*; *1776*; *Purlie*. But with the exception of *Hair*, *Company*, and perhaps *Jacques Brel* (which opened off-Broadway), they added nothing to the canon of musical art and did not help to repair the chasm between popular music and Broadway's musicals.

In his excellent book *The American Musical Theater*, Gerald Boardman calls the opening of *Hair* (music by Galt MacDermot, lyrics by Gerome Ragni and James Rado) on Broadway April 29, 1968, "in every respect—commercial, historic, esthetic—...far and away the most important musical offering of the season, possibly of an era." The plot of *Hair* is a believable combination of problems. Racial inequality, homosexuality, free love, poverty, and drug problems rear their heads, often without motivation, but long enough to allow the songs with strongly worded protests to shine through. The telling strength of *Hair* was its score, rich in melody, thoroughly contemporary in concept and lyrics, and orchestrated to allow the rock sound to come shining through and to fall on the ears of an audience, most of whom were twice the age of the show's creators.

Mr. Boardman calls *Hair* a failure because it did not spawn a trend, but I would deem it a success. For once, youth was having its say on Broadway, and although *Hair* did not possess the polished rhymes of the master lyricists, no matter; in one case, "Frank Mills," MacDermot had set simple but moving prose to music. Little of the score used the standard ABAC theater form or A^1, A^2, B, A^3. Most was like the contemporary rock form of verse, chorus.

Company feels like a '60s musical, although it opened in 1970. It was another departure, and another without emulators. It was a "conceptual" musical; music and lyrics served the concept of the alienated protagonist. It was also the most ambitious work thus far of the theater's great hope, Stephen Sondheim, who wrote music and lyrics to George Furth's plotless book. Contrary to *Hair*, it did not try to bring the rock and rollers back into the theater, but sought to appeal to an elite, cerebral group. Its songs and rhymes were brittle and literate, and its music was not hummable but ultrasophisticated. The protagonist, a bachelor named Bobby, envies his eight married friends. We spend most of the evening with these four couples, finding that their supposedly happy marriages are not that at all. One couple pass their nonalcoholic hours sniping; another is about to divorce; the wife in a third marriage proposes "keeping" Bobby, and so forth.

Meanwhile, Bobby lives in deceit and fantasy. He is confused throughout most of the musical. We feel he will remain a bachelor forever because he has become terrified of the kind of relationship he sees his friends embroiled in, but in a switch (a rewritten ending incorporated when the show was in tryouts), he reaffirms the case for loving in the final song — "Being Alive." The motivation doesn't work for me, but the plot change gives the show an affirmative ending and makes Bobby a more likable person. Perhaps this was the reason critics and public alike accepted the protagonist and welcomed the show, allowing it to run out the season and close with a profit.

Promises, Promises with music and lyrics by Burt Bacharach and Hal David, and a book based on the popular movie *The Apartment* by Neil Simon, contained the only song (except for those in *Hair*) of the decade to come near making the popularity charts. Written in soft rock, "I'll Never Fall in Love Again" has a contemporary feel. In fact, the whole show had a score that was more pop than it was Broadway.

The Seventies

Costs soared and producers were no longer willing to chance a two-million-dollar investment on an untried composer or lyricist. Broadway was becoming the home of lavish musical revivals of great composers long deceased: Duke Ellington (*Sophisticated Ladies*), Thomas "Fats" Waller (*Ain't Misbehavin'*), Jerome Kern (*Roberta*), Vincent Youmans (*No, No, Nanette*).

Superstar singers who could fill a stadium seating 25,000 for a one-shot concert could not be inveigled to sign the necessary contracts that would hold them for a six-month run of the play. They could earn many times what a Broadway producer would pay them by recording a best-selling album. Many went to Hollywood to make movies.

For songwriters trained in record studios, where they had complete autonomy over their own product, it would have been foolish to go to a drafty theater where some non-artistic producer would rearrange their lyrics or where their tunes were at the mercy of a dance director and a possibly superanuated "star."

That is not to say that the theater didn't give it a good try. Rock was introduced (*Godspell*; *The Wiz*; *Jesus Christ Superstar*; *Grease*; *Runaways*), but the tired businessman, the expense-accounted executive, and the liberal intellectual would not accept it. Amplification in the theater could never reach the level that one could create in one's own living room.

There were a few beacons. These were mostly lights shining on the American musical theater from a few composers and lyricists who had cut their teeth on Broadway in decades before.

Stephen Sondheim overwhelmed the musical theater with his brilliance. There were even two successful shows that excerpted his music. One cavalcaded his "hits" (*Side by Side by Sondheim*), and one (*Marry Me a Little*) was devoted to songs that had been dropped from his shows. Although most of his shows did not make money, they were succès d'estime. *Follies* (1970) concerned a group of showgirls who meet one last time on the stage of the theater where they had had their grandest success. The theater is about to be torn down and is crumbling as they and their lives are. This plot allows Sondheim to be nostalgic, bitter, loving, showbiz, raunchy, and sentimental by turns. (In one delicious list song he gives us the flavor of an era when he rhymes "Abie's Irish Rose" with "Dionne babies, Major Bowes.")

A Little Night Music (1972) is a musical version of Ingmar Bergman's film *Smiles of a Summer Night*. The plot concerns a middle-aged Scandinavian lawyer's attempt to free himself from an unwise, unconsummated second marriage to an eighteen-year-old. Along the way he falls in love with his former mistress, who abandons her own lover. At the end his petulant son runs off with his stepmother, leaving the lawyer and his mistress to resume their affair. The tender situation between these two middle-aged people allowed Sondheim his only "hit," "Send in the Clowns," a gentle melody with an ironic lyric. The form is not adventuresome — A^1, A^2, bridge, A^3, A^4.

In 1976 came *Pacific Overtures*, a story about the westernization of Japan, performed with a mostly Oriental cast. Largely influenced by haiku and Noh, the show was inaccessible. Since it made not the slightest concession to the tired businessman, its run was short and unprofitable.

Sweeney Todd (1979) is truly an opera in the Weill-Brecht tradition, and as such it demands a large orchestra, cast, theater. It received an excellent production on Broadway, but the plot, concerning a mad barber who slits his customer's throats in his insane pursuit of revenge, was not for Broadway. To further bloody the stage, the barber has a liaison with a woman who chops Sweeney's victims up and puts them into the "most delicious meat pies in London." In spite of the story, the music soars, the lyrics are brilliant, and the form daring. Since it is operatic, the construction (except for the "Ballad of Sweeney Todd"—rhyming couplets) is beyond the scope of this book.

Merrily We Roll Along (1982), although it contains some of Sondheim's most hummable music, was not successful, because of trouble with the book. The play starts with a lecture being given to a group of high school graduates by a successful songwriter—and we get the idea that he sold out to success somewhere along the way. Then the plot goes backward and we see the little compromises that finally add up to total sell-out. A beautiful ballad called "We Had a Good Thing Going" (see Punch-Line Songs, page 100) got several recordings.

It must seem strange that any book on songwriting spends so many paragraphs extolling a songwriter whose shows have almost invariably lost money, whose work has produced only one song that is a "semistandard," and who turns out a new show only every three years or so (Rodgers and Hart and Gershwin would have a new work on the boards every three months), but one has only to read a few lines of lyric to know that Sondheim is the greatest lyricist in American musical theater now, and perhaps of all time. Although England often leads us in the trends of pop music, most English critics acknowledge Sondheim as the leader of world musical theater as well.

In "The Miller's Son," a song sung by the servant in *A Little Night Music*, the form and even the basic rhythmic pulse are at the service of concept.

SLOW	I shall marry the miller's son
$\frac{3}{4}$	Pin my hat on a nice piece of property
	Friday nights for a bit of fun
	We'll go dancing. Meanwhile...
QUICK	It's a wink and a wiggle and a giggle in the grass
$\frac{2}{4}$	And I'll trip the light fandango.
	A pinch and a diddle in the middle of what passes by.

QUICK	It's a very short road from the pinch and the punch
$\frac{3}{8}$	To the paunch and the pouch and the pension.
	It's a very short road to the ten thousandth lunch
	And the belch and the grouch and the sigh
	In the meanwhile———
	There are mouths to be kissed before mouths to be fed
	And a lot in between
	In the meanwhile———
	And a girl has to celebrate what passes by.

There are two more sections to this song (I hesitate to call them verses or choruses) whose lyric constructions match the above. They build up the servant girl's fantasy about her future husband, and then the song ends as it began, with "I shall marry the miller's son."

It is obvious that in this kind of song, every syllable must be heard for full effect, and with all the meter changes, it is not a toe-tapper. It is closer to an operatic aria, without the pretension of opera.

The Eighties

Interestingly enough, the decade opened with a show called *Reggae*, which is, of course, the term for rhythmic black Jamaican soul music, showing that popular forms were becoming viable in the theater. Jazz, too, had taken its place with Duke Ellington's *Sophisticated Ladies*. Off-Broadway hits like *Joseph and the Amazing Technicolor Dreamcoat* and *Little Shop of Horrors* found a congenial home on the main stem. It was now permitted to write about homosexuality as *Falsettos*, *March of the Falsettos*, and *La Cage aux Folles* were eagerly accepted by the public. Pregnancy too, formerly verboten, could make a hit, even win a Tony, as *Baby*, a concept musical about the nine-month waiting period and birth, won all the awards. For "class," one could attend Sondheim's *Sunday in the Park with George*, a musical about an artist's struggle to capture his art. Two of the decade's biggest hits were *Les Miserables* and *The Phantom of the Opera*; the latter continues successfully, a generation later, in the twenty-first century, proving that huge romantic blockbusters can become so entrenched in our lives that they become part of our current history.

The Nineties

In the early nineties we could finally witness a show about male bonding and torture in a banana-republic prison cell. Called *Kiss of the Spider Woman*, it would be Kander and Ebb's finest work. But there were other gems. *Tommy*, billed as the first rock musical and created by The Who (mostly written by Pete Townshend), proved that hard rock could be successful on Broadway. By contrast, *Beauty and the Beast*, a Disney spinoff of the animated film, was an even greater success on stage and spawned a whole series of Disney theatrical adaptations. (It just closed in 2007). Lloyd Webber produced perhaps his best musical, *Sunset Boulevard* (based on Billy Wilder's film), which treated an aging silent film star with dignity. The grungy rock musical *Rent*, with the hit song "Seasons of Love" and an HIV-positive hero and heroine, was a Broadway smash hit of consequence.

The Twenty-first Century

Because of the enormous cost of producing them, truly inventive musicals were sparse in the new century, although *Hair* and *Tommy* had been appropriate to their times, had exhilarating music and lyrics, and had succeeded. Broadway, where a ticket to a musical now cost more than a hundred dollars, mostly stuck to revivals or family fare. Though the heavy-handed pop operas like Elton John's *Aida* were marginally successful, they did not start a trend. Other, similar efforts, including a pop opera about the Civil War and *Jekyll and Hyde*, were not successful (except for the well-entrenched *Phantom of the Opera*). The decade saw the emergence of the Disney Company musicals as a force, for *The Lion King*, *Beauty and the Beast*, and *Tarzan* would play well into the 2000s. Shows based on the songs of pop-music groups, like *Jersey Boys* and Abba's *Mamma Mia*, were successful. Mel Brooks, who had only a few songs to his credit, took the plunge and produced a splendid full score for the stage adaptation of his film *The Producers*. He has done it again, brilliantly, in the adaptation of his own *Young Frankenstein*. *Wicked*, perhaps the biggest hit of the decade, was based on Greogry Maguire's highly popular novel that told the story of *The Wizard of Oz* from the Wicked Witch of the West's point of view. *Wicked* proved that innate beauty and goodness have nothing to do with the color of your skin, just as *Hairspray* seconded the motion, adding that the size of your fanny didn't matter, either.

ROCK

Rock and Roll

In early 1952, a hard-of-hearing disc jockey named Alan Freed decided his program emanating from Cleveland over WJW needed a lift. His interest was piqued by the "race records" frequently played over obscure Harlem stations. In selecting records for his program, he frequently traveled to New York's esoteric record shops and noticed that white teenagers often requested shop owners to spin these elemental discs and wiggled and writhed to their strong downbeat. He brought many of their favorites back to Cleveland and played them on his program at highest volume.

The songs had short verses and hard, repetitive, driving choruses, which were raucously shouted. The images were blatantly sexual, even to the choice of the words *rock* (which was cleaned up on other stations to *dance*) and *roll* (*jelly-roll* had always been a black euphemism for sexual intercourse).

The inexorable intensity of the beat needed no setting of stage to make its full effect, so the verse was superfluous except as a way to create excitement before the entry of the chorus. That tension was further augmented by drawing out the verse and while the music waited for a chord that pulled into the chorus.

Jerry Lee Lewis and his imitators used the same driving beat and kept the decibel level of the mother instrument of rock and roll, the amplified guitar, at peak level. The sexuality continued and perhaps reached its zenith with Elvis Presley, who achieved the height of sentimentality with mawkish ballads and then quickly changed the pace with a rhythmic personal message like "Blue Suede Shoes." Through exposure of the two sides of his personality, he wowed his audience as few performers have done, and while most of the songs fade from memory, his utter sexuality is ever clear.

The proliferation of rock groups helped to make the lyric even less intelligible but added to the intensity and the overall sound level. The lyric seemed unimportant now. What mattered was how loud, how driving, the title (so I can buy my own), and especially, who was singing.

It is understandable that after the romantic lyrics of the thirties and forties, the new elementalism would be much sought for. Had the public accepted it, pure instrumentals might have been embraced and lyrics abandoned altogether. As it turned out, the lyrics of, say, "Shake, Rattle and Roll" are not unlike punk rock (see page 285). The concept of anger, sticking up for one's rights (don't step on my blue suede shoes; now or never) was compatible with the individualism that swept the teenagers along into the fifties and throughout the sixties.

"Shake, Rattle, and Roll" (Music and lyric by Charles Calhoun)

Get out from that kitchen and rattle those pots and pans
Get out from that kitchen and rattle those pots and pans
Well, roll my breakfast, 'cause I'm a hungry man.

SHAKE, RATTLE AND ROLL, SHAKE, RATTLE AND ROLL,
SHAKE, RATTLE AND ROLL, SHAKE, RATTLE AND ROLL,
YOU NEVER DO NOTHIN' TO SAVE YOUR DOGGONE SOUL.
Wearin' those dresses, your hair done up so right,
Wearin' those dresses, your hair done up so right,
You look so warm, but your heart is cold as ice.

(CHORUS)

I'm like a one-eyed cat, peepin' in a seafood store
I'm like a one-eyed cat, peepin' in a seafood store,
I can look at you, tell you don't love me no more.

(CHORUS)

I believe you're doin' me wrong, and now I know
I believe you're doin' me wrong, and now I know
The more I work, the faster my money goes.

(CHORUS)

The lyrics reveal a strong hostility on the part of the breadwinner, who wants his woman to tremble and to move sexually for him, and the shouting also expresses his anger.

Since the origins of rock and roll lyrics were in the blues it is not surprising that most rock and roll songs employed the 12-bar blues form. That is a longish line, setting up a premise (4 bars), followed by a repeat (4 bars) ending with a consequence of the premise (4 bars).

PREMISE	Get out from the kitchen and rattle those pots and pans (4 bars)
	Get out from the kitchen and rattle those pots and pans (4 bars)
CONSEQUENCE	Well, roll my breakfast, 'cause I'm a hungry man (4 bars)

The chorus often used the same blues construction, although the premise line was most often split into two parts, permitting the title to be brought solidly home.

TITLE	SHAKE, RATTLE AND ROLL, SHAKE RATTLE AND ROLL (4 bars)
AND	SHAKE, RATTLE, AND ROLL, SHAKE, RATTLE AND ROLL (4 bars)
PREMISE	
CONSEQUENCE	YOU NEVER DO NOTHIN' TO SAVE YOUR DOGGONE SOUL. (4 bars)

Additionally, since rock and roll often took a popular song of the day and transformed it through the use of an urgent triplet beat, we can expect to, and do, find much use of the A^1, A^2, bridge, A^3 form. This form is almost as accessible as the blues form, since the main theme is repeated immediately after it is first announced. Some of the important hits of this time that used the A^1, A^2, bridge, A^3 form were "Great Balls of Fire"; "Don't Be Cruel"; "Out of Sight, Out of Mind."

Although it may have no place in the scheme of this book, I cannot discuss the gigantic upheaval that the advent of rock brought to all pop music without adding that this was the decade, the fifties, that most critics consider the beginning of lyrical deterioration. It was the time when the star's charisma began to take over from the songwriter.

The shouting, the release of repression, the blatant sexuality, the violent (and necessarily non-touch) dancing, movement by performer and listener all contributed to the revolution that swept away craft and introduced raw feelings.

It was no longer necessary that rhymes be new, fresh, or even interesting; one could get away with

> Come on baby just cooperate,
> When I tell you we could have a date.
> Will you tell me that I'm not too late

or

> You can stop acting smart
> Don't keep breakin' my heart.
> I'm not tryin' to break your heart.

This was the time that Broadway and even Hollywood, with its well-trained songwriters, had to move over and take a back seat to those who had a few elemental chords and could handle a guitar. A natural voice and some elemental words, energy, and sexual presence meant more than a pocketful of rhymes. The enormous increase in amplification could now swell a simple blues pattern to the same decibel count as the thirty-piece orchestra of a Broadway musical. Lyrics no longer needed to be heard; in fact sometimes, because of the amplification, they were unintelligible. Raw power and the beat swept everything else away.

The Beatles and the Revolution in Form

The Beatles expanded the scope of rock and brought it respectability. They had their hair cut alike, not long but over the ears; they wore Cardin lapelless suits (of their manager Brian Epstein's design), but most of all, their music and lyrics were dedicated to the pursuit of excellence, and they refused to be involved in anything cheap or second-rate or déjà-vu. What they tried to do was push forward the frontiers of taste, and when they sang of love, it was intended to imply a real emotion and not, as their predecessors had implied, a swiveling pelvis in the back seat of a roadster.

Lennon, McCartney, and Harrison could sing in harmony or unison as they played. Thus, there was no immediately identifiable lead singer, for they frequently changed parts in mid-song. In contrast to all their imitators, they each had an individuality amid the unison.

No subject was too bizarre for them, and no form too familiar. They sang of tender love in "Michelle"—form AABA; middle-age nostalgia in "Yesterday"—form AABA; bitter relationships in "You Never Give Me Your Money"—form AAB; murdering the haughty, the teachers, and the judges in "Maxwell's Silver Hammer"—form verse-chorus; all the insane things government will tax in "Taxman"—form AABA; the utter hollowness of life and death in "Eleanor Rigby"—form ABABAB; misunderstandings in "She Said, She Said"—form ABAB; pure joy in "Good Day Sunshine"—form AA chorus, and many more.

The Beatles' output defies pigeonholing. Each song seems to have a different format and totally different concept. The moment they felt that they were succeeding and had one or two hits on the charts, they explored another avenue.

They paid their dues by working long and hard in Liverpool and then in Hamburg, where they sang songs written by other creators, adapting them perfectly to the much sought after "American" style, eventually, of course, writing all their own material.

Milton Okun, in his preface to a collection of *The Great Songs of Lennon and McCartney*, notes that they "made rock respectable, revolutionized the recording industry in general and the popular music industry in particular, set the precedent that a successful performer compose his own songs, and brought freedom to musical expression unprecedented in popular song. They took ideas from country & western, rhythm & blues, rock and roll. New musical terms were invented to describe their music: raga rock, baroque rock, white soul."

They created over two hundred songs of such irreverence, wisdom, cynicism, humor, and vulnerability—to say nothing of originality—that many people seriously thought they had other composers working for them. But no, most of the songs were created by John Lennon and Paul McCartney; the balance were the work of George Harrison.

Not only did they open new areas to the creation of music and lyrics, but they were known to spend months in a recording studio working out the special effects they favored on their albums. They treated the tape recorder as a musical instrument and tried recording an instrument at one speed and playing it back at another, sometimes distorted, sometimes slower or faster than the original recording. They tried recording a single instrument many times (overdubbing), altering the sound, and combining the tracks; playback would sometimes yield a never-before-created sound. Echo chambers, animal sounds, spoken dialogue, high frequencies, and static were sometimes used in their recordings.

But they created much more than gimmicks and special effects. In later years, when "sound" presence was often the difference between a hit record and a miss, we realized that their music was unique, the effects from their recording devices mere frosting.

In "Something," George Harrison's music does the job of finishing the section after the lyrics have ended. In "Here, There, and Everywhere," the music—this time credited to Lennon and McCartney—takes over. The form is AAB—what else could it be? Since the title divides itself in three parts, so does the song. If you look at a sheet copy of the song or listen to the Beatles' recording, you'll realize that never has form helped a song more.

The A^1 section gives us a feeling of what it's like to have the love object here or present. (Although the Beatles' lyrics always used "he" and "she," the emotions in their songs were suitable to either sex by a simple word change.)

The A^2 section discusses the longings that occur when two lovers are apart. There have been literally thousands of "apart" songs that wallow in sadness, but this one is unlike all of them because the tune and lyric seem to be pulling into a chorus. This is the B section that finds the lover, everywhere. Anyone who has been in love will recall the common situation where everyone we meet reminds us of our lover. A good concept hits us like unassailable truth.

"Here, There, and Everywhere" ends with the title, which seems to tie the three sections together into a neat package.

The dramatic story line of "She's Leaving Home," the freedom of its two and a half verses and three choruses, which are sung as counterpoint, are worthy of the most erudite composer-lyricists.

> "She's Leaving Home" (Music and lyric by John Lennon and
> Paul McCartney)

VERSE Wednesday morning at five o'clock as the day begins
Silently closing her bedroom door,
Leaving the note that she hoped would say more
She goes down the stairs to the kitchen clutching her handkerchief.
Quietly turning the back door key
Stepping outside, she is free.

CHORUS SHE
(WE GAVE HER MOST OF OUR LIVES)
IS LEAVING
(SACRIFICED MOST OF OUR LIVES)
HOME
(WE GAVE HER EV'RYTHING MONEY COULD BUY)
SHE'S LEAVING HOME AFTER LIVING ALONE FOR SO MANY YEARS
(BYE, BYE)

VERSE   Father snores as his wife gets into her dressing gown,
Picks up the letter that's lying there.
Standing alone at the top of the stairs,
She breaks down and cries to her husband
"Daddy, our baby's gone!"
Why would she treat us so thoughtlessly?
"How could she do this to me?"

CHORUS   SHE
    (WE NEVER THOUGHT OF OURSELVES)
IS LEAVING
    (NEVER A THOUGHT FOR OURSELVES)
HOME
    (WE STRUGGLED HARD ALL OUR LIVES TO GET BY)
SHE'S LEAVING HOME AFTER LIVING ALONE FOR SO MANY YEARS
    (BYE, BYE)

VERSE   Friday morning at nine o'clock
She is far away,
Waiting to keep the appointment she made
Meeting a man from the motor trade.

CHORUS   SHE
    (WHAT DID WE DO THAT WAS WRONG)
IS HAVING
    (WE DIDN'T KNOW IT WAS WRONG)
FUN
    (FUN IS THE ONE THING THAT MONEY CAN'T BUY)
SOMETHING INSIDE THAT WAS ALWAYS DENIED
FOR SO MANY YEARS,
SHE'S LEAVING HOME.

As it appears in the work of the Beatles, the prevailing anger of the times is directed at society, but it is a benevolent anger and everything comes out all right in the end. Even though their work may suggest arson ("Norwegian Wood") or murder ("Maxwell's Silver Hammer") or isolation ("Yellow Submarine"), it is a cartoon anger. Gone are the petulance, the personal sense of frustration, that characterized the rock and rollers. Gone too is the frenzy.

Rock

The late sixties were a time of great change for pop songs. Most musicologists feel that this was the time when rock and roll became simply rock. The young were no longer interested in shoobie-doobie-wah-wah-doo or dooby-dum-dooby-dum-doo-dow. Life had to be valid, meaningful, and relevant. The most important groups, the Beach Boys, with their wholesome harmony, and the Beatles, whom the critics were now recognizing as leaders in the avant-garde, were evolving into different musicians than had previously been imagined. George Harrison, who had added the sitar (a strange-sounding Indian native instrument), now offered a song based on an Indian raga called "Love You To." Records were no longer three minutes of hummable and foot-tappable tunes. The melodies had to sound fresh, and the lyric had to be open to many interpretations. Although the Beach Boys' two albums in the middle-late sixties did not have new-sounding lyrics, their harmonic language was lush and their manager, Brian Epstein, had seen that the production of the records was all new. The album *Good Vibrations* had an extremely sensual, almost erotic feel, a sound montage combining the mystical with the sexual. It made all groups aware that *a recording was not merely a collection of songs—it could be produced in such a way that it became an experience.* Song after song was arranged in precise order.

Meanwhile, the Beatles were producing new albums, and taking many months in the studio to create their sounds. Although Lennon and McCartney published all their songs under both names, interviews with them have since revealed that at the time McCartney was writing light, almost tender, romantic songs, while Lennon's were grittier, raunchier, hard-edged, with some unusual phrases sounding like symphonic chords that crashed and then disappeared. The sounds on their *Revolver* album were, says Jeremy Pascall in *The Illustrated History of Rock Music* "like running along the dial of a radio and catching brief snips of foreign stations, hearing an orchestra here, an announcer there, some drama in an unrecognized language, a screech, a roar, a crackle of static."

The effect of making the voice purposely *not beautiful* was totally new. (This has spawned a whole generation of emotional singers like Lou Rawls and Bette Midler, to whom the emotion is more important than voice, a situation impossible in the Crosby-Sinatra era.)

In the last cut on *Revolver*, a song called "Tomorrow Never Knows" makes us feel we are in a smoky harem or a Far Eastern cafe. The Beatles bombard us with their message, which now sounds as though it's been shouted over a bullhorn. And the message? It merely tries to calm our fears. They speak of relaxing and surrender; they want us to drift and float. There is nothing wrong, they tell us, in entering the world of the void and observing its colors.

Acid Rock

Of course they are talking about drugs. LSD (Lysergic acid diethylamide), a hallucinogenic that had been known for years, now became a part of the rock culture. The music that it spawned was known as acid rock.

Dr. Albert Hofman, who synthesized it in 1938, took some by accident in 1943 and wrote about his experiences on a "hallucinogenic trip." Clinical tests had proved that LSD could contribute to the cure of schizophrenia, and it was also used to cure alcoholics. The British writer Aldous Huxley wrote that this drug seemed to open "the doors of perception." Gradually a cult developed, most of whom felt that "acid" was perception-altering and mind-expanding.

People like the Beatles, rich, young, curious, were always looking for the novel. They had embraced occult religions, yoga, marijuana, and alcohol. According to "The Love You Make," some of the group tried sex with multiple partners, homosexuality, and even sexual contact with the wife of another member of the group. All these experiments were supposed to have been entered upon to widen one's experience, and since it was generally believed in the late sixties that LSD produced the most extraordinary mental and perceptual experiences, they tried it too. Many people believed that acid obliterated the ego, transforming the taker into a kinder, more loving, helpful, and creative person. LSD was supposed to open your eyes to the beauty around you. Dr. Timothy Leary, high spokesman for "acid tripping" had preached: "It is necessary for us to go out of our minds in order to use our heads," and many in those days listened and followed his suggestion.

The Beatles (who had been turned on to acid by their dentist) found that with its use they could hear clapping as showers of sparks or feel a mild electric shock as a bolt through the whole body. Now they wished the world to know about their experiences under acid, especially the importance of colors. That is why Lennon/McCartney wrote, "Listen to the colors of your dreams." It was said that LSD enlarged colors gigantically so they could actually be felt. (Rock concerts today still spend most of their budgets on flashing lights and lasers of various colors. Music and color have been entwined since Scriabin and his color wheel early in the twentieth century.)

LSD was being manufactured and distributed quite legally in the late sixties, and it is estimated that 300,000 "trips" (a "trip" was a few drops of liquid on a cube of sugar) were disseminated in the Haight-Ashbury district of San Francisco in 1966 in a period of three days! Many, like Ken Kesey and his Merry Pranksters, were handing it out without realizing the consequences, which were now becoming clear—LSD was a dangerous drug. Its effects on the brain were not merely charming and whimsical.

Suddenly it was reported young people were dying under the effects of acid. Taking the drug made youths believe they were invincible. Many believed they could fly and launched themselves off rooftops, and of course, it became illegal to manufacture or possess LSD in Great Britain or the United States. Peter Laurie, in his book on drugs, states that a physical analogy for this "mind enhancing" drug would be "spraying salt water inside a television set"—corrosive and erosive.

It may seem inappropriate in a book devoted to the craft of writing songs to spend time and analyze the acid trips of the sixties, but I believe their influence has continued to pervade popular music. When the Beatles came down from a trip, they were always critical of the work they had done while on acid, because they were always devoted to excellence. But other groups, not so gifted or so fussy, performed on the record what was created under the influence of drugs. Most of the successful groups had their followings, and the record buyers purchased the latest disc because of their charisma.

The form of acid rock wasn't important. The best of Lennon/McCartney seems to use AABA. Of course the contemporary verse-chorus form often shows, as in their "Lucy in the Sky with Diamonds." This alleged tribute to LSD changes meter between the verse, which is written with 3 strong pulses per unit on bar, and chorus, which has 4 pulses per bar. It does another curious thing—it has a happy ending.

"Lucy in the Sky with Diamonds" (Music and lyric by John Lennon and Paul McCartney)

Picture yourself in a boat on a river with tangerine trees, and marmalade skies.
Somebody calls you, you answer quite slowly a girl with kaleidoscope eyes.
Cellophane flowers of yellow and green towering over your head
Look for the girl with the sun in her eyes and she's gone————
LUCY IN THE SKY WITH DIAMONDS
LUCY IN THE SKY WITH DIAMONDS
LUCY IN THE SKY WITH DIAMONDS, AH————
Follow her down to a bridge by a fountain where rocking horse people eat marshmallow pies
Everyone smiles as you drift past the flowers that grow so incredibly high
Newspaper taxis appear on the shore waiting to take you away.
Climb in the back with your head in the clouds and you're gone————
LUCY IN THE SKY WITH DIAMONDS...
Picture yourself on a train to the station with plasticene porters with looking glass ties.
Suddenly someone is there at the turnstile, the girl with kaleidoscope eyes.
LUCY IN THE SKY WITH DIAMONDS...

The title uses the initials of the drug that the songwriters are celebrating, but is inoffensive to those who are not in the know since the image is so fanciful.

L ucy in the
S ky with
D iamonds

Hard Rock

As the Beatles preached their "love everybody" sermons, other groups had an inner violence. These hard-rock groups had strange names like Jefferson Airplane, The Holding Company, the Grateful Dead, and Blood, Sweat and Tears. Some of their members were shy men who said everything through their music. Jimi Hendrix's offstage voice was so soft as to be barely distinguishable. Here is a description of his manner onstage, from Jeremy Pascall's *Illustrated History of Rock Music* (New York: Galahad Books, 1978):

> … Hendrix was a magician. Anyone who saw him would tell you that. He looked like a magician, an afreet. He was a black Heathcliff, wild, maniacal, soaring. He laughed madly on stage as he conjured magic with his guitar. His guitar was this familiar. He made sex magic with it. The notes spun, shot, tumbled, cascaded, pitched, flew, glided, spat, whined, snarled, stuttered, sang and whistled from that guitar. Hendrix made music that no one had heard before. He took ugly tones and made them beautiful. He loved the guitar, he balled it right there on stage, and then flung it from him in disgust, crashed it into the stage. He caressed it, picked its strings with his teeth. He tossed it carefully over his shoulder and still played it. He had complete mastery over it and on stage he was all-powerful. He was the high priest at a pagan ritual, and he conducted the perverse liturgy orchestrating the responses of us his acolytes, building us to a peak of fervor, calming us down, incanting and casting spells, stimulating us to another climax, wringing out our emotions, demanding our utter involvement. He brought us to an orgasm of sacrilegious worship and then he offered his guitar — his magic wand, his staff of life, his phallus — as a sacrifice. He set fire to it and abruptly quit the stage with all the amplifiers howling like tormented djinns. We subsided into our seats. Drained, exalted, emptied, triumphant.

Hendrix's fervor in smashing instruments seems to have been genuine, but it started a whole vogue of rock stars losing control. They are sometimes faking, and sometimes carried away, but even today, no self-respecting hard rock concert is over until at least one guitar has been destroyed.

In the seventies, Kiss was the most popular "gimmick" group. Although their rock was hard, they decided to call attention to themselves through outlandish special effects: explosive devices, snow machines, police lights, rocket-firing guitars, levitating drums, bizarre makeup, outrageous costumes, and a bass player who ate fire and spat blood.

The form of hard rock is generally verse-chorus, often with lyrics that have the same impulsive beat. Often the rhythm takes over from the melodic ideas, and rhyme becomes the most important lyrical device, overshadowing the meaning, as in the excerpt below from Bruce Springsteen's "Blinded by the Light":

Some brimstone baritone, anticyclone rolling stone preacher from the east.
He says "Dethrone the dictaphone, hit it in its funnybone where they expect it least."
And some new-mown chaperone was standin' in the corner all alone
Watching the young girls dance.
And some fresh-sown moonstone was messin' with his frozen zone
To remind him of the feelin' of romance.

BLINDED BY THE LIGHT

OH CUT LOOSE LIKE A DEUCE, ANOTHER RUNNER IN THE NIGHT.

BLINDED BY THE LIGHT

SHE GOT DOWN BUT SHE NEVER GOT TIGHT

BUT SHE'LL MAKE IT

ALRIGHT ...

Bubblegum

To every action there is a reaction. The lyric of "Blinded by the Light," whether you like it or not, does make you think. In the seventies, the reaction to this exercise in interpretation was an interest in juvenile things like puppy love or sweets. Confectionary songs like "Yummy, Yummy, Yummy" (I've got love in my tummy, etc.), "Na, Na, Hey, Hey, Kiss Him Goodbye," and "Chewy Chewy," caught on with the preteens, who now were demanding their own music by their own, generally twelve-year-old, stars. Unfortunately, the trend continued throughout the decade.

Generally in a bubblegum song, the lyrics, the chords, and the harmonic design are naïve. Typical of the period is the song quoted below:

"Sweet Pea" (Music and lyric by Tommy Roe)

Oh, Sweet Pea, come on and dance with me,
Come, on, come on, come on
And dance with me.
Oh Sweet Pea, won't you be my girl?
Won't, you, won't you, won't you be
My girl?
I went to a dance just the other night.
I saw a girl there, she was out of sight.
I asked a friend of mine who she could be,
He said that her friends just call her Sweet Pea.

OH SWEET PEA, I LOVE YOU CAN'T YOU SEE?

LOVE YOU, LOVE YOU, LOVE YOU, CAN'T YOU SEE?

OH, SWEET PEA, WON'T YOU BE MY GIRL?

WON'T YOU, WON'T YOU, WON'T YOU BE MY GIRL.

In the second verse, the young Romeo asks Sweet Pea to dance, and in the third, he gets her away from the dance and takes her out under the stars, where he holds her close. The form and content are typical of this kind of song.

Folk-Rock

Folk-rock is almost a redundancy, since most of the music written since the fifties has been in the rock idiom. Those artists whose roots were in folk would have had to embrace some sort of "folk sound" to keep up with the contemporary. By the mid-sixties they had exchanged their acoustic guitars for amplified ones, raised their concert decibel levels, added more percussion and thus more rhythm to their work, substituted a synthesizer for their acoustic keyboards. All this was relatively easy for them. What was difficult was changing the concepts from the themes of group action or ecology to the more personal ones of rock.

If it is true, as has often been said, that the major figures in rock have been Elvis Presley, the Beatles, and Bob Dylan (some would add the Rolling Stones and The Who), the major figure in the trinity who influenced folk-rock was Dylan.

This man, who had asked where the flowers had gone and how many years were to pass before people were allowed to be free, was a likely candidate to let his lyrics wander into the realm of rock. As he had been influenced by the Beatles, he began in turn to influence them. He told John Lennon that rock should be more than a series of love songs or a group of pleasant tunes with a beat. He eschewed the spaced-out, drugged-out culture and demanded to know "how does it feel to be without purpose? to be like a rolling stone? to have no religion?" The Byrds, the Rolling Stones, and even the Beatles were affected by his questioning, and if they were never able to answer his questions, at least they were aware of the issues.

Bob Dylan signed a group of musicians he'd found playing in New Jersey bars and organized them into a tight rock group called the Band. After the demise of folk-rock in the late sixties, they went on to become a respected name in rock.

Other groups who were influenced were Simon and Garfunkel ("The Sounds of Silence") and Sonny and Cher ("I Got You, Babe"). These led to later groups like the Lovin' Spoonful and the Mamas and the Papas and solo singers like John Sebastian and John Denver.

While they went beyond the bounds of folk-rock, Buffalo Springfield (Neil Young, Stephen Stills, and Jim Messina, among others) had to have been influenced by Dylan. And one cannot imagine the later emergence of an important group like Jefferson Airplane, the other San Francisco bands, the flower children, country rock (into which Dylan was to drift later), the Youngbloods, and even the Eagles had there been no Dylan and no folk-rock.

Folk-rock used the verse-chorus form almost exclusively. It generally limited its message to no more than two verses with an ever-repeating short chorus.

The Seventies

Splintered best describes an era where rock went in many directions. Except for a small amount of theater music (see page 49) all the popular music used rock as its foundation. When an old standard like "I Only Have Eyes for You" was revived, a rock beat was added. There were punk rock, reggae rock, rockabilly, soft rock, Tex-Mex, and a few holdovers from the previous decade—hard rock, acid rock, bubblegum, and folk-rock.

It was not unlike the revolution that occurred when men started removing their ties and women began varying the height of their hemlines. The public was as eclectic as the styles. A woman could dress in jeans one day and the next in mini-skirt, maxi-skirt or floor-length hemline. It was perfectly okay to be sloppy one day, casual the next, and formally elegant on the third. And it was acceptable to enjoy various kinds of music.

The decade began badly, with the death of Janis Joplin and then, barely a month later, of Jimi Hendrix. Also, the Beatles disbanded in 1970, and although Simon and Garfunkel had a big success with "Bridge Over Troubled Water," they too separated shortly after.

In a reaction to the drug and acid rock world, family groups rose to the top: the Osmonds (Mormons who wouldn't even drink coffee) the Jacksons (Jehovah's Witnesses, whose religion forbade liquor, meat, and sex), and the Carpenters (brother and sister, and their sound told you they were "pure").

Perhaps the greatest departure in the seventies was the emergence of many androgynous performers. Of the males, David Bowie freely admitted his homosexuality, Elton John revealed his bisexuality, and Alice Cooper carried transvestitism to absurd lengths with pillows stuffed beneath his clothing. It was definitely a time of sexual confusion.

Some talented women emerged in this decade. It seemed that women, so embroiled in the struggle for equality, did not have to stoop to farce, weird makeup, or bizarre effects; they simply sang. Emmylou Harris, Linda Ronstadt, Olivia Newton-John, Melanie, Helen Reddy, Gladys Knight, even Barbra Streisand seemed to select the best songs of the era.

But the overwhelming influence on the era was disco. It seems to have gotten a stranglehold on and stifled the creativity of the entire decade. I quote again from Jeremy Pascall's *The Illustrated History of Rock Music*:

> ... this was the nadir of music—either black or white. It was precisely the rubbish played in those hellholes to young people of regrettable limited taste. They demanded nothing more than a bland beat to which they could mindlessly gyrate. Disco was this. It chunked along at precisely the same rhythm (to precisely the same tune, most of us would say), with precisely the same instrumentation and precisely the same voices intoning approximately the same words. I said it left its mark on the decade. This is wrong. It slid over the decade like a slug slides across glass and

left the same glistening slime. You didn't notice its arrival and you didn't remark on its departure. Disco was the music of the "dreary decade" in that it was nothing at all. It was the bastardized child of miscegenation between a metronome and a computer. To anyone with the slightest ear it signified the paucity of the times.

Mr. Pascall notwithstanding, disco in the seventies did have a few exciting moments, when the dance and its mesmerizing rhythm became part of the concept. Barry Manilow's "Copacabana," with its verse, chorus form and minor then major melody seemed to create a Latin rock. The Streisand-Summer collaboration on "Enough Is Enough" had an original build-up of volume and excitement.

Reggae, a strong rhythmic pulse similar to bossa nova, had spread from Jamaica and was a revitalizing influence on black performers.

There were of course established creators who followed their own stars — Stevie Wonder, The Rolling Stones, The Who. They emerged from this dismal decade with their creativity flowing as strongly as when they entered it.

One cannot leave any discussion of the decade without mentioning the emergence of the heavy metal sound. Heavy metal implies an improvised blues line (see page 224), with the volume turned way up; the addition of a strong bass line, which is also played at loud decibels; and an amplified drum. It was an attempt to simulate the overamplified stadium sound that occurred at a live rock concert.

The Eighties

It is hard to pinpoint a trend that sums up the eighties because the era was so splintered, but certain movements seem to have occurred that sum up that era's sound.

By the time we reached the 1980s, popular music had adopted rock and roll, and the old pop sound, with its doo-wop back-up and sentimental style, was being sung only by the older generation. "It was a time," an artist like Todd Rundgren tells us, "when music had become secondary to a personality. We became an art of the personality or a personality cult as embodied by people like Madonna and Michael Jackson. This is not to demean their music, although much of it is demeanable, but the music was an adjunct to the selling of their personality." Concepts seem to have broadened, with some new ones surfacing. Major themes that creators in the 1980s explored include technology ("Mister Roboto"); neo-patriotism ("They're Coming to America"); paranoia ("Somebody's Watching Me," "Gloria"); the media ("Dirty Laundry"); and class inequality ("Uptown Girl").

Splintering continued with some big hits reverting to the old-fashioned love song ("Hello," "Truly"); the old rock 'n' roll ("Rock This Town"); pure sexuality ("Muscles," "Rapture," "Sexual Healing"); and machismo ("To All the Girls I Loved Before," "Maneater").

Form remained traditional with the most popular constructions by far being: a) verse, chorus, verse, chorus with a bridge sometimes added before a return to the final chorus; b) 12-bar Blues; and c) A, A, Bridge A, especially constructed on the "Heart and Soul" or rock and roll (I, VI, II, V) harmonic pattern.

Rhyme, influenced by new wave, punk, and childlike rap, became singsongy, a bit pretentious, with omitted or padded words to maintain its even quality.

Recorded sound and MTV became much more vital to a record's popularity. The synthesizer, which is capable of echoless cut-off, seemed largely to have replaced acoustic instruments. Background groups with unusual rhythmic clapping were prevalent. (Knowledgable songwriters were aware of this and left room in their phrases for a rhythmic answer.)

Superstar duos were especially popular: Kenny Rogers with Dolly Parton or Sheena Easton; Julio Iglesias with Willie Nelson; Michael Jackson with Paul McCartney.

Androgyny reached a new high, with Culture Club's Boy George, Michael Jackson, and David Bowie its foremost practitioners.

Gone were the seventies' obsessions with feminism and ecology (although we were aware of the possibility of nuclear holocaust, songwriters seemed to avoid this concept), and rap, speaking over a rhythmic line, had not yet become as popular as it was to become in succeeding decades.

For music and lyrics of the 1990s and beyond 2000, see the Appendix.

COUNTRY

Since the mid-sixties, country music, (the additional "and western" is rarely used now) has had a steady rise in popularity. It has outlasted the disco vogue and even outdistanced blues. Country songs are no longer parochial, and they no longer need a western lope. Radio stations in all urban centers that formerly played only the latest jazz and rock are now switching to country.

The borders of country are stretching. Rockabilly, country-rock, and country-funk are being explored. While those words refer more to musical and rhythmic departures than they do to lyric construction, they often influence the form into which the song is cast.

Concept is fast changing and abandoning its old-fashioned ways. Multiple rape is avenged in "The Coward of the County"; infanticide is suggested in "Ode to Billy Joe"; an older white man's seduction of a young black woman is approved in "We've Got Tonight." These concepts would have been taboo in previous decades.

The cowboy song, formerly the archetypical country song, has been replaced by the country-style song that lauds or complains about life in the big city. Billy Joel tells us (replete with harmonica) that he is in a "New York State of Mind," and discusses a sleazy piano bar in an urban center in "Piano Man." In "Billy the

Kid" he enlarges the canvas, emerging from "West Virginia with a six shooter in his hand" to "from Oyster Bay, Long Island, rode a boy with a six-pack in his hand." Even Dolly Parton, purely a country lass, talks about working in the city — nine to five.

Although all forms are now saleable, the verse-chorus form is still the most popular. An accessible chorus, repeated many times, is the quickest way to popularize a song. I'll illustrate by using an old chestnut whose third verse gives a clue to the romanticism in the cowboy's soul. The concept of home is still most prevalent — from leaving home to be free, to going home for love and acceptance.

"Home on the Range" (Traditional)

Oh, give me a home where the buffalo roam,
Where the deer and the antelope play
Where seldom is heard a discouraging word,
And the skies are not cloudy all day.

HOME, HOME ON THE RANGE,
WHERE THE DEER AND THE ANTELOPE PLAY,
WHERE SELDOM IS HEARD A DISCOURAGING WORD,
AND THE SKIES ARE NOT CLOUDY ALL DAY.

Where the air is so pure and the zephyrs so free
And the breezes so balmy and light
That I would not exchange my home on the range
For all of the cities so bright.

(CHORUS)

How often at night when the heavens are bright
With the light from the glittering stars,
Have I stood there amazed and asked as I gazed
If their glory exceeds that of ours.

(CHORUS)

Although in a famous lawsuit "Home on the Range" was judged to be in the public domain, a ninety-year-old woman having sung it through in court and sworn that her husband and companions had sung it while riding herd long before the turn of the century, it feels to me more like a composed song. The chorus might have "just grown," but the verses, with their inner rhymes (*heard, word; exchange, range; amazed, gazed*) and non-cowboy language (*zephyrs, balmy, glittering, glory*), seem to have been constructed in a studio rather than on the prairies.

In addition to the popular verse-chorus form, there is a certain kind of country song with simple melody that merely repeats verses. This is often a narrative song, as well illustrated by an old American folk tune, "Down in the Valley." A large slice of Americana is wrapped in the story of the young man waiting in jail to be executed, hoping his true love (for whom he attacked and inadvertently killed another suitor) will send him some sign of her feelings. The castle "forty feet high" refers to the gallows.

"Down in the Valley"

Down in the valley, valley so low,
Hang your head over, hear the wind blow.

Hear the wind blow, love, hear the wind blow
Hang your head over, hear the wind blow.

If you don't love me, love whom you please;
Throw your arms 'round me, give my heart ease.

Give my heart ease, love, give my heart ease;
Throw your arms 'round me, give my heart ease.

Write me a letter, send it by mail,
Send it in care of Birmingham Jail.

Birmingham Jail, love, Birmingham Jail.
Send it in care of Birmingham Jail.

Write me a letter, only three lines
Answer my question, "Will you be mine?"

Will you be mine, dear, will you be mine?
Answer this question, "Will you be mine?"

Build me a castle forty feet high
So I can see her as she goes by.

As she goes by, dear, as she goes by,
So I can see her as she goes by.

Roses love sunshine, vi'lets love dew;
Angels in heaven know I love you.

Know I love you, dear, know I love you,
Angels in heaven know I love you.

Unity and accessibility are achieved in this form by the repetition of the last few words, making every other verse sound like a kind of chorus. (In fact the song is most effective when performed this way.)

Johnny Cash's "Folsom Prison Blues" features a series of verses, in this case 4-line. Like "Down in the Valley" it uses a simple melody that makes a chorus unnecessary.

I hear that train a-comin', it's rollin' round the bend
And I ain't seen the sun shine since I don't know when,
I'm stuck in Folsom Prison and time keeps draggin' on
But that train keeps rollin' on down to San Antone.

When I was just a baby my mama tole me, son
Always be a good boy, don't ever play with guns
But I shot a man in Reno, just to watch him die.
When I hear that whistle blowin' I hang my head and cry.

I bet there's rich folks in a fancy dinin' car,
They're probably drinkin' coffee and smokin' big cigars.
But I know I had it comin', and I know I can't be free
But those people keep a-movin' and that's what tortures me.

Well, if they freed me from this prison, if that railroad train was mine,
I bet I'd move it over a little farther down the line
Far from Folsom Prison, that's where I want to stay,
And I'd let that lonesome whistle blow my blues away.

The theme of wanderlust is beautifully set out in Jimmy Webb's "By the Time I Get to Phoenix." Three verses are a necessary part of the plan of the work: morning, when the wanderer leaves for Phoenix; noontime in Albuquerque; and evening, when he crosses the Oklahoma border. I quote the last, moving, verse:

By the time I make Oklahoma she'll be sleepin'.
She'll turn softly and call my name out low.
And she'll cry just to think I'd really leave her,
Tho' time and time I tried to tell her so.
She just didn't know
I would really go.

The A^1, A^2, Bridge, A^3 form is much used in country music. It is illustrated by Kris Kristofferson's "Help Me Make It Through the Night" and in "Don't It Make My Brown Eyes Blue?" (music and lyric by Richard Leigh).

Don't know when I've been so blue,
Don't know what's come over you.
You've found someone new
And don't it make my brown eyes blue?

I'll be fine when you're gone,
I'll just cry all night long,
Say it isn't true
And don't it make my brown eyes blue?

Tell me no secrets, tell me some lies.
Give me no reasons, give me alibis,
Tell me you love me and don't let me cry
Say anything, but don't say goodbye.

I didn't mean to treat you bad.
I didn't know just what I had
But, honey, now I do
And don't it make my brown eyes blue?

In the mid-eighties, country music seemed to be heading into 3/4 rhythm, something like a slow waltz, creating a lilt that is missing from rock, which is always in 4/4. Something naïve, or old-fashioned, about this triple time appeals to the audience of country music.

The most popular form by far is verse, chorus, verse, chorus. Next in frequency would be A^1, A^2, Bridge, A^3, and rarely the theatrical ABAC.

YOUR STYLE

In the early twenty-first century, there are so many styles and trends open for any songwriter's creation. Certainly the major trends, like pop, rock, punk rock, hip-hop, and country, are all hitting the tops of the charts. But I urge you as songwriters to be true to your own aesthetic. Frank Sinatra sang the same kind of songs he sang in the forties decades later, and he still sold a heap of records. Country stars like Ernest Tubb did not alter their style in years, and perhaps that is the very reason for their success.

There is no doubt that the role of a popular songwriter (except for those writing for the musical theater) has changed in the last fifty years. Today's pop songwriters generally perform their own material. They must be conversant with sound mixing, amplification, instrumental accompaniment onstage and in studio. If you are writing in current fashion, you will need to know a great deal about studio-created sounds.

In choosing the style that you will write in, I'd advise you to:

1. Write in a style that is comfortable to you.
2. Choose a suitable form for that style (A^1, A^2, Bridge, A^3 for a ballad; verse-chorus for country; etc.).
3. Learn to sing your song yourself. (Put it into a suitable key for your voice; find some kind of instrumental backing.)
4. Make a home recording demo and listen to it critically.

2 TYPES OF SONGS

THE FIRST SECTION analyzed form and the different styles of song lyrics so that when you wrote something, it would sound professional. This section will be devoted to the different types of songs that professional composer-lyricists write. Sometimes it is an assignment for an industrial show, sometimes a needed flip side of a record. Occasionally, a performer asks for a piece of special material. Sometimes a songwriter goes beyond the purely creative because of a desire for a record that will hit the charts.

I believe, and would suggest, that the beginning songwriter should create several songs in each of the following categories. Advanced songwriters may use this section when they are scrounging around for ideas or looking for a concept.

STARTING WITH PARODIES

I have found in my classes that the easiest way to approach lyric writing for the first time is through writing parodies. Parody is a wonderful exercise for putting the correct number of syllables against a given melody.

So many lyricists are fascinated with word games (after all, they are constantly fitting syllables into a given number of notes). They fall naturally into parody. Anyone interested in working in advertising will need to be able to write parodies, for many commercials are parodies of songs we know. If you are an amateur lyricist, parody is useful for organization meetings, goodbye luncheons, and other occasions. Parodies to melodies that are in the public domain (not under copyright) can be published but must have the approval of the original creator.

Things to Remember When Writing Parody

1. The song you parodize *must* be well known. There is no sense parodizing an obscure song like "London in July" because the listener must be able to imagine the original song as the parody goes by. "Hello, Dolly" could become "Goodbye, Ronnie" or "Bonsoir, Fifi," or "Shalom, Molly." "New York, New York" could become "L.A., L.A." or "Detroit, Detroit."
2. The accents *must match*. Nothing is worse than humor handled clumsily. "Newark, Newark" as a parody for "New York, New York" would make any listener cringe.
3. The rhymes must come in the same places as the original. Analyze the rhyme scheme of the song you are parodizing, and be sure your song follows it (see below).
4. As a general rule, treat your subject with humor or irony. Topical references make amusing parodies, but of course they don't have a long life. Nothing is duller than yesterday's news.

"New York, New York" (Music by
    John Kander, Lyric by Fred Ebb)

"Attack Iraq" (Lyric by Lizanne Feller)

Start spreadin' the news (1)
I'm leavin' today (2)
I want to be a part of it (3)
New (4) York, New York.

When critics chimed in (1)
Complained I talk bad (2)
Found me a way to make 'em quit (3)
A(4)ttack Iraq.

These vagabond shoes (1)
Are longin' to stray (2)
And step around the heart of it (3)
New (4) York, New York.

Convinced 'em I'd win (1)
Outdo dear old dad (2)
While TV spread the news of it (3)
A(4)ttack Iraq.

I want to wake up in the City that
    doesn't sleep (5)
To find I'm king of the hill, Top of the
    heap (5)

Got re-elected with a mandate for
    four more years (5)
By simply wavin' the flag; playin' on
    fears (5)

My little town blues (1)
Are meltin' away (2)
I'll make a brand new start of it (3)
In old New (4) York.

My schoolboyish grin (1)
Still makes folks feel glad (2)
The press don't guess the ruse of it, (3)
A(4)ttack Iraq.

If I can make it there (6)
I'd make it anywhere (6)
Come on, come through (4)
New (4) York, New York.

To get a first-class war (6)
You'll be remembered for (6)
I tell you, suh, (4)
A(4)ttack Iraq!

WRITING LYRICS TO SONGS IN THE PUBLIC DOMAIN

As will be discussed in more detail in the section on copyright, every song goes into public domain (that is when its music or lyrics or both can be used by anyone without payment of royalty) seventy years after the death of its author. If the song is a cooperative effort, it remains under copyright until seventy years after the death of the last collaborator (see note on public-domain songs in the Appendix). To you, the lyricist, this means there are thousands of melodies written by classical or long-since-deceased composers that are fair game for popular songs.

This idea was born way back in the nineteenth century, when French words were added to Chopin's theme for his Etude in E Major (Op. 10, #3), and "Tristesse," as it was called, became a favorite of the Parisian salon. Chopin would have cringed, especially had he realized the amount of money being made from the sheet sale of his music, but of course this was a time before copyright laws.

Early in the twenties, "I'm Always Chasing Rainbows" was adapted from Chopin's *Fantasie-Impromptu*. Then the favorite composer for music stealing became Tchaikovsky. His "Moon Love" (Fifth Symphony), "Our Love" (Romeo and Juliet Overture), "Tonight We Love" (Piano Concerto), "This Is the Story of a Starry Night" (Sixth Symphony) were all well-known hits of the forties and fifties. This Russian composer's mine of melody was the basis of all the songs used in Walt Disney's full-length animated feature *Sleeping Beauty* as well. "The Anniversary Song," one of the big hits of the forties, is a Russian waltz by Ivanovici to which words have been appended. Nor were French composers immune. Debussy was tapped for his "Reverie," which became "My Reverie." Ravel's "Pavane (for a Dead Princess)" became "The Lamp Is Low."

When Wright and Forrest succeeded with "Song of Norway," using the music of Edvard Grieg, they were launched into the big time. They continued with *Kismet*, using Borodin's music, and had a song that hit the charts—"Stranger in Paradise." They followed this with an adaptation of the Anastasia story, using Rachmaninoff's music, but by this time both the vogue and their inspiration had flown.

Classically trained singers have always enjoyed classical melodies whose range shows off the breadth of their voices. For Mario Lanza, the traditional Neopolitan folk song "O Sole Mio!" was adapted to become "There's No Tomorrow."

Simon and Garfunkel had one of their greatest successes with "Scarborough Fair," although this was a revival of a medieval melody, and not strictly in the realm of adaptation. The most successful of all is probably Elvis Presley's "Love Me Tender," which is merely a new lyric for the old song "Aura Lee."

More recent adaptations have included Barry Manilow's "Could It Be Magic," which is based on the chords of Chopin's Prelude in C Minor; Walter Murphy's "A Fifth of Beethoven;" and Eric Carmen's adaptation of Rachmaninoff called "Never Gonna Fall in Love Again."

Things to Remember When Writing Lyrics to Songs in the Public Domain

1. Check with the Library of Congress in Washington, D.C., to be sure the song *is* in the public domain. Very old songs like "Tea for Two," "Alexander's Ragtime Band," and "Happy Birthday" are, surprisingly, still under copyright. Don't risk a lawsuit.
2. Check for singability. Some songs may be in the public domain, but have too broad a range for successful adaptation (Puccini arias). They may have too many notes per square inch, which makes them more instrumental than vocal (Scott Joplin's "The Entertainer" or "Maple Leaf Rag").
3. Go back to the *original* melody and adapt your lyric to this, *not* to some other lyricist's or composer's version, which may be different enough from the original to be under copyright. If you follow the published version of "Down in the Valley," which varies slightly from the original folk tune, you would be liable for copyright infringement.
4. Do not use the entire melody of a classical piece. Be sure you adapt by taking out any sections difficult to sing. Adapt means *simplify*.
5. Give credit to the original composer (under the title). Too many songwriters are shy about mentioning that their original melody came from another source. I believe it takes a certain sense of originality and a great feeling for what is timely to create an adaptation. Most musicians will know the origin of the melody anyway, so be big about it, and approach adaptation as an art.

WRITING A LYRIC TO ALREADY EXISTING MUSIC

Throughout the forties and fifties, movie themes were wordless. Every one of the big bands had its own wordless theme song. Sometimes the public clamored to sing some purely instrumental songs, and lyricists were assigned (with varying degrees of success) to versify the music. The technique is not easy to master, for instrumental music can often have wide skips that are hard to sing, or a bunch of notes strung together that sound marvelous as part of a saxophone riff but make words impossible to understand.

"Laura" (music by David Raksin, lyric by Johnny Mercer) has become a standard of the jazz repertoire, and it started life as a movie theme. Johnny Mercer aimed to distill the leading character's fabulous beauty and mystery, and he succeeded notably:

Laura, is the face in the misty night
Footsteps that you hear down the hall,
The laugh that floats on a summer night

That you can never quite recall.
And you see Laura on a train that is passing by
Those eyes, how familiar they seem
She gave your very first kiss to you
That was Laura,
But she's only a dream!

The theme from a successful Bette Davis movie, *Now, Voyager*, became a song entitled "Wrong, Could It Be Wrong to Love?" and the expansive theme from *Gone with the Wind* became "My Own True Love." Of course, today movie songs come complete with lyrics, but there are still successful instrumentals that need words.

Johnny Mercer did a masterful job of setting Erroll Garner's theme song "Misty," noteworthy in the section where Garner's melody sweeps up to a sustained note. He handles these spots cleverly by using throw-away words on the quick notes leading to strong words like *clinging, sound,* and *right foot.*

In the "One-Note Samba," his task is even more complicated, because he must get so many notes into the rapid tempo. I print the bridge opposite.

All these rapid-fire pitches are intelligible because Mercer has chosen short syllables.

TRANSLATIONS

When a song becomes successful in one country, its record may be released internationally. Aware that most people want to sing it in a language they understand, the publisher and the recording company will hire a lyricist to translate the song. (It is rare indeed for a song like "Volare (Nel Blu, Di Pinto Di Blu)" to reach the top of the charts when sung in its original Italian, as was the case in 1958.)

The lyricist is provided with a literal translation. If you are ever hired to translate a foreign song, I hope you will approach the project as most professional lyricists do. They use the original lyric as a point of departure and often take off from there. They get their ideas from the title and the musical line.

Johnny Mercer turned Jacques Prévert's rueful poem *Les Feuilles Mortes* (The Dead Leaves) into a splendid lyric called "The Autumn Leaves." He observed all the rules of lyric writing by starting with the hook or title and closing with it. In addition, he assembled all the images to make a chronological climax at the peak of the music. He was setting Prévert's concept, and *not* translating exactly. Most important, he was being led by the balance in the music and its emotion. Kosma, the composer, had set the place where the rhymes should come. I quote from the beginning and end of the song.

"Les Feuilles Mortes"	"The Dead Leaves" (literal translation)	"The Autumn Leaves"
C'est un chanson		The autumn leaves
Qui nous rassemble,	This is a song	Drift by my window
Toi, tu m'aimais	That resembles us.	The falling leaves
Et je t'amais	You, you loved me	Of red and gold
	And I loved you	
Et la mer efface		But I miss you
Sur le sable	And the sea erases	Most of all, my darling,
Les pas des amants	On the sand	When autumn leaves
Désunis.	The footsteps of the	Start to fall.
	Disunited lovers.	

It is rare indeed, and usually sounds dreadful, when the translator uses a literal translation, but it is advisable to come close to the original title, to capitalize on whatever success the song may so far have achieved. "Two Loves Have I" is an exact translation of "J'ai Deux Amours"; "Mon Homme" translates to "My Man." Conversely, "Duerme?," which became "Feelings," and "Que Reste-t'il" (literally, "what remains"), which became "I Wish You Love," have nothing to do with their original foreign titles and were hits anyway. Perhaps they are the exceptions that prove the rule.

Often it is better to leave evidence of the song's foreign roots in the lyric. Edith Piaf's "La Vie en Rose" was retitled "You're Too Dangerous, Chérie" and flopped miserably, but when the intriguing French title was retained and a new, more intimate lyric was written, it became a standard.

Other well-known translations are "Speak to Me of Love"; "Mack the Knife"; "If You Love Me, Really Love Me"; "The Girl from Ipanema"; "Love Is Blue"; "Pigalle"; "El Rancho Grande"; "What Now, My Love?"; and "Gloria."

STORY SONGS

After parody, where the rhythm is laid out for the lyricist and even the subject to be parodized is suggested, the next kind of song to try is a story song. Every one of us has the ability to make up some sort of story. Sometimes the point of departure can be folklore or fairy tale or even an intriguing article in a newspaper. Often the story will need a twist, like the "Piña Colada Song" ("Escape"), in which he doesn't know that his "lovely lady" likes piña coladas; he advertises for someone who does, and his "lovely lady" answers the ad. This switch makes the story interesting. It also lends itself to three choruses. Country songs are frequently story songs. "The Coward of the County" is a good example.

An original gem is Cole Porter's "The Tale of the Oyster."

A¹ **THEME**	Down by the sea lived a lonesome oyster, Ev'ry day getting sadder and moister He found his home life awf'lly wet And longed to travel with the upper set Poor little oyster!
REPEAT OF **A¹ THEME**	Fate was kind to that oyster, we know, When one day the chef from the Park Casino Saw that oyster lying there And said, "I'll put you on my bill of fare." Lucky little oyster!
A¹ THEME **ALTERED** **HARMONICALLY**	See him on his silver platter Watching the queens of fashion chatter, Hearing the wives of millionaires Discuss their marriages and their love affairs. Thrilled little oyster!
A¹ THEME **ALTERED** **MELODICALLY**	See that bivalve social climber Feeding the rich Mrs. Hoggenheimer; Think of his joy as he gaily glides Down to the middle of her gilded insides. Proud little oyster!
BRIDGE	After lunch Mrs. H. complains And says to her hostess, "I've got such pains! I came to town on my yacht today, But I think I'd better hurry back to Oyster Bay." Scared little oyster!

REPEAT	Off they go through the troubled tide
OF	The yacht rolling madly from side to side.
BRIDGE	They've tossed about till that poor young oyster
	Finds that it's time he should leave his cloister
	Up comes the oyster!

RETURN OF	Back again where he started from
A¹ THEME	He murmured, "I haven't a single qualm,
	For I've had a taste of society,
	And society has had a taste of me."
	Wise little oyster!

John Kander and Fred Ebb, who are masters of the story song, wrote one for Liza Minnelli that has a New York flavor while at the same time suiting Miss Minnelli's personality. It is of the contemporary form verse-chorus, with lots of repeats.

"Ring Them Bells"

VERSE	Gather around, I've got a story to tell
	About a Manhattan lady that I know very well.
	She lives at 5 Riverside, her name is Shirley DeVore,
	And she traveled round the world to meet the guy next door.

VERSE 2	Well, there was trouble inside Apartment 29E
	Cause Shirley's mother and dad were as upset as can be.
	They said, "We hate to complain, dear, and we don't like to grouse,
	But you're nearly thirty-two, you should get out of the house!"

CHORUS	YOU GOTTA RING THEM BELLS
	YOU GOTTA RING THEM BELLS
	YOU GOTTA MAKE THEM SING,
	YOU GOTTA RING THEM BELLS
	IT'S SUCH A HAPPY THING
	TO HEAR THEM TING-A-LING
	YOU GOTTA RING THEM BELLS

In succeeding verses, Mr. Ebb goes on to tell us about how Shirley borrowed some money and flew to Europe, where, after "bombing out" in several countries, she was steered toward Yugoslavia. There on the beach she met a guy who "took her reason away" and was stunned to find out that he lived in the same Riverside Drive apartment building—actually right next door. Of course the title "Ring Them Bells" (which we assumed to be imaginary wedding bells) now takes on a new meaning. Kander and Ebb meant *doorbells*! The revelation makes everyone smile. And then before a final chorus, the lyricist hits us with a moral:

> Well, there's a moral to learn from little Shirley DeVore
> Who had to borrow a thou to find a lover next door—
> You girls who live in apartments, don't just stare at the walls
> Open up the door and hurry out in the hall—
>
> AND RING THEM BELLS
> COME ON AND RING THEM BELLS ...

The verse-chorus form can get a little tiresome in a long song with lots of verses, so to maintain the interest of chorus, I wrote the following, where each succeeding chorus is different.

"Raffetin et Nicolette" (Music and lyric by Stephen Citron)

> They had just turned sixteen when they met in Marseilles
> They fell madly in love and they hurried away
> To Paree where they opened a tiny cafe
> With a few extra seats
> That were out on the street.
> He managed the kitchen while she tended bar,
> And inside of a year Michelin gave them a "star."
>
> RAFFETIN ET NICOLETTE
> IT IS KNOWN AS THE PLACE FOR THE BEST BOUILLABAISSE
> AND THEY GIVE YOU WINE
> WHILE YOU STAND IN LINE
> AT CHEZ RAFFETIN ET NICOLETTE.
>
> After counting the till they'd sit down for a drink
> Then a scheming Parisienne in diamonds and mink
> Said to Raffetin, "Chéri, I really do think
> You could charge a lot more with a smarter decor."
> So she mirrored the walls, and before she was through
> She replaced all the dishes, and Nicolette too.
>
> NOW IT'S RAFFETIN ET DOMINIQUE
> AND IT'S QUAIL'S EGGS IN ASPIC AND TERRIBLY CHIC;
> YOU DON'T EAT — YOU DINE
> AND THERE IS NO LINE
> AT CHEZ RAFFETIN ET DOMINIQUE.

Well, that left Nicolette in a shaky condition
But like all the French, she had lots of ambition.
She called on a friend with a clear proposition
"Your profits are vast when your turnover's fast"
He had plenty of money he couldn't explain
And he gambled it all on a crêperie chain

NOW IT'S MANUEL ET NICOLETTE
AND WHEREVER YOU GO FROM CALAIS TO BORDEAUX
THERE ARE NEON SIGNS AND ENORMOUS LINES
AT CHEZ MANUEL ET NICOLETTE.

When she heard Dominique had abandoned her man
Nicolette left Manuel and sought out Raffetin,
But insisted he'd have to agree to her plan—
Change the sign on the door, rip the rug from the floor.
He would now work the kitchen while she tended bar
And she watched like a hawk so he never strayed far.

BACK TO NICOLETTE ET RAFFETIN
AND IT'S KNOWN AS THE PLACE FOR THE BEST BOUILLABAISSE
AND SHE CALLS THE SHOTS WHILE HE SCRUBS THE POTS
AT CHEZ NICOLETTE ET RAFFETIN
NICOLETTE ET RAFFETIN
NOW SHE'S GOT THE TOP BILLING
THE FISH SOUP IS THRILLING.
THEY GIVE YOU WINE, WHILE YOU WAIT IN LINE
AT CHEZ NICOLETTE ET RAFFETIN.

Dos and Don'ts for Story Songs

1. Use verse-chorus form.
2. Most story songs are in the third person; the singer pulls the audience in by telling what happened to so-and-so.
3. Take your time. Most story songs are three or more verses.
4. A good method of working is to write your story in prose first, *then* write the chorus, which will comment on the action.
5. Last of all, write the verses.

DESCRIPTIVE SONGS

After the story-song concept, I find the descriptive song the easiest to write. All of us have encountered some intriguing person or can make up a fictional character worth writing about. Since in the song the person is usually fixed in time, with little character development, I'd advise you to find as interesting a person as possible. The person need not be real. Often, in lyrics, we make our protagonists larger than life.

Billy Joel describes himself (when young) in "Piano Man"—he tells us what the pianist in the bar is thinking and especially how he reacts to his customers. In the end, with the line "man, what are you doing here?" we know that the piano man will someday break out of this sleazy bar. The same songwriter describes an uptown girl in his song of that name, and we get a picture of both the downtown boy and the uptown girl, because we see how he imagines her. As I said above, the picture may not be real—all that matters is that the lyricist gets us to believe it.

Along the way, the song may digress from the title person to make a point; in fact, the songs with an extra dimension—like "Eleanor Rigby," which not only talks about Eleanor, but Father McKenzie and mostly about alienation—are most successful. "Gloria," a song that made the charts in the early eighties, told us about Gloria's *illusions* of popularity and asked the question "Why is nobody calling?" This is more interesting than a mere listing of the subject's traits. "Mickey" is sung by a girl who thinks Mickey is fine. We assume from the lyric that Mickey is gay, and although she dotes on him, he will not give her a tumble. She says, almost angrily, "It's guys like you—" This is putting the person written about in a social situation. Analyze "Eleanor Rigby" and you'll see what I mean.

"Eleanor Rigby" (Music and lyric by John Lennon and Paul McCartney)

Ah! Look at all the lonely people
Ah! Look at all the lonely people.
Eleanor Rigby picks up the rice in the church where a wedding has been,
Lives in a dream
Waits at the window
Wearing the face that she keeps in a jar by the door,
Who is it for?

ALL THE LONELY PEOPLE
WHERE DO THEY ALL COME FROM
ALL THE LONELY PEOPLE
WHERE DO THEY ALL BELONG?

Father McKenzie writing the words of a sermon that no one will hear,
No one comes near.
Look at him working,
Darning his socks in the night when there's nobody there,
What does he care?

(CHORUS)

Eleanor Rigby died in the church and was buried along with her name.
Nobody came.
Father McKenzie
Wiping the dirt from his hands as he walks from the grave,
No one was saved.

(CHORUS)

In 1981, a song that topped the charts described a person with fascinating eyes; even though they were beautiful, the concept tells us to beware since the girl is a tease and has "Bette Davis Eyes." Notice how this song zeroes in on that one important feature just as Gilbert and Sullivan spoofed a Victorian major-general in *The Pirates of Penzance* and concentrated on his tremendous knowledge of useless and outdated facts. I quote from the second chorus:

I'm very good at integral and differential calculus
I know the scientific names of beings animalculous,

and later

I know our mythic history, King Arthur's and Sir Caradoc's
I answer hard acrostics, I've a pretty taste for paradox
I quote in elegaics all the crimes of Heliogabalus
In conics I can floor peculiarities parabolous.

In the last verse they decide to face the problem straight on and have the major-general say, "For my military knowledge, though I'm plucky and adventury/ Has only been brought down to the beginning of the century." Of course this makes a much more interesting song than mere description. It puts the major-general in his times.

"Sunny" is a curious kind of descriptive song. I'm sure its melody, which is fresh and bright, had the greatest influence on its success. But "Sunny" has a few other things going for it. It has a dark melody, which is always an intriguing idea with a bright lyric; it can be sung by either man or woman; it repeats the title many times and its words describe an especially bright and *sincere* young person, whom the singer loves.

The next three choruses (and I call this song with no verse all choruses because they are so short) are in the same vein [as the above;] they tell us a bit more about the reaction of the singer to Sunny.

Descriptive songs are all about us. In addition to the ones listed above, the lyricist can instantly recall oldies like "Dolores"; "Charmaine"; "Nina"; "Laura";

"Nancy with the Laughing Face"; "The Girl That I Marry"; "Rio Rita"; "Lydia the Tattooed Lady"; and later ones like "Maybellene"; "Venus"; "Mame"; "Michelle." Songs about men are fewer, but there are "Jim"; "Vincent"; "Bill"; "Jude"; "Frank Mills."

The descriptive song need not be limited to a person. Any place that interests you is suitable for description. As with the personal song, if you add another dimension besides a travelogue description of the area, your song will have another dimension. Jim Webb's "Galveston" is successful partly because it describes the city, but mostly because it mentions the girl who is missed and the soldier's fear of death. The contrast between "My Blue Heaven" and "The Hive," both songs about newlyweds' homes, is enormous; the former is happy pictorial, the latter is trenchant statement.

"My Blue Heaven" (Music and lyric by Walter Donaldson)

When whipporwills call
And ev'ning is nigh
I hurry to my blue heaven.

A turn to the right
A little white light,
Will lead you to my blue heaven.

You'll see a smiling face,
A fireplace, a cozy room
A little nest that's nestled
Where the roses bloom.

Just Molly and me,
And Baby makes three,
We're happy in my blue heaven.

"The Hive" (Music and lyric by Jim Webb)

See her walkin' whitely,
As though she really was a virgin
With her tiny feet precisely on the line.
And she thinks her whitely thoughts
About the whitely things she bought
And the altar crouches silently

Waiting for the virgin to arrive.
And you can almost hear her buzzin' in the hive!

They play the whitely music
As though it was really music
In the parking lot they're lettering a sign.
The preacher says the proper thing,
And then the rusty alto sings,
And now they'll all get roaring drunk
Pretendin' they're essentially alive,
While the grand procession leads into the hive!

God bless our happy cubicle,
Keep it safe and sanitized
Homogenized and pasteurized.
There's no place like numb.
Behold the female disappearing through the doorway
She never really fought it
And now, by God she's got it
And the altar crouches silently,
Waiting for the virgin to arrive,
And you can almost hear her screamin'
In the hive!

Some examples of the descriptive place song are: "Chicago"; "I Left My Heart in San Francisco"; "Manchester, England"; "New York, New York"; "New York State of Mind"; "I Happen to Like New York"; "Do You Know What it Means to Miss New Orleans"; "Between Eighteenth and Nineteenth on Chestnut Street"; "Shenandoah"; "Autumn in New York"; "April in Paris"; "Memphis in June"; "Gary, Indiana." The best of these express a longing to return, because of either homesickness or an uncompleted love affair.

SITUATION SONGS

The situation song differs from the story song in that the protagonist is fixed in a period of time, and it differs from the descriptive song in that it does much more than describe a person or place. It creates a dramatic situation, and it tells only part of a story by painting a dramatic scene. Often the hero or heroine is trapped in a desperate situation. What could be more pessimistic than "Ten Cents a Dance," written by Richard Rodgers with lyrics by Larry Hart in 1930, at the onset of the Great Depression. (I have numbered the lines for easy referral in the analysis that immediately follows.)

"Ten Cents a Dance"

VERSE	1	I work at the Palace Ballroom
		But, gee, that Palace is cheap.
		When I get back to my chilly hallroom
		I'm much too tired to sleep.
	5	I'm one of those lady teachers
		A beautiful hostess, you know.
		One that the Palace features
		At exactly a dime a throw.
A¹		Ten cents a dance,
	10	That's what they pay me,
		Gosh, how they weigh me down.
A²		Ten cents a dance
		Pansies and rough guys
		Tough guys who tear my gown.
BRIDGE	15	Seven to midnight I hear drums
		Loudly the saxophone blows
		Trumpets are tearing my eardrums,
		Customers crush my toes.
A³		Sometimes I think
	20	I've found my hero
		But it's a queer romance.
		All that you need is a ticket
(WITH		Come on, big boy,
EXTENSION)		Ten cents a dance.
INTERLUDE	25	Fighters and sailors, and bow-legged tailors
		Can pay for their tickets and rent me.
		Butchers and barbers and rats from the harbors
		Are sweethearts my "good luck" has sent me.
		Though I've a chorus of elderly beaus,
	30	Stockings are porous with holes at the toes
		I'm here till closing time,
		Dance and be merry — it's only a dime!

REPEAT		Sometimes I think
OF		I've found my hero
A³ WITH	35	But it's a queer romance.
EXTENSION		All that you need is a ticket,
		Come on, big boy,
		Ten cents a dance.

Although many of the topics that follow will not be discussed until later chapters, it is impossible for me not to comment on this song, which I believe to be one of the best *and worst* ever written. Remember — in studying songwriting, you can learn more from someone else's mistakes than from their successes.

line 2: *gee* gives us an immediate social class of the hostess.

line 3: *hallroom* — there is no such word, obviously inserted to rhyme with *ballroom*.

lines 1-5: these tell us much about the singer, her work, her educational background, her dislike of her job.

line 6: an ironic or sarcastic statement, one that will occur again in line 28.

line 8: it's very good to end the verse with "a dime a throw," for it's always more interesting to use a synonym for what you wish to say in a verse, saving the title line for the chorus.

line 9: wonderful title; it sings.

line 13: *pansies* is the wrong word; at that time it was a derogatory term for *gays*, and you would never have found a male homosexual in a dance hall.

line 15: "hear drums": the accent is wrong, it is obviously thrown in to rhyme with "eardrums"

line 16: "Loudly the saxophone blows" would never be said by the same girl who says "gee" and "gosh."

line 20: "hero and queer ro-(mance) are intended to rhyme, but the rhyme is hollow, for the lyricist never tells us what's queer about her romance.

line 29: "elderly beaus" (actually spelled *beaux* in the sheet copy); the term is much too elegant for the girl who is singing.

line 30: "stockings are porous" makes an inner rhyme (see page 113) with "chorus," and is both forced and difficult to understand when sung.

One of the best situation songs I know is Irving Berlin's "Suppertime," which concerns a mother who has to tell her children that their father won't be coming home anymore. The song was written in response to a lynching. The situation is a most moving one, for the mother fears she must walk the line of telling the children without destroying their faith in God. Other situation songs are:

"Killing Me Softly": audience member embarrassed because the artist on stage sings so knowingly

"Tie a Yellow Ribbon": Ex-prison inmate wonders if the girl he left behind will still want him

"You'd Better Sit Down, Kids": divorcing parent departing, trying not to make the kids bitter

"Hello in There": old folks stuck in a situation with not much to do, hoping someone will talk to them

Some Situations for Song

1. man or woman bored with job or housework
2. boss or employee who wants to get out of a job situation
3. person trapped in well, mine, subway, elevator, or held hostage by political situation or mugger or rapist
4. person entering or being released from hospital, prison, new job, heaven or hell, first extramarital affair
5. plight or joy of scuba diver, circus performer, actor, salesman, seamstress, sculptor, park attendant, unsuccessful songwriter, new homeowner, terminally ill, expectant father or mother

If you consider these few situations you might be able to come up with a song where the protagonist is at some sort of crossroads. He or she does not have to handle it to its conclusion. Merely being there makes it a situation song.

LIST SONGS

In his notes for *Company*, Stephen Sondheim writes, "I started a list of what's company. Then I started to expand the lines. "Love is what you need is company. What I've got as friends is company. Good friends, weird friends, married friends, days go, years go, full of company ... Phones ring, bells buzz, door clicks, company, call back, get a bite," then the whole notion of short, staccato phrases occurred to him. And he states that by the time he had listed his general thoughts, he had the smell of the rhythm of the vocal line.

In "Gee, Officer Krupke," with music by Leonard Bernstein, Sondheim uses one of his favorite techniques, a list of parallel lines.

My father is a bastard,
My ma's an S.O.B.
My grandpa's always plastered
My grandma pushes tea.
My sister wears a moustache
My brother wears a dress
Goodness, gracious, that's why I'm a mess!

The list song is as old as Gilbert and Sullivan, for even "A Modern Major-General" is merely a list of facts (see page 86). Cole Porter, who had such glib humor, was, besides Sondheim, its most prolific practitioner. From "I Get a Kick out of You," in which he talks about all the things that bore him, to "Let's Do It," which mentions all the categories of animals that can fall in love, to "All of You," in which the lover mentions (quite harmlessly) all the parts of the opposite body that he'd like to make love to. But of all his list songs I know, my favorite is "The Physician (But He Never Said He Loved Me)," because it adds another dimension to the list—unrequited love. Notice the typical AABA form.

VERSE	Once I loved such a shattering physician,
	Quite the best looking doctor in the state.
	He looked after my physical condition
	And his bedside manner was great.
	When I'd gaze up and see him there above me
	Looking less like a doctor than a Turk
	I was tempted to whisper, "Do you love me,
	Or do you merely love your work?"
CHORUS	He said my bronchial tubes were entrancing,
A¹	My epiglottis filled him with glee.
	He simply loved my larynx
	And went wild about my pharynx,
	But he never said he loved me.
A²	He said my epidermis was darling,
	And found my blood as blue as could be,
	He went through wild ecstatics,
	When I showed him my lymphatics,
	But he never said he loved me.
BRIDGE	And though no doubt,
	It was not very smart of me,
	I kept on a-wracking my soul
	To figure out
	Why he loved ev'ry part of me,
	And yet not me as a whole.

A³   With my esophagus he was ravished.
Enthusiastic to a degree,
He said 'twas just enormous,
My appendix vermiformis,
But he never said he loved me.

2ND CHORUS   He said my cerebellum was brilliant,
And my cerebrum far from N.G.
I know he thought a lotta
My medulla oblongata
But he never said he loved me.
He said my maxillaries were marvels,
And found my sternum stunning to see,
He did a double hurdle
When I shook my pelvic girdle
But he never said he loved me.
He seemed amused
When he first made a test of me
To further his medical art,
Yet he refused
When he'd fixed up the rest of me
To cure that ache in my heart.
I know he thought my pancreas perfect,
And for my spleen was keen as could be
He said of all his sweeties,
I'd the sweetest diabetes
But he never said he loved me.

3RD CHORUS   He said my vertebrae were "sehr schöne"
And called my coccyx "plus que gentil"
He murmured "molto bella,"
When I sat on his patella
But he never said he loved me.
He took a fleeting look at my thorax
And started singing slightly off key.
He cried, "May Heaven strike us,"
When I played my umbilicus
But he never said he loved me
As it was dark
I suggested we walk about
Before he returned to his post.
Once in the park,
I induced him to talk about
The thing I wanted the most.

He lingered on with me until morning
Yet when I tried to pay him his fee,
He said, "Why, don't be funny,
It is I who owe you money,"
But he never said he loved me.

Tips on the List Song

1. Use more than a mere list. "The Surrey with the Fringe on Top" lists the parts of the automobile but also talks about what will be happening on the date. It's the combination that's important.
2. List songs are usually fairly long, in order to get a decent sized list and the addition of another concept.
3. Stay within your list. Don't go adding other lists. (Think of "The Windmills of Your Mind," in which all the images are about circles — (carousels, wheels, rings).

Other list songs are "Let's Get Away from It All"; "I'm Still Here"; "Monday's Child"; "The Twelve Days of Christmas"; "If I Ruled the World"; "Second Hand Rose"; "A Hundred Ways to Lose a Man"; "Sadie, Sadie"; "The Christmas Song"; "50 Ways to Leave Your Lover"; "Calendar Girl"; "Short People"; "Love Train"; "Season's Greetings"; "Give Peace a Chance."

SOCIAL MESSAGE SONGS

Most lyricists are bursting with things to say. Stop any one and he or she will tell you what's wrong with this country and the world. Generally, this social conscience can be put to good use in songwriting. Ecology, war, the fight for sexual equality, struggles to unionize, and the lowly employee's reach for upward mobility are all interesting subjects. Of course the sixties and seventies were the heyday for social message songs, but I'm sure you could look and find things that trouble you about the world "out there" that *your* song could repair.

Randy Newman, who often writes social message songs, is frequently misunderstood. His message may be so heavily disguised that it works for both the bigot and the liberal. His "Short People" caused a furor because many thought he was casting a slur on all short people, when actually he was castigating those who *put down* short people. Similarly, in the less cryptic "Sail Away," he is able to expose an old wound. This song is not about slaves but about the oily, supersalesman slave trader.

When you are writing your own, try to approach the lyric obliquely. Don't merely say that enslaving people is wrong, but let us see the stupid, uneducated trader.

Other good subjects are feminism ("I Am Woman"); integrated schools ("Black and White"); civil rights ("Blowin' in the Wind"); making it alone ("I Will Survive"); divorce ("Custody"); ecology ("They Paved Paradise"); war ("Where Have All the Flowers Gone?"); interracial relationships ("Society's Child"); police brutality ("Ohio"); the draft ("Alice's Restaurant"); sexual preference ("I Am What I Am"); and nuclear war ("Eve of Destruction").

BIRTHDAY SONGS

Lyricists who are looking for "something to write about" frequently look inward. Everybody has a birthdate, and the inspiration can travel from there. One could write about zodiac signs ("Aquarius"; "Gemini") or philosophize on the passing years ("Is That All There Is"). Another birthday could trigger happiness ("Happy Birthday to Me") or hate ("Today Is My Birthday and Nobody Sent Me a Card").

"Little Lamb," to which Stephen Sondheim wrote lyrics, for *Gypsy* in 1960, is an unusual birthday song. The singer is talking to her stuffed animals, gifts from her mother on previous birthdays, purposely selected to keep the girl a juvenile. It approaches the birthday song from a fresh angle.

"Little Lamb" (Music by Jule Styne, Lyric by Stephen Sondheim)

Little lamb, little lamb,
My birthday is here at last,
Little lamb, little lamb,
A birthday goes by so fast.

Little bear, little bear,
You sit on my right, right there.
Little hen, little hen,
What game shall we play, and when?

Little cat, little cat,
Ah, why do you look so blue?
Did somebody paint you like that
Or is it your birthday too?

Little fish, little fish
Do you think I'll get my wish?
Little lamb, little lamb,
I wonder how old I am?

FOREIGN OR PSEUDO-FOREIGN SONGS

Foreign lands used to be exotic enough to catch the public fancy. In the past many songs using a few foreign phrases hit the charts, but with the accessibility of travel, their appeal diminished. Still there is some mileage to be gained from the idea, especially when mixed with another concept like love, hate, or prejudice. "Darling, Je Vous Aime Beaucoup" has become a standard because of its charmingly sentimental melody as well as its pidgin French, which allows almost anyone to *feel* like he is singing in French.

"Darling, Je Vous Aime Beaucoup" (Music and lyric by Anna Sosenko)

Darling, je vous aime beaucoup.
Je ne sais pas what to do,
Darling, you've completely stolen my heart.
Morning, noon, and nighttime too,
Toujours wond'ring what to do.
That's the way I've felt right from the start.
Ah, chérie, my love for you is très, très, fort.
Wish my French were good enough,
I'd tell you so much more.
But I hope that you compree
All the things you mean to me
Darling, je vous aime beaucoup,
I love you, yes I do.

Most of today's foreign songs are written for the theater or geared toward the novelty market ("Istanbul Is Constantinople"), and many are concerned with the *method* of transportation ("Leavin' on a Jet Plane"; "Rocket Man"). Don't confuse the foreign song with a translation. The former is a concept, the latter is a craft.

PATRIOTIC SONGS

We have only to think of "Yankee Doodle Dandy," "You're a Grand Old Flag," and "God Bless America" to be aware of how many standards are patriotic songs. For any beginning songwriter these are generally easy to create. Make sure you can march to them and that they move along at a fairly good clip.

"Only in America" (Music and Lyric by Jerry Leiber, Cynthia Weil, Mike Stoller, and Barry Mann)

Only in America can a guy from anywhere
Go to sleep a pauper and wake up a millionaire!

Only in America can a kid without a cent
Get a break, and maybe grow up to be President!
Only in America, land of opportunity,
Would a classy girl like you
Fall for a poor boy like me.

Only in America can a kid who's washing cars
Take a giant step and reach right up and touch the stars.
Only in America could a dream like this come true.
Could a boy like me start with nothing,
And end up with you.

Patriotic songs are similar to descriptive songs, but the canvas is larger. As in so many other categories, the mixture of patriotism with another element is sure-fire. "You're a Grand Old Flag" mixes patriotism with the flag; "God Bless America" mixes patriotism with God; "Yankee Doodle Dandy" mixes patriotism with personal description.

Sometimes called the antipatriotic song, the social message song (page 94) may have the opposite concept.

HOLIDAY SONGS

Holidays, especially Christmas, can often be successful concepts for songs. The old concept of "home for the holidays" has been worn to death, but there might be some life left in it if you couple it with bringing a new love partner with you, coming home after the war, being home where there's no one there, visiting where the house has been torn down, or any other idea that occurs to you. As a point of departure into novelty songs Christmas again makes it, with titles like: "I Saw Mommy Kissing Santa Claus"; "Rudolph the Red-Nosed Reindeer"; "All I Want for Christmas Is My Two Front Teeth." The rest of the year is often neglected by songwriters, and so I generally suggest that you don't ignore Thanksgiving Day, Valentine's Day, St. Patrick's Day, the first day of spring, the Fourth of July, and all the other holidays that might make excellent song concepts.

The seasons, as well as directions (North, South) are often used in song. Stephen Sondheim says he spends the whole of Alan Lerner's "If Ever I Would Leave You" wondering what will happen in the other seasons after "it wouldn't be in summer," and indeed the formula can lead to predictability. But don't forget that it also creates unity, a much desired commodity. However, you should be careful with obvious things like the months of the year; nothing could be duller than a recounting of all twelve, or all seven days of the week. Ira Gershwin handled the days in a beautiful, almost abstract fashion in a section of "The Man I Love"; as in all good writing, it's what you omit that creates interest.

Maybe I shall meet him Sunday,
Maybe Monday, maybe not.
Still I'm sure to meet him one day,
Maybe Tuesday will be my good news day.

Imagine how boring this would be had the lyricist continued with Wednesday, Thursday, Friday, and Saturday. My advice on handling the holiday song is to select a holiday that appeals to you, combine it with another concept, and then cast it into one of the older forms like A^1, A^2, bridge, A^3, or ABAC.

GIMMICK SONGS

In a gimmick song, a lyricist arrives at an idea *before* beginning to write the song. The lyric can be built about a single note ("One-Note Samba," "Johnny One Note") or a scale ("Doe, a Deer"; "All of a Sudden My Heart Sings"). Although the two most obvious musical tricks, the single note and the scale, have been used, you might find a new way to handle them imaginatively or perhaps to build a concept on a broken chord or a pair of notes. The gimmick of "All of a Sudden My Heart Sings" is so amazingly universal—16 lines, each line a succeeding member of an ascending scale, and then of a descending scale—as to make us wonder at its success. It's utterly predictable.

"All of a Sudden My Heart Sings" (Music by Jamblin, Lyric by Harold Rome, Jamblin, and Herpin)

ASCENDING	C or do	All of a sudden my heart sings
	D or re	When I remember little things
	E or mi	The way you dance and hold me tight
	F or fa	The way we kiss and say goodnight
	G or sol	The crazy things you say and do
	A or la	The fun it is to be with you
	B or ti	The magic thrill that's in your touch
	C or do	Oh! Darling, I love you so much!
DESCENDING	C or do	The secret way you press my hand
	B or ti	To let me know you understand
	A or la	The wind and rain upon your face
	G or sol	The breathless world of your embrace
	F or fa	Your little laugh and half surprise
	E or mi	The love light gleaming in your eyes
	D or re	Rememb'ring all those little things
	C or do	All of a sudden my heart sings.

NONSENSE SONGS

This kind of song used to be called a novelty. Its roots can be traced as far back as "Shoo, Fly, Shoo" and "Jimmy Crack Corn" to the gay nineties' "Ta-Ra-Ra-Boom-De-Aye." This last was a kind of can-can with an obvious accent on the boom. Mostly it was a way of letting off steam.

Every era has had its own nonsense songs. The turn of the century had "Row, Row, Row," with lines like:

And then he'd row, row, row,
A little further he would row,
Oh, oh, oh, oh
And then he'd drop both his oars,
Take a few more encores
And then he'd row, row, row.

The Charleston era created many nonsense songs. Perhaps the one that's the most fun to roll off the tongue is "Ja-Da." Say the words aloud as you read, and you'll hear the rhythm in them.

Ja-da, ja-da
Ja-da, ja-da, jig, jig, jig.

Ja-da, ja-da
Ja-da, ja-da, jig, jig, jig.

That's a funny bit of melody,
It's so soothing and appealing to me.

Ja-da, ja-da
Ja-da, ja-da, jig, jig, jig.

Other songs, the mere listing of whose titles bring to mind strange and enjoyable sounds are "Zing, Went the Strings of My Heart"; "The Boogely-Woogely Piggy with the Oink-Oink"; "Three Little Fishies" (this was sung with a lisp, to approximate a child's singing; the adults *loved* it); "Marezy Doats" (a sort of riddle which, when slowed down, explained that "mares eat oats"); "Itsy Bitsy, Teeny Weeny, Yellow Polka-Dot Bikini" (that title says it all); "Hi-Lili, Hi-Lo" (a charmer that was created for a young girl and a finger puppet); "The Purple People Eater"; "Chim-Chim-Cheree"; "Chitty-Chitty Bang-Bang" (describing the sound made by an old Model-T automobile). As you can see, all these songs are in lively tempo and their literary idea is always at the service of the sheer joy of singing. The fifties had perhaps the greatest vogue of singing nonsense songs, but when scat singing came into prominence (improvising on a melodic line), this kind of singing began to wane. It disappeared almost entirely in the "meaningful" sixties and seventies. Except for the Beatles' "Ob-la-Di, Ob-la-Da," I know of no other recent successful nonsense songs. Perhaps it's time for a revival?

Suggestions for Writing Nonsense Songs

1. use quick or fairly quick tempo
2. create chorus *first* (select nonsense syllables that sing easily)
3. get a fanciful verse idea
4. create a *very* simple melody
5. record the song and listen to see if it's catchy

PUNCH-LINE SONGS

In a famous de Maupassant story, a woman works all her life to repay the cost of a diamond necklace she borrowed and lost, only to be told by the owner in the ultimate punch line, "But, my dear, the diamonds were only paste." The punch-line song is similarly shocking and often unforgettable. This kind of song was the mainstay of the revue, intimate or Broadway, and is still being created for sophisticated revues and cabaret acts.

The greatest punch-line songs have the surprise at the very last word—if possible, on the very last syllable. In the song below, Oscar Hammerstein sets up a devil-may-care situation, which he destroys with the final syllable. I quote it in its entirety because, with its three-part verse and standard ABAC chorus, it is a typical forties theater song.

"All in Fun" (Music by Jerome Kern, Lyric by Oscar Hammerstein II)

VERSE   We are seen about New York,
El Morocco and the "Stork"
And the other stay-up-late cafés
I am on the town with you these days
That's the way it stands.

We have had our little while
Just a fellow and a girl
And our feet have left the ground a bit
We've played around a bit.
That's the way it stands.
For we are strictly "Good-time Charlies"
Who love to play and dance about

And maybe kick romance about,
And that's the way it stands.

CHORUS   All in fun, this thing is all in fun
When all is said and done,
How far can it go?
Some orchids, some cocktails,
A show or two
A line in a column
That links me with you,

Just for laughs,
You're with me night and day
And so the dopes all say
That I'm that way about you.
Here's a laugh
And when I tell you this will kill you;
What they say
Is true!

The current master of the punch-line song is indisputably Stephen Sondheim. In the "Echo Song" (*A Funny Thing Happened on the Way to the Forum*), "Barcelona" (*Company*), and especially "Could I Leave You" (*Follies*), the listener waits on the end of his seat. The songs are so expertly constructed, with such clever rhymes along the way, that we relish rehearing them, contrary to most punch-line songs, which suffer from diminishing returns, not unlike a joke whose ending we know.

Lyricist Howard Dietz succeeded in making a growing punch line song by putting a surprise at the end of each A section, of course saving his best zinger for the last. This song is supposed to be sung by a country girl newly arrived in the city.

"Confession" (Music by Arthur Schwartz, Lyric by Howard Dietz)

I never kissed a boy before
Now isn't that a shame,
I never kissed a boy before—
Before I knew his name,

I never had a taste for wine,
Now isn't that a sin?
I never had a taste for wine
It can't compare to gin!

It's nice as nice can be
Our faith is at last restored
To know that vice can be
Its own reward.

I always go to bed at ten
Now, isn't that a bore?
I always go to bed at ten.
But I go home at four!

Some punch-line songs you might investigate are "I Said No!"; "She Had to Go and Lose It at the Astor"; "And Her Mother Came Too"; "Guess Who I Saw Today"; "Meeskite"; "Goodbye. John"; and "Nothing."

INSPIRATIONAL SONGS

Ever since "Look for the Silver Lining" (lyric by Buddy DeSylva), lyricists have been cheering up the down-hearted with optimistic songs. Sometimes the message was that God or Jesus would ease one's troubles, sometimes that we should have faith in a brighter tomorrow, or sometimes merely that time heals all wounds.

From the advice-filled twenties through the gloomy thirties, there were an abundance of titles like "Let a Smile Be Your Umbrella"; "With a Shine on Your Shoes"; "Smile"; "When You're Smiling"; "Get Happy"; "Great Day"; and "There's a Great Day Coming—Manana." Later songs in this tradition are "You'll Never Walk Alone"; "I Believe"; and "Bridge Over Troubled Water."

GOSPEL SONGS

The designation gospel song was coined by Thomas A. Dorsey, born in 1899 and still composing into the 1980s. He started as accompanist for the great blues artists Ma Rainey and Bessie Smith, but with the coming of the Depression, he abandoned that music and began to write "pop-religiosos"—religious songs with popular rather than religious orientation.

These were a far cry from the hymns that were the mainstay of the black church in the mid-thirties and an even greater distance from the responsive spirituals of earlier decades. Throughout the Depression era, groups like the Golden Gate Quartette and the Deep River Boys sang their gentle four-part harmony, but Dorsey's songs soon won the congregation over and were adopted by the "shouters" like Sallie Martin.

As rhythm and blues developed into rock and roll, gospel, which had shaped rhythm and blues, went on to be called soul. That's why so many of our major soul singers have strong gospel or church feeling. Aretha Franklin, Sam Cooke, LaVern Baker, Della Reese, Dionne Warwick, and Lou Rawls all began their careers by singing gospel music.

Do not confuse gospel music with blues. Gospel singers maintain that their music is the music of the Lord while blues is the music of the devil. A true gospel singer like Mahalia Jackson would never sing a blues song, but many artists like Ray Charles *did* take gospel songs transforming them into rhythm and blues by secularizing the lyric. "This Little Light of Mine" became "This Little Love of Mine" in Charles's version; "How Jesus Died" became "Lonely Avenue."

Those songs were successful on the gospel charts, but if you want to write a really successful pop-gospel song, one that might have a chance to make the Top 40 chart, I'd advise you to think of writing a love song that can be interpreted personally or religiously. Use "You" or "He" or "Him" to mean either the lover or Jesus, God, or faith, as in "You Light Up My Life" or "He Makes Me Feel Alive" or "I Don't Know How to Love Him."

Certain phrases appear again and again in gospel songs, such as "I was fallen," "cold, icy hands," "took me to Calvary," "the blood of my Savior," and "lightning flashes." But don't be misled into believing that merely throwing in the phrases will make a successful gospel song. To be successful, every gospel song must have honest scriptural roots and be written with faith.

Recently, they have been more oblique. The concept could be something like how Jesus sheds His light in the same way as the Statue of Liberty, both acting as beacons to the homeless, or "I saw a man yesterday who made me feel as though I was in the presence of the Lord."

Some gospel titles will give you an idea of areas that are logical to explore: "The Lord Will Make a Way"; "With My Song I Will Praise Him"; "You Gave Me Love (When Nobody Gave Me a Prayer)"; "Lift Up the Name of Jesus"; and "Just a Little Talk with Jesus."

LOVE SONGS

By far the greatest number of songs written (and successful) today are love songs, so much so that when anyone thinks of writing a song, this is usually the concept in mind. Songs with the word *love* in the title are generally passé, but in recent years there have been "This Love"; "I Believe in Love"; "Love Fool"; "I Will Love Again"; "Crazy in Love"; and many more. Yet I think the best love songs are those that talk about love without saying it. The "First Time Ever I Saw Your Face" (music and lyric by Ewan MacColl) is a good example.

The first time ever I saw your face
I thought the sun rose in your eyes
And the moon and stars were the gifts you gave
To the dark and empty skies, my love,
To the dark and empty skies.

The first time ever I kissed your mouth
I felt the earth move in my hand
Like the trembling heart of a captive bird
That was there at my command, my love
That was there at my command.

The first time ever I lay with you
I felt your heart beat close to mine,
I thought our joy would fill the earth,
And last till the end of time, my love,
And last till the end of time.

The language is poetic and *loving*. The repeated words *my love* are almost unnecessary. Any more talk of loving would be soupy. A case in point is "Little Green Apples," by Bobby Russell, whose verse talks about waking up next to the one beloved and goes on to list the chores she does, how she's always ready to drop her work and meet him, always ready with a big smile even though he may be late. The chorus and title come from the cliché "sure as God made little green apples," which in this case is inverted to "If that's not loving me, then all I've got to say is God didn't make little green apples and it don't rain in Indianapolis in the summertime."

"Just the Way You Are" saves its few words about loving until the very end. Billy Joel's long and beautiful lyric ardently pleads with the loved one to stay the same, not to change the color of her hair or to try to fit into fashion's mold.

In short, in all the best love songs, the message is gotten across without being obvious. Here are some kinds of things you might write about.

1. what friends say about the loved one
2. how different the two are, or how much alike
3. what it's like to travel along with someone you love
4. going through hard times with a loved one
5. what happens when two strongwilled people collide
6. cheating on one's lover—guilty conscience or rationalizing
7. how tragic it is that the lovers will never meet again
8. waiting for that one person to enter one's life
9. in love with the city; the ocean; one's career; a married person; a friend
10. envy of another's love relationship

UNSUITABLE CONCEPTS

No kind of song has to be unsalable. None. Some unsavory subjects like rape, cannibalism, diseases, and the like appear unsuitable, but handled sensitively, nothing that you feel deeply about should be taboo.

3 RHYME

Is RHYME NECESSARY? No. Can we write good lyrics without rhyme? Yes. Then why do we knock ourselves out to try to fit words together like a jigsaw puzzle so that they can have a singsong rhyme?

Songs feel "righter" when the lyricist uses rhyme. Although a favorite classic standard, "Moonlight in Vermont," avoids rhyme entirely and John Denver's "Annie's Song" and Ewen MacColl's "The First Time Ever I Saw Your Face" use it sparingly, they are exceptions.

We feel comfortable when words rhyme. Ever since childhood, whether calling names or skipping rope, most children love to sing and create rhymes. Perhaps rhyming brings a bit of order to those chaotic years. How often have we heard "Sticks and stones may break my bones," or "Little Tommy Tucker sings for his supper" (a bad rhyme) or made-up rhymes like "In jumps Alice, fat as a palace; Out comes Jane, skinny as a train."

What we adults call singsong comes to us naturally, for as children we derive a sense of pleasure from speaking in rhythm, and as we mature, we tie the package together with rhyme. So we always long for the balance and order that rhymes give. Besides, an incomplete thought that terminates in rhyme *seems* more profound.

You have what I lack myself
And now I even have to scratch my back myself.

(Rodgers and Hart "It Never Entered My Mind")

or

If happy little bluebirds fly
Beyond the rainbow why, oh, why can't I?

(Arlen and Harburg "Over the Rainbow")

Another reason we rhyme is that music relies so heavily upon repetition that we feel the corresponding accents and pulses in the lyrics, or want to feel them. If you sing

In a cavern, in a canyon,
Excavating for a mine,
Lived a miner, 'Forty-niner
And his daughter, Lulubelle

you will feel dissatisfied, not only because you are used to ending with the word *Clementine* (although Lulubelle has exactly the same accents), but because it bothers your inborn sense of order. The simple melody gives us a lift on the word *mine* and settles us peacefully down on the "-tine" syllable. And we demand that the words follow suit.

In ancient times, before most people could read, sagas and legends were related in rhyme. All classical poetry was written in rhyming couplets. This was not done for "artiness," but to make the story more dramatic and weighty. It also helped to make the lines easier to memorize.

If in your schoolwork you were ever obliged to commit a poem to memory, I'm sure you could remember it better *because* it rhymed. Anyone who has ever heard children spout a poetic assignment couplet after couplet will be aware that rhyme is a strong mnemonic crutch.

Rhyming can be an asset when the rhyme intrigues us or a bore when it has a "june-moon" predictability. Stephen Sondheim does not disappoint us in his bitter tirade of a song called "Could I Leave You?" when he rhymes "confess" not with an expected "Yes!" but an unexpected punch line, more thrilling because it is in rhyme — "Guess!"

One more asset of rhyme is known to all singers. Most of them (especially those who have had some training) will tell you that they "sing" on the vowels and "cut off" on the consonants. If you sing aloud any high note on the word *heart*, you will see that the *ah* lets the sound continue, while the *rt* cuts off the air.

It is because of this that rhyme often solves the problem of intelligibility. If we hear a phrase like "you are fi —" for an example, we might assume the word the lyricist intended was *fifth, first, fire, filthy, finish,* or many other *fi*-sounds. But if the songwriter precedes the "fi-" with "I always speak the best of what is *mine,*" then we know from the rhyme that the thought will not continue with "and you are fire" or anything else but "and you are fine."

No matter how new or daring your concept, how outlandish and original your harmony, most listeners feel more comfortable with rhymed lyrics because:

1. rhyme gives weight to our thoughts
2. rhyme follows the natural contours of the melody
3. rhyme creates a musical effect with words that have similar sounds
4. rhyme jogs our memory and helps us remember the song
5. rhyme helps the listener guess and understand our message

WHAT MAKES RHYME?

To satisfy the ear as a rhyme, words must have identical vowel sounds and different consonant sounds. *Make* and *rake* rhyme. *Lack* and *park* do not; the vowel is the same, but the pronunciation, or vowel sound, is different. Words that have the same consonants plus an extra one are still rhymes, although the poets' manuals say they are not. They satisfy the ear and as such are perfectly legitimate in songs. *Rake* and *brake* are fine, as are *sleep* and *leap*.

It almost goes without saying that to be a satisfactory rhyme, the rhythmic accents of the words must match. *Tender* and *refer* seem to match, but nothing could *sound* worse.

PAPER RHYMES

Poets often use what songwriters call paper rhymes. These look perfectly good on the page, but unless you bend the sound of the words, they make dreadful rhymes. *Find* and *wind*; *naked* and *baked*; and (unless you are British) *queen* and *been*; *rain* and *again*.

IDENTICAL RHYMES

What about words like *fair* and *fare*? Lorenz Hart and Ira Gershwin used to enjoy using them, and indeed to good effect, for they do pique the intellect. But they never satisfy the ear. We have come far beyond the stage where lyrics could be used as a display of the creator's cleverness. Even in the theater, which allows for some intellectual stimulation, this trick should be avoided.

John Denver's otherwise adequately rhymed "I'm Sorry" seems to let us down when the lyricist lapses into identical words in the last verse. In his first verse he rhymes "didn't say" with "went away." This satisfies the ear. His second verse lacks punch because he rhymes "put on you" with "without you."

REGIONAL RHYMES

Throughout this big world there are great differences in the way residents of various countries pronounce the same words. In America alone many regionalisms exist. *Girl* will be *girrll* if you come from New Jersey, *gal* if you have an Oklahoma accent, *gull* if you hail from New Orleans, *gahl* in Boston, and *goil* in Brooklynese (Larry Hart actually rhymed *goil* and *spoil* in "Manhattan" as well as Bronyx and Onyx).

Regionalisms in speech patterns can give an authenticity to your lyric providing you stick to the same area in your choice of rhymes. You can make your work sound western or eastern or country or disco or even English by your choice of words. For example, *been* is pronounced *bin* and rhymes with *sin* in America, but the same word is pronounced *bean* and rhymes with *scene* in England. Stephen Sondheim gave his stripper "Miss Mazeppa" a Brooklyn background by rhyming "Mazeppa" with "schlepper" (pronounced "schleppa" in Brooklyn).

IMPERFECT AND FALSE RHYMES

The great classic lyricists like Hart, Hammerstein, Porter, Mercer, Lerner, and so many others of the pre-rock era aimed always for exact rhymes. They would not countenance false or inexact rhymes in their work and constantly rewrote until all false sound was eliminated.

It is true that this insistence on perfect rhyme sometimes led to "overrhyme," without regard to concept. Often the lyricist ended up being clever and arch at the sacrifice of character honesty (see "Ten Cents a Dance" on page 89).

We are speaking about a different era, when songs generally originated in the theater or in movies. There, every syllable had to be part of the fabric of the entire show. Later, in the big band era, a recording needed clarity and understandable diction before even the smallest record company would release it. With the advent of heavy amplification, distortion sometimes set in and often the words were indistinguishable. The total decibel count became the raison d'être of many recordings, and chorus after chorus of the *same* lyric was performed, so eventually the audience came to understand the words. Those who had a need to know the lyric could find it on the album-liner notes or go out and buy a sheet copy. But no longer was *what* was said as important as *how* it was said.

Popular singers began searching for intimacy, and the trained voice was a problem on the market. *Going* always was sung *goin'* and sometimes *gohne*. All the final *-ed* sounds were swallowed and nobody pronounced the final *s*, so of course you could rhyme *cream* with *dreams*; *hash* with *lashed*.

All this was an effort to make the singer sound like a friend next door. The "non-trained singer" became the only successful one in the popular field.

These days, the song itself is only one element in a record's rise to the top of the charts. Concept, arrangement, production, publicity, the artist's charisma, sound, and vogue all seem to be as vital to record sales as words and music. Being aware of this, so many songwriters trying to seem contemporary have never developed their sense of rhyme. Others, citing their colleagues as examples, have been able to squeak by with "almost rhymes." After all, why cogitate for hours, perhaps days, to get perfect rhymes when near enough will do? Isn't everyone doing it? Won't "perfect rhymes" sound too crafted and old-fashioned?

The sixties and seventies produced remarkably few standards. Even though the record market exploded, very little of what was played is of lasting value.

Below are some imperfect rhymes from songs that were at the top of the charts, sometimes for several weeks. I have selected line endings where the music sounds as if a rhyme would make it more symmetrical. The indiscriminate selection is from well-known songs of the seventies like "Gonna Fly Now," "Fame," "Band on the Run," "I Write the Songs," and "How Can You Mend a Broken Heart."

move — lose	come — run
brain — flame	down — found
change — insane	forever — together
mine — line	sing — things
time — crime	soul — old
breeze — leave	rain — again

The seventies were rife with rhymes like *fine* and *time*, and it is my feeling that the least offensive of the false rhymes is the *m* and *n* sounds when juxtaposed.

It is still possible in these times to write for the popular market and to use perfect rhymes. The songs of Billy Joel, Marty Panzer, Randy Newman, John Prine, Jim Webb, Neil Diamond, Barry Manilow and Alan and Marilyn Bergman, among others, always seem to use perfect rhymes. Theater composers like Edward Kleban, Stephen Sondheim, and Stephen Schwartz set high standards and insist their rhymes be perfect.

You should expect no less from yourself. Remember, people memorize your phrases! They sing your rhymes! Don't give them what is trite or second-rate.

ONE-, TWO-, AND THREE-RHYMES

A one-rhyme (ultimate rhyme, masculine rhyme) must have its accent on the last syllable of the line. It does not matter how many non-accented syllables precede the final accent.

Some one-rhymes are: greed — heed; through — you; fright — trite; complete — defeat; condense — suspense; saloon — brigadoon; misinform — thunderstorm;

and raid—afraid. Replace—outer space are still one-rhymes because the last syllable is accented.

One-rhymes are sometimes called ultimate rhymes, because the accent is on the last syllable. Sometimes they are referred to as masculine rhymes. In Latin and the Romance languages French, Spanish, and Italian, gender is built into nouns by adding suffixes that often add another unaccented syllable to the word. For example, in French, a male dog is *chien* while a female dog is *chienne*. Classical scholars called one-rhymes masculine rhymes because in Latin poetry, the masculine form of a noun was pronounced in one syllable and the feminine form was pronounced with two syllables.

Today *one-rhyme* is the preferred term, because *masculine rhyme* seems chauvinistic and *ultimate rhyme* is unwieldy.

In a two-rhyme (penultimate rhyme, feminine rhyme), the accent is on the next-to-last syllable.

Some two-rhymes are: action—traction (liquefaction); Daddy–caddy—FinanHaddy; candy—dandy; tango—mango; confusion—illusion; and infection—injection.

Three-rhymes (pen-penultimate rhymes, dactyl) have an accented syllable followed by two unaccented ones.

Some three-rhymes are: laboring—neighboring; Hungarian—barbarian; speediest—neediest; conventional—intentional; priority—inferiority; muttering—stuttering.

Four-, five-, and six-rhymes, although rare, are possible and are identified by the distance between the accented or rhyming word and the end of the line.

Although most rock abjures two-and three-rhymes, rhyme itself has been a necessary part of songs, and it will continue to be an integral part of songwriting for many years to come.

The one-rhyme is most direct. A strong, driving song like "Footloose" (lyric by Loggins-Pitchford) uses "Please, Louise, pull me off my knees" (all one-rhymes). Lionel Richie in "Hello" rhymes "outside my door" with "is it me you're looking for?" One could find thousands of examples of songs that use one-rhymes almost exclusively, but the songs I find most rewarding are those that use a variety of rhyme.

Culture Club's "Miss Me Blind" uses "gun" and "fun" and later "then" rhyming with "men"—all one-rhymes, but in the second verse, we get some two-rhymes in the rhyming of "forever" with "clever." Lorenz Hart handled one-, two- and three-rhymes with such ease that the listener didn't know they were there. In the verse of "Bewitched," which is set to Richard Rodgers's music, he uses two-rhymes—"know it" and "show it" alternating with one-rhymes "charms" and "arms." Later, in the chorus, he avoids dullness by using mostly three-rhymes.

Cole Porter, who was a rhyming genius, sometimes used unisyllabic lines that in lesser hands would create a series of boring one-rhymes. By placing the rhymes sometimes at the beginning and sometimes at the end of a line, he varied the accent. The song below uses only deceptively simple one-and two-rhymes but sounds ten times more intricate and amusing because of their placement.

"Ace in the Hole" (Music and lyric by Cole Porter)

Sad times	(TWO-RHYME)
May follow your *tracks,*	(ONE-RHYME)
Bad times	(TWO-RHYME)
May bar you from *Sacks,*	(ONE-RHYME)
Add times	(TWO-RHYME)
When Satan in *slacks*	(ONE-RHYME)
Breaks down your self-con*trol.*	(ONE-RHYME)
*May*be	(TWO-RHYME)
As often it *goes*	(ONE-RHYME)
Your *A*bie	(TWO-RHYME)
May tire of his *Rose,*	(ONE-RHYME)
So, *baby,*	(TWO-RHYME)
This rule I pro*pose*	(ONE-RHYME)
Always have an ace in the *hole!*	(ONE-RHYME)

To help you identify the various types of rhymes, I've prepared a simple and perhaps obvious chart.

thirst	(ONE-RHYME)
worst	
*thirst*ing	(TWO-RHYME)
*burst*ing	
first of all	(THREE-RHYME)
worst of all	
first of the lot	(FOUR-RHYME)
worst of the lot	

INNER RHYMES

In "All of a Sudden My Heart Sings" (page 98), when we noticed the lines

Your little laugh and half surprise
The love light gleaming in your eyes.

we may have been struck with the one-rhyme of "surprise" and "eyes" and slipped over the "laugh" and "half," which is a perfect inner rhyme. Inner rhymes almost always fall on *un*accented syllables, and give the line a graceful curve.

The record for inner rhymes is probably held by Cole Porter, whose "I Get a Kick Out of You" has six in a row, comprising most of the A³ section:

I get no kick in a plane
*Fly*ing too *high* with some *guy* in the *sky*
Is *my* idea of nothing to do
But I get a kick out of you.

In "It's De-Lovely," he wrote:

You can *tell* at a glance
What a *swell* night this is for romance
You can *hear dear* mother nature murmuring low
"Let yourself go!"

Sometimes the inner rhyme is so subtle that listeners may think the words were chosen by accident. Generally, it is not accident but the lyricist's poetic speech that creates the inner rhyme. In "Knock Three Times" (music and lyric by Levine and Brown), the line "and only in my dreams did that wall between us come apart" might not appear to have an inner rhyme, but these days, songwriters often rhyme "dream" and "between," and we must consider this planned. In "Through the Years" (music and lyric by S. Dorff and M. Panzer), in the line "As long as it's O.K. I'll stay with you through the years," the "K" and the word "stay" make a lovely, tender inner rhyme.

The lyricist intent on improving technique is advised to study all music, noticing where the inner rhymes help or hinder the mood of the song.

NON-RHYMED LYRICS

When a lyricist does not use rhyme, is it because of a lack of technique or is it by design? I hope it is because of a conscious wish to avoid the rhyme, but one can never be sure.

What *is* essential when a lyricist decides not to rhyme is a strong rhythmic feeling to the words. "Moonlight in Vermont" (music by Karl Suessdorf, lyric by John Blackborn) is poetic and also uses a strong rhythmic pulse, especially in the bridge.

*Pe*nnies in a stream
*Fa*lling leaves of sycamore
*Moon*light in Vermont

*I*cy fingerwaves
Ski trails on a mountainside
*Moon*light in Vermont.

*Te*legraph cables they *sing* down the highway
And *trav*el each bend in the *road*.
*Pe*ople who meet in this *ro*mantic setting
Are *so* hypnotized by the *love*ly

*Ev'*ning summer breeze
*War*bling of a meadowlark,
*Moon*light in Vermont
You and I and
*Moon*light in Vermont

I've added accents so you may observe that the song was created with a careful rhythmic plan and is not as arbitrary as it looks.

My advice to fledgling songwriters on whether to use or avoid rhyme and what kinds of rhymes to use:

1. Don't avoid rhyme. You have to prove that you know how to use it before the public will believe you are avoiding it by design.
2. Don't ever use rhyme just for the sake of rhyming.
3. If you are working in the theater, no less than perfect rhymes will do. If you are working in the pop field, seek perfect rhymes, but understand you have some leeway.
4. Inner rhymes are a bit old-fashioned in pop music, but they still are useful in the theater.

RHYME SCHEMES

Assuming you are going to use rhyme, which lines will rhyme? Every line, every other line? Every fourth line?

You may create your own scheme, but the ones most often used are below:

A A B B

First and second lines rhyme, third and fourth lines rhyme. By far the most common scheme.

"Love Will Keep Us Together" (Music and lyric by Neil Sedaka and Howard Greenfield)

Love will keep us together
Think of me babe whenever
Some sweet talkin' guy comes along,
Singin' his song

A B A B

First and third lines rhyme; second and fourth lines rhyme.

"Love for Sale" (Music and lyric by Cole Porter)

Let the poets pipe of love
In their childish way,
I know ev'ry type of love
Better far than they

A B C B

Only the second and fourth lines rhyme. Generally has same effect as ABAB. In the lyric below, we sometimes find ABAB and ABCB.

"The Night Chicago Died" (Lyric by Pete Callander)

In the heat of the summer night
In the land of the dollar bill
When the town of Chicago died
And they talk about it still

And the sound of the battle rang
Through the streets of the old east side
Till the last of the hoodlum gang
Had surrendered up, or died.

A A B C C B

First two and fourth and fifth lines rhyme, but the memorable rhyme is the third and sixth lines. A very common scheme for theater songs because of its unity.

"Some People" (Music by Jule Styne, Lyric by Stephen Sondheim)

Some people can get a thrill
Knitting sweaters and sitting still
That's okay for some people who don't know they're alive!

Some people can thrive and bloom
Living life in a living room
That's perfect for some people of one hundred and five!

A A A B C C C B

Rather a complicated scheme, but a wonderful one for a ballad.

"What Are You Doing the Rest of Your Life?" (Music by Michel Legrand, Lyric by Alan and Marilyn Bergman)

What are you doing the rest of your life?
North and south and east and west of your life
I have only one request of your life.
That you spend it all with me.

All the seasons and the times of your days
All the nickels and the dimes of your days,
Let the reasons and the rhymes of your days
All begin and end with me.

ORIGINAL RHYME SCHEMES

Sometimes (especially if you write both music and lyrics) your lyric thought will not conform to the four-or six-line verse. In this case, you may create your own design. John Prine did just that in his well-known "Hello in There." The rhyme scheme, being A B C C C, creates the boring end that suits the concept beautifully.

Edward Kleban chose a beautiful scheme for "What I Did for Love." The form is A¹, A², release, A³ and the rhyme scheme is A B C D. What's that, you say? Nothing rhymes? Look at the sheet music or replay the lyric in your head, and you will see that the repeat of the first section has the same scheme, and we recall the lines from four lines above. The same thing happens after the release in the final section.

In my own song called "Joey," I chose a dramatic scheme to balance the concept, which deals with a father who is about to go off to prison saying goodbye to his young son.

Joey,
I should have told you yesterday
But I just was too ashamed to say
That in a little while I'm goin' away
Joey.

Joey,
I know that this is bound to upset you
But it's the kind of place that's so hard to get to
And I wouldn't want you visitin' even if they'd let you
Joey.
Punch me in the belly the way we do in play,
But this time make it real.
Give me some pain that I can take away,
A wound that never will heal.
God knows, that inside of me I'm battered and torn
But I never let it show through.
I've been shattered and festering since I was born
But none of my scars came from you.

No, Joey,
I guess nothing worked out as I planned,
And maybe you're too young to understand,
But now you'll have to do the best you can.
Joey,
Joey, Joey,
The next time I see you————
You'll be
A man.

Sometimes the rhyme scheme will be dictated by the final line. In a song called "I'll Take Care of You," not wanting to end on an "oooh" sound, which has been done ad nauseam, I approached the rhyme with:

So don't reject these arms that yearn for you
Cause I'm your lucky break,
And I'll take
Care of you.

When setting David Shire's music for "I'll Never Say Goodbye," Alan and Marilyn Bergman headed for their important rhyme with a line about "today," which of course rhymes with the "say" in "I'll Never *Say* Goodbye." If the music is intense enough, this kind of treatment can be very effective and we will never miss the rhyme for the dangling last words.

WORDS THAT WILL NOT RHYME

No word in the English language is taboo (even the "four-letter" words have been used), but certain words are better avoided because there are so few rhymes for them or because they don't "sing." I'd certainly try to avoid "non-rhymers" at the end of a line.

"Love" has so few rhymes that it complicates the lyricist's task, since more songs are written about love than any other subject. "Love" rhymes only with "dove," "glove," "shove," "above," and (stretching it a bit) "of." In most cases the "glove, shove, and dove" rhymes come out sounding forced. "Skies above" or, worse, "all else above" is shopworn. Compound words like "lady-love," "belove," "turtle-dove," "fox-glove" are usable only by nineteenth-century poets. That leaves only "of" (which is not, by the way, a perfect rhyme, but close enough), and so many songwriters have used the "dreaming of," "thinking of" rhyme that I see little freshness possible. The answer? If you use the word *love*, put it in the middle of the line or find a synonym for that emotion that will rhyme.

Other words prominent in love songs that you should avoid at line's end are: "self" (myself), which only rhymes with "elf," "shelf," and "pelf"(?); "mouth," which only rhymes with "south"; "rhythm," which seems only to rhyme (when forced) with "with 'em."

I must also caution you about the use of the "ee" sound, so often misaccented in American popular music. "Me" rhymes with all the one-rhymes like "see," "be," and "free," but this word so necessary to any lyric is frequently rhymed with "memory" (which comes out sounding "memor*ee*") instead of "*mem*ory" or "suddenly" (sounding like "sudden*lee*"). I'm aware that many of today's successes use "memoree," but it still sounds amateurish. So be careful about any "ee" sound at the end of a line.

There are many words in our language that do not rhyme, but almost all of them can be used at the end of a line when the lyricist handles them with compounds. For example, Hart used "hero" and "queer ro" (-mance) in "Ten Cents a Dance";

Lee Adams rhymed "tragedy" with what sounds like "gladjedy" in the lines below, quoted from "Put on a Happy Face" (music by Charles Strouse):

Take off that gloomy mask of tragedy
It's not your style
You'll look so good that you'll be glad you de-
Cided to smile.

Sometimes the lyricist in search of rhyme will be forced to use slang, which has an unfortunate tendency to date quickly, seeking a rhyme for "rouge" with "stooge." Another resort is regionalism, "rhumba" rhyming with "number" in New Yorkese.

What follows is a list of words that do not rhyme. I'm sure you will find others that do not rhyme to your ear, as well as find ones on the list for which you have discovered rhymes.

absence	employee	language	puss
absent	evening	license	pussy
accent	every	lilac	
access			refuge
almost	film	manhood	reluctant
angel	filthy	margin	
April	fondle	method	Sabbath
ardent	fragment	mischief	safest
August	fullness	modern	sarcasm
		monarch	satire
bargain	goodness	monster	sausage
bishop	gorgeous	month	scarce
budget	gossip		scoundrel
bulb		noisy	sculpt
	handsome		serpent
cabbage	homely	ogre	shindig
cactus	hostage	okra	signal
charcoal	hundred	olive	softly
chemist	hungry	orchid	stalwart
cockeyed		omelet	stubborn
Cockney	infant	polka	substance
common	item	portrait	sudden
costly		postage	sugar
	joyous	poverty	sunrise
dampen	junior	princess	sunset
damage		profile	
druggist	kitchen	proverb	tailspin

target   vaguest   violinist   whoopee
tidied   valve   volcano   wolf
tinsel   vengeance   wasp   woman
topaz   vampire   weapon
travail   victim   watchword   xylophone
tyranny   violin   welfare   zebra

4 WORD USAGE

Poets (and lyricists too) have always used imaginative language. Even our word *prosaic* refers to a just ordinary description, whereas *poetic* intrigues the imagination. If "Johnny One Note" held on to his note for a long time, that's prosaic, but if he held that high note "until he was blue in the face," we get a visual image. You may say "I love you a lot," but that is not memorable; however, if you say "I love you a bushel and a peck" and you are, as in Frank Loesser's *Guys and Dolls*, costumed as a farmer, your words will be remembered. So it would be wise to avoid ordinary, prosaic language in your lyric and always to seek a colorful way of getting your message across. What follows are some ways to make your lyric more memorable.

SIMILE AND METAPHOR

The dictionary defines *simile* as "a figure of speech in which one thing is likened to another, dissimilar, thing by the use of 'like' or 'as'" (e.g., a heart as big as a whale, her tears flowed like wine) and *metaphor* as "a figure of speech in which one thing is likened to another, different, thing by being spoken of as if it *were* that other" (e.g., a mighty fortress is our God; all the world's a stage). In short, a simile uses the words "like" or "as," while a metaphor avoids them. Both are useful in songwriting.

"All the Things You Are" (music by Jerome Kern, lyric by Oscar Hammerstein II) is an example of pure metaphor because the beloved has *become* the various things the lyricist writes about:

You are the promised kiss of springtime
That makes the lonely winter seem long.
You are the breathless hush of ev'ning
That trembles on the brink of a lovely song.
You are the angelglow that lights a star
The dearest things I know are what you are.
Some day my happy arms will hold you
And some day, I'll know that moment divine
When all the things you are, are mine.

Every songwriter needs to develop a talent for comparing things to other things but should try to avoid hackneyed phrases like "You make me feel like a king (queen)" [SIMILE] or "With you I'm a king (queen)" [METAPHOR].

Cole Porter's "You're the Top" is one continuous stream of glittering metaphors transforming the loved one into "the Colosseum," "the Tower of Pisa," the "Mona Lisa," "the nimble feet of Fred Astaire," and "Camembert." Dorothy Fields, in *Sweet Charity*, equated life with "frozen peaches and cream" in one of my favorite metaphors. Other metaphors are: "I am music"; "You are my ace in the hole"; "You are love"; "War is Hell"; and "You are the sunshine of my life."

Similes seem to be a bit easier to create than metaphors because the comparisons can be more far-fetched and still remain clear. Some similes are: You take my breath away like water from a spring; the world is like an apple whirling silently in space; I set by myself like a cobweb on a shelf; your lips, like cherries, or roses or berries; the sun streaming in like butterscotch; my heart feels like a spring that's overflowing.

ALLITERATION

Using the same letter to begin several words is called alliteration. "Bad, Bad, Leroy Brown" would not be nearly as good a title if it were Bad, Bad, Leroy Green. "Delta Dawn," "The Shadow of Your Smile," "Different Drum," and old standards like "Love Me or Leave Me," "Got a Lot of Living to Do," "Bye Bye Blues," "Live for Life," and "Winter Wonderland" would not be so catchy without their alliteration.

Alliteration is excellent when used in a title, but unless it is truly poetic, I would avoid it in the body of the song. I quote from Stephen Sondheim's lecture at a "Lyrics and Lyricists" (itself an alliteration) meeting:

"As for alliteration, my counterpoint teacher had a phrase 'the refuge of the destitute.' Any time you hear alliteration in a lyric, get suspicious. For example, when you hear 'I Feel Pretty' and she sings 'I feel fizzy and funny and fine,' somebody doesn't have something to say."

But that is not always true. When Cole Porter's "love" states that his kiss is "delicious, delightful, delectable, delirious, dilemma, delimit, de-luxe, and delovely," it's a tour de force. In his last verse he uses alliteration equally amusingly to describe his son as appalling, appealing, a polywog, a paragon, a Popeye, a panic, and a pip. More recent pop songs have used phrases such as "Cadillac car," "frightened frog," "cryin' in my cornflakes," "stop and smell the roses," "another day down the drain," "like a sailboat sailin' on the sea," and "sweet surrender," among others. My advice is to use alliteration sparingly, and *never* in place of a truly original thought.

ONOMATOPOEIA

This multisyllable word stands for the formation of a word by imitating the natural sound associated with the object or action involved (e.g. tinkle, buzz, whisper).

Somewhat like alliteration, a little of this goes far. Words like *zip* and *zing* are frequently used in pop songs. The clang! clang! clang! in the "Trolley Song" (Martin and Blane) is an integral part of the song, just as the word *shuffle* in the "Old Soft Shoe" makes us practically hear the artist tapping on sand. But the best thing about onomatopoeia is that it forces us to listen to our lyrics to create colorful language. It urges us to try to make our listener *see* and *feel* what we're singing about. The screech of chalk on a blackboard, the drumming of fingernails on a table, and the grinding of teeth are recreated for us in onomatopoetic speech.

WORDS THAT DO NOT SING

Oscar Hammerstein often mentioned how dissatisfied he was with the last line of "What's the Use of Wond'rin'," a song from *Carousel*. Even though most professional lyricists have great respect for this song, Mr. Hammerstein attributed the song's commercial failure to his choice of the final words. The A³ lyric goes:

So when he wants your kisses
You will give them to the lad,
And anywhere he leads you, you will walk;
And anytime he needs you
You'll go running there like mad.
He's your fella and you love him.
And all the rest is talk.

Hammerstein maintained that the final "k" sound, being impossible for the voice to sustain, cut the song off abruptly, before the singer had a chance to "sell" it. Indeed he was right, for the *k* is one consonant that is impossible to maintain. The others are *b*, *p*, *d*, *t*, and *g*.

Stated simply, it would be foolish of you to end a song whose melody you wish to sustain with any of the above. *Fight, night, right* (unless you hold onto the "i" sound) will cut their sounds completely, as will *trap, climb, read, bed,* and *bring.*

Any of the aforementioned words may be used if the singer sings *on the vowel,* but this makes the words unintelligible. This is the reason opera singers' lyrics are rarely understandable; concert singers are always taught to sing on vowels, for the voice is more beautiful and high notes more easily achieved when sung on vowels. Pop singers, on the other hand, often draw out certain consonants—not the ones mentioned above: they are impossible. But we have all heard Sinatra sing *alllll* or *nothing at alllll,* and Peggy Lee always sang *Kissss* me. Rock singers, unfortunately, swallow the ends of syllables. (And that explains why we sometimes see singulars rhyming with plurals and words that rhyme only vaguely.)

CONNECTING THE WORDS

If you have ever tried to set words to a rapidly moving melody, you must have discovered that not all syllables are created equal. Some unisyllables like *fraught, through, bombed,* and *smiled* take several different motions of lips and tongue; while others, like *a, we,* and *Oh* take merely one. If you string a bunch of "long syllables" together, you will find the singer has difficulty making *your* message clear. "Love" is one of the difficult ones to say, and unfortunately so, because it must be so prevalent in songdom. It requires three separate motions; ul, uh, vuh, and so when Stephen Sondheim uses "Don't you love farce?" in "Send in the Clowns," the singer is obliged to come to a complete halt between the latter two words or else the phrase will emerge as "Don't you lovearce?"

The prohibition is therefore not so much of long syllables as much as of using the same consonant in succeeding words. "Big girl" comes out sounding like "bigirl" and "hot tamale" emerges as "hotamale." All these may be clear on the page, but try saying them aloud and notice how ambiguous they sound.

It is almost as bad to use *any* two consonants in adjacent words because the singer must take special care to make them intelligible. "Deep lake" is harder to sing than "blue lake"; "ripe grape" requires more effort than "ripe apple."

So, remember:

1. Don't string a group of long syllables together.
2. Don't use adjacent words ending and beginning with the same consonant.
3. Use adjacent words ending and beginning with any consonant sparingly.

INVERTED LANGUAGE

Back in the discussion of operetta lyrics, I mentioned the inverted manner of an operetta phrase. This is frequently achieved by placing the verb at the end of the sentence. "As to and from her work she goes" or "when I a certain party saw" are inversions that have no place in songwriting today, and I'm sure you would avoid them. But what about lines like "and when myself is feelin' low, I think about her face aglow" from "Little Green Apples" (music and lyric by Bobby Russell) or "In the mirror I saw him" from "Lucille" (Roger Bowling and Hal Bynam)? Inverted language always comes off sounding like you couldn't fit your phrase into the rhythmic scheme right side up.

FILLING OUT OR TELESCOPING A LYRIC

When a melody has been written before its lyric, the one who adds words may sometimes use more or fewer syllables than desirable to conform to the melody. This will always sound forced, and its use invariably betrays an amateur lyricist.

Before 1950 it was common to encounter "dear" ("I would be a king, dear, uncrowned") as the crutch, while in the last several decades it has been "babe"; "hon"; and especially, and chauvinistically, "girl." "Just" and "very" are two other words that fill space while adding nothing to your lyric. Exclamatory words like "ah" and "oh" likewise only clutter your lyric. "Ah, Sweet Mystery of Life"; "Oh, My Papa"; and "Oh, What a Beautiful Morning" would all be better without their first ejaculation.

When there were too few pitches for their lyric, though, lyricists used to resort to contractions: "'Twas then heaven bles't me"; "O'er the sea of mem'ry"; "'Tis said"; "'Twill be." Less offensive, but still to be avoided, are omissions like "Glass that's full of tinkle" for "*A* glass ..."

Getting the exact number of syllables without padding or contracting may be a difficult chore, but it is part of the lyricist's craft and a technique you should master. One has a bit more leeway in contemporary music and folk music to add to or subtract from the melodic line instead, but this is a crutch I'd advise you to use sparingly.

MATCHING ACCENTS AND MEANING

Music, as you know, has accents. They create our basic urge to dance. And a lyric has its own accents, similar to poetry. When the two conform perfectly, we have a memorable wedding of music and lyric. Too often that is not the case.

A musical accent will be created when a composer puts a note on the downbeat, a heavily accented beat, or a high pitch, which causes our voice to ascend to reach that note. If you sing through the last phrases of "Killing Me Softly with His Song," you will hear:

> killing me softly with *his* song,
> killing me *softly* with his *song*.

The first time the title is announced, it lacks emotion because we know already whose song it is and find the word *his* redundant. But the second time, we are moved because the musical *and* lyrical accents match. Conversely, the last announcement that "You Deco*rat*ed My Life" and "Leavin' *on* a Jet Plane" (with high pitch on the italicized syllables) seem less than good to me.

Lyricists should also be careful, when using high pitch, to make sure that upper notes do not occur on unimportant words. I'm sure Cole Porter did not mean *the* night is young, *the* skies are clear, but those high pitches accent the throwaway words. Similarly, Ira Gershwin who wrote the lyrics for "The Man That Got Away" may not have intended Judy Garland to belt out "*The* writing's on the wall, *the* dreams you've dreamed," but those *the*'s take over the entire section. It is always advisable to sing through a completed lyric to check for unimportant words that receive musical accent and intrude on your concept.

INAPPROPRIATE SPEECH

In Rodgers and Hart's "Ten Cents a Dance" when the lyricist's dance-hall hostess mentions her "chorus of elderly beaux" we lose credibility that the same girl who said "Gee! that Palace is cheap" is speaking. Good lyrics, like good writing, will have an authentic ring. One of songdom's most unbelievable cowboys sings in "El Rancho Grande," "for I just love herding cattle." Writers of country music are rarely guilty of this crime of pretension, but I have found many new songwriters using fancy language or words they did not quite understand.

Inappropriate speech is most dangerous when used in the theater, for all the plot devices depend on our belief in the character. It is hard enough for us to accept someone suddenly bursting into song, let alone stepping out of the role. Stephen Sondheim has often mentioned his inappropriate line for Maria in *West Side Story*. In "I Feel Pretty," she says, "It's alarming how charming I feel," a line that Mr. Sondheim admits would be more acceptably sung by a Park Avenue debutante than by a Puerto Rican immigrant.

POETS' HANDBOOKS AND RHYMING DICTIONARIES

You should also invest in a rhyming dictionary. One of my favorites is Gene Lee's *Modern Rhyming Dictionary: How to Write Lyrics* (Cherry Lane Books, 1981) because it has so much about songwriting in general. *The New Comprehensive American Rhyming Dictionary* by Sue Young (Morrow, 1991) is also most valuable. It not only lists one-rhymes, but also adds two-, three-, four- and sometimes five-rhymes. For example, it lists simple "a" rhymes like "lay," "neigh" and follows them with two-rhymes like "dismay," "entrée," and "hearsay." The next column goes to three-rhymes with "consommée," "castaway," and so forth and then on to four-rhymes such as "cabriolet," "catch-of-the-day," "naïveté." These extended rhymes can almost suggest a concept for a song. A rhyme such as "prima donna" and "Rosh HaShanna," which this book lists, could spark a fertile mind to write an amusing song about a devout opera singer who refused to perform on Jewish holidays. Rhymes like "Tijuana" and "marijuana" are an obvious beginning for a song.

Other rhyming dictionaries include the *New Rhyming Dictionary and Poet's Handbook* by Burges Johnson (Harper and Row, 1957) and *The Complete Rhyming Dictionary: The Essential Handbook for Poets and Songwriters* by Clement Wood (Doubleday, 1936). Neither of these has any information on songwriting, despite the subtitle of the latter. One dictionary aimed specifically at the songwriter is *The Songwriter's Rhyming Dictionary* (NAL, 1983) by Sammy Cahn, a most respected lyricist. Every lyricist I know refers to a rhyming dictionary from time to time, not so much for rhymes, but to open one's mind and to direct one's thought processes to associated words.

Things to Check for in a Completed Lyric

No amount of technique and perfect rhymes and balanced form can mean anything if your song is hackneyed or old-fashioned. But if you have created an original statement, don't put it aside until you check the following things:

- TITLE: Make sure it is interesting and that it is used several times in the chorus of the song.
- HOOK: This is a strong, short melodic and/or rhythmic idea. Often repeated, this is what the listener will remember after the first hearing.
- OPENING GRABBER: The first words should intrigue us to go into the song. "I've been alive forever"; "I learned the truth at seventeen"; "Don't go changin' and try to please me."
- MAKE YOUR POINT EARLY: The first fifteen seconds of the song are crucial. Don't ramble or you'll lose your audience.
- DON'T COUNT ON THE ARRANGEMENT TO STRENGTHEN YOUR SONG: The song must stand alone, words and music, so you'd better not delude yourself by thinking that a beautiful voice or a smashing recording will save it. They can only enhance what must be a good product to begin with.
- KEEP CONSISTENT TONE: If you're writing country, be sure every word sounds like a country person would sing.
- USE CONTEMPORARY LANGUAGE: Scan the newspapers and TV for current phrases if you want the song to sound of these times.
- DON'T GO ON ANY LONGER THAN NECESSARY: Don't rush through, but don't go on and on. Try to get your total message across within two minutes, allowing the other two minutes of recording time for repetition and instrumental.

PART II

MUSIC

5 MELODY

A SONG, of course, is made up of lyrics and music. No one can say which is more important, but we can say that in a slow ballad, the melody line will predominate, and if songs like "Feelings," "More," or "Hello" appeal to us, it is generally because we like their melodies. With a novelty song like "Splish-Splash" or a punch-line song like "Guess Who I Saw Today," the lyric is more important. And in a song like "All Night Long," it's the reggae rhythm that gets to us. But whether the lyrical message is less or more important than the music, *they must help each other*. A high note on a punch-line syllable or a jumpy line in a lullabye is equivalent to sabotage.

It is then the composer's job to make the words *sing*. This is accomplished by combining the elements that add up to what we call music. Each is a special art, and the amazing thing is that they all are used simultaneously! Rhythm can be a lifelong study. Percussionists and drummers will tell you that they are not concerned with melody or harmony. Their major attention is directed to subdividing their beat in the subtlest proportions. One has only to listen to the big-band recordings of Buddy Rich or Gene Krupa to understand how rhythm *alone* can be a satisfying experience. Add to it melody, and you will begin to imagine the complex fabric that the musician weaves. Of course even the simplest melody must be divided into its elements of pitch and rhythm, for mere tones (pitches) do not make a melody. Once the melody is created, the composer sets it off with harmony.

THE BASICS OF NOTATING A MELODY

Many memorable melodies have been created without their composers' knowing anything of the paraphernalia of musical composition. It has long been rumored, (though I've never believed it) that one of our doyen songwriters has a piano equipped with a lever to change keys, for the man, they say, plays only in the key of C. I know a theater composer who wrote an entire Broadway musical (a hit that ran for two years) without once setting a note to paper, for he sang his songs into a tape recorder. Of the Beatles, only Paul McCartney could read music. I have often played through musical albums written by friends, composers whose names are too well known to be mentioned here, whose work has been transcribed by someone in their publishing house from recordings into sheet music. So there is a precedent for many young and gifted songwriters to proclaim that it is a waste of time to learn to write music in the aural world in which we live. Who needs to care about lines and spaces and slurs and rests in a world dominated by thousands of hours of recordings?

You do! The majority of songwriters—almost invariably those who are more than a one- or two-record success—*can* read music. Many of them don't do it well, others are expert, but most still use the printed pages as an *added way of improving their songs.*

Stephen Sondheim, Stephen Schwartz, Marvin Hamlisch and Andrew Lloyd Webber (composers of *A Little Night Music, Pippin, A Chorus Line*, and *Cats*, respectively) still write out complete scores. Gershwin and Ellington in the past, and André Previn and Randy Newman in the present, can or could work in either classical or pop fields and are masters of orchestration as well. Joni Mitchell, Joan Baez, John Prine, Jimmy Webb, John Kander, Billy Joel, Barry Manilow, Neil Sedaka, and many others are able to notate the music they compose.

Having a song on paper will help you improve it, for the faults will glare at you from the page. You'll see at once if the vocal range is too wide for anyone but a hyena. You might not know why the song bores even you, but a glance at the paper could show you that you keep returning to the same pitch, a sure way to create the yawns. You may wonder, after performing the song, why your listeners take a few moments to realize the song is finished and to applaud, but your manuscript might show you that your melody peters off *downward*, a clue that you have missed the climax that should come near the song's end.

Writing down a melody is not easy. But if you really want to be a total songwriter, for the reasons above, you should learn to do it. Many songwriters are able to write their melodies with no aid from any instrument, and indeed, this is an ideal situation, but I would advise all beginners to take as much help as they can get. *Use a keyboard instrument at first*—piano (acoustic or electric) or organ, and *persist!* (A keyboard instrument will also help your understanding of scales, for they are most easy to visualize on anything from an 18-note electronic keyboard to a concert grand.) Music manuscript may have more "rules" than written language, but the page *always* sounds like it looks (unlike languages with words like *through* and *bomb*, which don't sound the way they look).

Since this is a book about song*writing* rather than song *taping*, I shall be obliged to introduce and analyze some musical terms that comprise the language of music. All terms will be defined in the Glossary. So don't stumble around words like *bars, pitches, time signatures, segues,* or *tessitura* expecting to grasp their meanings in context. Look up any term you don't understand, for if you are derailed by technical terms, it is difficult to regain the track. And you had better be sure-footed to withstand the layers that will be added to the melody — rhythm and harmony.

In my classes in songwriting, when I introduce melody writing, everybody groans. But after they have successfully notated their first tune, the groans become less audible. Once they have practiced writing melodies for a while, they become like anyone in any craft, more and more proficient, and what took hours in the beginning takes minutes and eventually seconds.

A few "givens" follow. I could never call them rules. Most of these might have been taught to you in music appreciation class in school.

The Staff

The grand staff, used for centuries, is a canvas for the circles and stems that we call pitches. When we wish to create high sounds, we indicate them on the top lines or spaces, and when we wish low tones, we use the bottom or even go below the staff. Songwriting usually involves only the upper five lines called the treble clef, even though the bass voices may sing down below.

THE GRAND STAFF

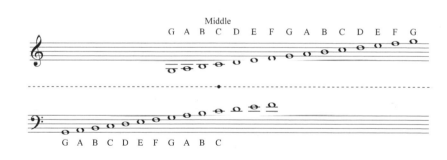

Because songwriting involves only the treble clef, you will not need to memorize the lines and spaces of the lower part of the grand staff. That section, called the bass clef, would be essential to you if you were a classical musician playing one of the low instruments like double bass or cello, but for all popular music (even if you play a low instrument like bass guitar), your music will be written in the treble clef.

It would be wise, then, to memorize the meanings of the various lines and spaces of the treble clef. The spaces are easily recalled because they spell face, and the lines reading upward, E, G, B, D, and F, are brought to mind by the familiar doggerel E(very) G(ood) B(oy) D(oes) F(ine). (In England, Every Good Boy Deserves Favour.)

THE TREBLE CLEF

When the pitches go above or below the staff, we create little pieces of lines and spaces to indicate them. These may be more difficult for the eye to accommodate, but eventually one recognizes them as quickly as the pitches that are squarely on the staff.

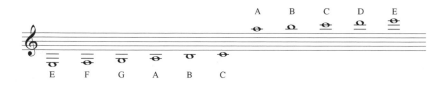

Sharps, Flats, and Naturals

Knowing the lines and spaces will give you access to only seven out of the twelve possible pitches into which our musical distance is divided. In our musical system, the sound between tones with the same letter name is divided into twelve equal parts. This division, which can be created on any instrument, fretted or valved, is perhaps most easily grasped by looking at a keyboard. The five black keys and their seven adjacent white keys comprise what is called an octave. In our musical system we divide this octave into twelve *equal* parts, called half tones. And to refer to these added subdivisions of the octave, we employ the terms *sharp* and *flat*, lumped together as *accidentals*. You will need to understand these if you intend to notate anything more involved than a simple folk tune. Put simply:

Sharp (♯) means to raise the indicated pitch a half tone.
Flat (♭) means to lower the indicated pitch by a half tone.
Natural (♮) means to cancel a foregoing sharp or flat.

1. Sharps and flats need not necessarily be black keys on the keyboard. E sharp is created by striking the same white key as F; C flat is the same as B.

2. A sharp or flat once indicated is in force throughout the measure or bar, (see below) unless cancelled by a natural.

3. In notating with accidentals, seek to choose the fewest possible for ease of reading.

which is much easier to read than

4. In speaking of these accidentals, we let the *letter name* precede and we say F sharp or B flat or A natural, but when we write them, the *sign* must precede the letter name. This is done so that anyone reading from a page will alter the pitch before it is struck.

Armed with a knowledge of pitches, you could almost make music, but before setting down your first melodies, you will need to know more than the tones involved in treble clef. You will need to understand: bar lines, time signatures, note values, and the major scale.

Bar Lines

The bar line is a musical division. Just as poetry is divided into pentameter and trimeter and as a story is made up of sentences, so a musical composition is comprised of bars. (Bars and measures are synonymous; *measures* is the term more often used in concert music, while *bars* is preferred by jazz and pop musicians.)

But before you can concern yourself with the divisions of the bar line, you will have to discover the regular pulsations found in the music. The regularity maintained by all music will be indicated in the time signature. It will say how many pulsations exist between accents.

Serious composers, especially contemporary ones, change the number of pulses in succeeding bars frequently. Stravinsky will use 3 beats in a bar followed by 7 in the next, succeeded by 4. This gives his music a rhythmic excitement and unpredictability, but this kind of shift is quite out of place in popular music, where most songs use a regular beat. Here the excitement is achieved by putting an accent on an unexpected part of the bar, usually 4 beats to the bar, or less frequently 3 beats to the bar.

Time Signature

A rundown of time signatures, in the context of popular-music rhythms, begins on page 236. I would suggest you don't even look at it until you have mastered the simple songs in this section. Time signatures are indicated by *two* numbers looking like a fraction (but never pronounced that way). The upper number indicates how many beats in each bar; the lower number indicates what *kind* of note gets *one* beat.

For most popular music and the simple songs that comprise this section, the time signature will be either 3/4 or 4/4. In 3/4 there will be three pulses (beats) to each bar; in the more common 4/4, there will be 4 pulses (beats) to each bar. In both cases, the quarter note will be equal to one pulse.

Taking a simple song, "Are You Sleeping?" ("Frère Jacques"), here is a way to discover the all-important time signature.

1. Sing the song aloud at a slower than usual tempo.
2. Clap your hands heavily on the outstanding beats and weakly on the light ones. Exaggerate.
3. Anytime your song conforms to *hard*, weak, weak, weak, you are creating four pulses, with the accent on the first one. The upper number in such a time signature would always be 4.
4. Remember to keep clapping even though there may be no syllable. Pulse and rhythm are constant as your heartbeat. And, like your heartbeat, the pulse goes on even though you may be silent or sleeping.

ARE	YOU	SLEEP	ING?	ARE	YOU	SLEEP	ING?
Hard				Hard			
clap	clap	clap	clap	clap	clap	clap	clap

BRO-	THER	JOHN,		BRO-	THER	JOHN	
Hard				Hard			
clap	clap	clap	clap	clap	clap	clap	clap

MORN-	ING	BELLS	ARE	RING-		ING	(repeat)
Hard							
clap		clap		clap		clap	

DING		DONG		DING		(repeat)	
Hard							
clap		clap		clap		clap	

Like any song whose pulsebeat is *hard clap, clap, clap, clap,* "Are You Sleeping?" would have a time signature of 4/4. Of course, the hard clap is the first beat of the bar, and the bar line (when you write it down) will be placed directly in front of the *hard clap.*

If you understand the above, you will be able to write the song with very little difficulty. At worst, you could "hunt and peck" at some keyboard instrument to discover the pitches you need, but the thing that's hardest for most neophytes—writing down the rhythm—will be practically solved.

At this point, rather than writing the melody, resist the urge to set pen to music paper and check back on some of the rhythmic facts we have discovered in "Are You Sleeping?"

In the first line, every syllable got *one* clap, while in the second, the word *John* got *two* claps. Moreover, in the third line, "Morning Bells Are" (four syllables) took only two claps. In music, the basic pulse is the quarter note, and syllables that get more or less than one pulse are indicated by the appropriate time values.

Time Values

o	**WHOLE NOTE**	4 pulses
𝅗𝅥	**HALF NOTE**	2 pulses
𝅘𝅥	**QUARTER NOTE**	1 pulse
𝅘𝅥𝅮	**EIGHTH NOTE**	½ pulse

A rhythmic sketch for "Are You Sleeping?" should make these time values clear. (In modern usage, groups of eighth notes are banded together for easier visualizing of the basic pulses.)

Before completing "Are You Sleeping?" by adding the melodic pitches, there is more to be understood about time values. Writing Richard Rodgers's "I'm in Love with a Wonderful Guy" will clarify what I mean. The A¹ section of the lyric is:

I'm as corny as Kansas in August
I'm as normal as blueberry pie
No more a smart little girl with no heart
I have found me a wonderful guy.

Clapping out the pulses, we arrive at:

I'M		AS	COR-	NY	AS
Hard			Hard		
clap	clap	clap	clap	clap	clap

KAN-	SAS	IN	AUG-		UST
Hard			Hard		
clap	clap	clap	clap	clap	clap

I'M		AS	NOR-	MAL	AS
Hard			Hard		
clap	clap	clap	clap	clap	clap

BLUE-	BER-	RY	PIE		
Hard			Hard		
clap	clap	clap	clap	clap	clap

NO	MORE	A	SMART	LIT-	TLE
Hard			Hard		
clap	clap	clap	clap	clap	clap

GIRL	WITH	NO	HEART,	I	HAVE
Hard			Hard		
clap	clap	clap	clap	clap	clap

FOUND	ME	A	WON-	DER-	FUL
Hard			Hard		
clap	clap	clap	clap	clap	clap

GUY.					
Hard			Hard		
clap	clap	clap	clap	clap	clap

The rhythmic impulse *hard clap*, clap, clap will always indicate 3/4 time. If you count the hard claps, you will find 16 of them, signalling the familiar 16-bar period. Three-quarter time is often erroneously called waltztime. Actually a song in 3/4 often is a WALTZ, but there are many 3/4 songs, especially gospel or country ones, that are far from waltzes.

Most of the clapping in "I'm in Love with a Wonderful Guy" is straightforward. The first syllable has two claps, which indicate a half note, and the rest of the song has one clap per syllable—except for the end of the second line, on the word "pie," and at the last line of the quotation, on the word "guy." "Pie" has three claps and "guy" has six. These examples introduce two new aspects of musical notation: the dot and the tie.

The dot is a useful tool that increases the note it follows by half. The tie, or slur, can also be used to prolong a note. The tie is most often used to carry a pitch *over* the bar in a case like the word "guy," since it is impossible to put six beats into one bar. The tie is especially useful when a composer wishes to hold a note for a long time.

A rhythmic sketch of "I'm in Love with a Wonderful Guy" would look like this:

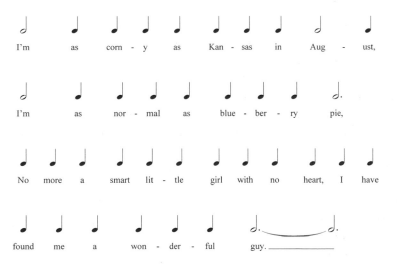

If you add bar lines to the rhythmic sketch (that is, insert a bar line before every hard clap), it actually begins to look like music! The sense of the lyric does not always match the division into bars.

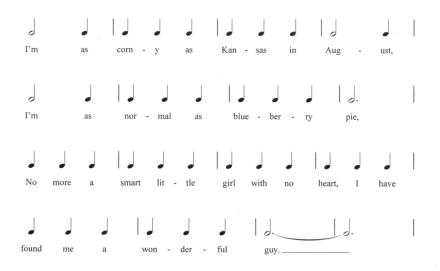

The Major Scale

Perhaps we could set down the pitches and rhythm of "Are You Sleeping?" and "I'm in Love with a Wonderful Guy," but it would be better first to know something about scales, for then we would set those songs down in a vocal range that is singable. This introduction will enable you to write simple tunes. The complete section on scales will be found on page 193.

A knowledge of major, minor, modal, and blues scales is essential to every songwriter. Chromatic, pentatonic, whole-tone, and exotic scales are occasionally called into play for special ethnic effects, and I would advise any advanced composer to study them.

All that can come later, but for this section on basics you must be familiar only with the major scale. In the last 150 years, the great majority of songs published and recorded in the United States have been in major keys, which means they have been constructed on a major scale.

How did we arrive at the major scale? And what, indeed, is a scale?

Historians have lately advanced the theory that early man's desire to approximate woman's voice resulted in the creation of the first scales. If a man sings a pitch and asks a woman to echo it, she will usually sing the same pitch in a register that is more comfortable for her voice, the two notes spanning an octave. Once the octave was achieved, the ladder from male to female had to follow naturally. Primitive man, aiming to fill the gaps between himself and his mate, created a series of grunts that led up to her voice.

If the theory is true, the experience must have been sublime, for the scale remains the basis of every musical system in the world. In the Far East, in classical times, the male-female rapprochement was divided into 5 equal parts (pentatonic); a Hungarian divided it into 24 equal parts by tuning two pianos a little bit (1/4 tone) apart, and centuries ago, long after it had been much used, an anonymous genius in ancient Ionia codified his region's scale. He made seven different steps of the Ionian octave ladder and varied the distances from rung to rung. It satisfied him and the Ionians to have a smaller pitch differential between the third and fourth tones on the ladder and also between the next to last and last.

In nearby Doria, they preferred having their shorter distances between the second and third rungs and the sixth and seventh of their ladder, while each of the other provinces of ancient Greece had its own home rules for scale-building. The one that conquered all — the one we use and find satisfying — is the Ionian. It has other names; some call it the first mode, others call it the "happy scale," but mostly it is known simply as the major scale.

To play one, you merely have to start on any C on any keyboard instrument, (the white key to the left of a group of two black keys), then follow the white keys on the instrument until you arrive at the next "C." You will have played the C major scale. Here it is notated.

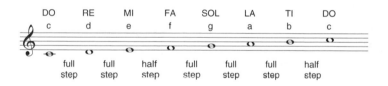

On the keyboard there is no difference between E and F and any of the other white keys in the gamut, but if you listen to the pitch, you will hear a closeness between E and F that does not exist between any of the "full step" keys. You could hear another "half step" closeness by striking, say, D♯ to E.

The members of the scale were given syllable names (extracted from the first syllables of the Latin Mass). In Europe, these are more familiar than the alphabet letter names. In the United States, letters are used almost exclusively. I suggest you familiarize yourself with both letter and syllable names.

Putting It All Together

Returning to where we left Brother John sleeping, we can now insert the melody to make a completed song. I always suggest beginners enter *only* the pitches at first, adding the accents, bar lines, and final rhythmic values later.

1. Notate the Pitches

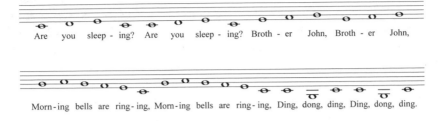

Are you sleep - ing? Are you sleep - ing? Broth - er John, Broth - er John,

Morn-ing bells are ring-ing, Morn-ing bells are ring-ing, Ding, dong, ding, Ding, dong, ding.

2. Put Accents on the Hard Claps

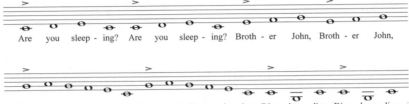

Are you sleep - ing? Are you sleep - ing? Broth - er John, Broth - er John,

Morn-ing bells are ring-ing, Morn-ing bells are ring-ing, Ding, dong, ding, Ding, dong, ding.

3. Put Bar Lines Before the Hard Claps

Are you sleep - ing? Are you sleep - ing? Broth - er John, Broth - er John,

Morn-ing bells are ring-ing, Morn-ing bells are ring-ing, Ding, dong, ding, Ding, dong, ding.

4. Complete by Adding Rhythmic Values, Clef Sign, and Time Signatures

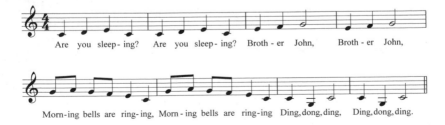

Are you sleep- ing? Are you sleep- ing? Broth - er John, Broth - er John,

Morn-ing bells are ring-ing, Morn - ing bells are ring-ing Ding, dong, ding, Ding, dong, ding.

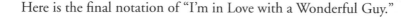

Here is the final notation of "I'm in Love with a Wonderful Guy."

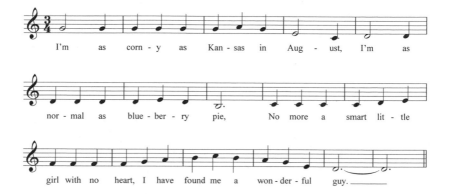

Each of these melodies is now complete. If you are a pop or rock composer, they may sound unfinished because they lack chord indications (in the United States, these chord names are printed above the melody; abroad, they're printed below). If you are a concert musician, you will miss the harmony that composers recreate for you by adding other pitches *below* the melody, and perhaps adding additional harmony in the bass clef (see page 202 for two-chord harmonizations).

You may have noticed that "I'm in Love with a Wonderful Guy" fits neatly into the lines and spaces of the treble clef, but in "Are You Sleeping?" many pitches wander below the staff. Not only does this make the song more difficult to read and to write, but it is harder for the garden-variety singer to perform. The song would be more singable if we lifted it a few tones, or *transposed* it.

TRANSPOSITION

Most music stores sell an inexpensive slide rule to tell you what notes you need when going from one preselected key to another. I believe this device is both impractical (it takes so long to look up each pitch that you waste many hours) and unprofessional (obviously you can't call yourself a songwriter if you need to refer to a crutch with each pitch). Nothing could be easier than transposition. Select simple keys and simple tunes until you get the hang of it. Once you do, you may find it boring, but never difficult. I have chosen to transpose "Are You Sleeping?" into F from the "lowish" (for it) key of C. Now it will fall mostly within the five lines of the staff.

In transposing from C to F, any C merely becomes F, and like in algebra, all D's become G's. This merely means *all pitches will be lifted a space and a line* (or *a line and a space*) as we move into the new key.

WILL EQUAL

Bar lines, note values, all other aspects remain the same. Here is "Are You Sleeping?" in the original and transposed.

IN C

Are you sleep-ing? Are you sleep-ing? Broth-er John, Broth-er John,

IN F

Are you sleep-ing? Are you sleep-ing? Broth-er John, Broth-er John,

IN C

Morn-ing bells are ring-ing, Morn-ing bells are ring-ing, Ding, dong, ding, Ding, dong, ding.

IN F

Morn-ing bells are ring-ing, Morn-ing bells are ring-ing, Ding, dong, ding, Ding, dong, ding.

KEY SIGNATURE

Because of the Ionian construction, with its half step between 3 and 4 and again between 7 and 8, if you move everything up in the scale and play the white keys from F to the next higher F, you would create a "sour" scale. Your ear would want to "fix" the B (4th tone of the scale) and change it to the black key directly to its left (called B♭—B flat). Had you lived centuries ago in Lydia, you might have enjoyed this scale, which, because of its bizarre 4th tone, most of us find humorous. On that Aegean island it would merely have been your native tool, the basis of all your composition (see modes—Lydian, page 197). But today, since our ears are accustomed to the major scale or Ionian mode, all others seem exotic at best; at worst, downright wrong.

In our system, it was decided that rather than constantly correct those B's by indicating them as "B♭'s," it made more sense to state the fact at the very beginning of the piece, immediately after the clef sign and before the time signature. This key signature means *all B's will be B♭'s until further notice.* (Composers of concert music indicate this key signature at the beginning of each line; popular composers indicate it only once at the beginning of the song, unless there is a change within the song.)

The key signature for the scale of F is B♭. What follows is a list of others. You will notice that there are fifteen key signatures even though there are only twelve different keys on the keyboard. This is because scales with many sharps can be spelled equally well as though they had many flats. C♯ major uses the same keyboard keys as D♭ major.

Memorizing fifteen key signatures is no easy task, and in the beginning is rather unnecessary. There is a simple rule for telling the key or scale merely by a glance at the key signature. (Incidentally, don't confuse *key* on the keyboard with key, or scale.)

In the sharps the key or scale is a half tone above the last sharp. For example, take a look at the key with 4 sharps. The last is on the fourth line (meaning D♯); the scale then is a half tone above the D♯, meaning E. *In the flats*, the key or scale is indicated by the next to last flat (of course, F, which has only one flat, will have to be memorized, but you know that one already). For example, take a look at the one with four flats. The next to last flat is on the second space A♭, and indeed that is the scale. Remember, these rules apply only to major keys. For songs constructed in minor or other modes, check the appropriate section.

IN WHICH KEY SHALL I WRITE MY SONG?

I always advise beginning songwriters to *write in the key of C.* Let the pitches stick out above or below your staff—I believe you will create better songs if you work in a simple key. Later, certainly, transpose it to any scale that is comfortable for your voice if *you* are the singer, or to a medium voice range for another's eventual performance.

I have found, however, that certain genres and eras have preferred certain keys, so if you wish to conform to a style or period, once you have composed your song in a simple key, it might be wise to transpose it.

Preferred Keys

Operetta Music	D♭	A♭	
Russian and gypsy music	G Minor	C Minor	
French chansons	D Minor	F	B♭
Spanish songs	F Minor	B♭	D Minor
American composers of the forties and fifties	E♭	A♭	B♭
Country	A	D	
Blues (classic)	B♭	C	G
Marches	G	D	
Hard Rock	D	A	E
Punk Rock	G	F	C

ACCIDENTALS

I have never meant to imply in my use of simple melodies like "Are You Sleeping?" or "I'm in Love with a Wonderful Guy" that all music stays within the scale. On the contrary, most of the melodies we find interesting frequently leave the seven different pitches of the scale for an accidental note. (They usually come right back in—if they don't, that is called modulation—see page 213.)

Transposing a melody that has accidentals is slightly more involved than transposing one with none. Also, songs in keys with many sharps or flats are a bit more difficult.

- A SHARP BECOMES A NATURAL WHEN TRANSPOSING TO FLATS.
- A SHARP STAYS A SHARP OR BECOMES A DOUBLE SHARP WHEN TRANSPOSING TO SHARPS.
- A FLAT BECOMES A NATURAL WHEN TRANSPOSING TO SHARPS.
- A FLAT STAYS A FLAT OR BECOMES A DOUBLE FLAT WHEN TRANSPOSING TO FLATS.

Study the two examples on the next page.

"CAN'T HELP LOVIN' DAT MAN" (MUSIC BY JEROME KERN, LYRIC BY OSCAR HAMMERSTEIN II)

"MARIA" (MUSIC BY LEONARD BERNSTEIN, LYRIC BY STEPHEN SONDHEIM)

INTERVALS

What makes "Over the Rainbow," "Maria," and "People" so instantly recognizable and so different from each other? Their opening intervals, the distances between their first two pitches. "Over the Rainbow" uses an expansive interval, an octave; "Maria" uses an exotic one, the augmented fourth; and "People" uses a comfortably homey one, a major second.

Composers should know the characters of intervals, because a melody is, in a way, a series of connect the dots. Every song is a collection of hundreds of intervals. If the series is logical and repetitive enough, the song will satisfy us. If the intervals vary wildly, the melody will be jagged. In the extreme, the music will sound dissonant and disorganized.

Intervals are divided into two categories, perfect and imperfect. The perfect ones used to sound correct before the sixteenth century. They sound hollow and empty to us today. They are the fourths and fifths and octaves. You can create their sound by striking C and F or C and G on any keyboard instrument. You will hear the "tuning up" sound often considered harsh.

What antiquity categorized as imperfect intervals are known as seconds, thirds, sixths, and sevenths. Although the seconds and sevenths still sound dissonant to most of us the thirds and sixths sound smooth and romantic. Most people would consider them closer to perfection than the perfect intervals. This is because we are closer to classic and romantic music of the nineteenth century, which relied heavily on the lushness of thirds and sixths. You may savor the sound of thirds by striking C and E; turn the notes upside down, E below the C, and you will have a sixth.

The names given intervals can confuse a beginner, but one must merely examine, say, C and D, which keys are adjacent on the keyboard and whose pitches are adjacently notated on the staff and remember that this is called an interval of a *second*—not a first. Similarly, C to E is called an interval of a *third*, not a second.

Intervals may be altered according to the following rules regardless of whether they ascend or descend.

- Increasing the span of a perfect interval by a half step results in an augmented interval.
- Decreasing the span of a perfect interval by a half step results in a diminished interval.
- Increasing the span of a major interval by a half step results in an augmented interval.
- Decreasing the span of a major interval by a half step results in a minor interval.
- Increasing the span of a minor interval by a half step results in a major interval.
- Decreasing the span of a minor interval by a half step results in a diminished interval.

The following chart should help you understand all intervals:

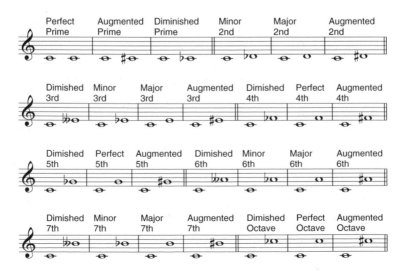

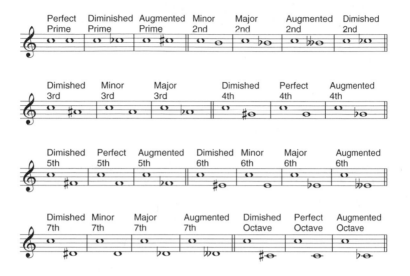

The chart above will help you recall intervals. Select a song from each group and you will easily be able to summon to memory all the distances between pitches. Notice that there are no examples of the augmented fourth downward or the major seventh downward. This writer could find none existing at the beginning of a well-known song. Perhaps you can find one or, lacking that, write a song using one. The syllables that are italicized indicate where the interval occurs.

Going Upward

MINOR SECOND—ONE HALF STEP

"The Windmills of Your Mind"   Like *a cir*-cle
"Everything's Coming Up Roses"   *Things look* grand
"Temptation"   You *came, I* was alone

MAJOR SECOND—TWO HALF STEPS

"People"   *Peo-ple*

MINOR THIRD—THREE HALF STEPS

"Alone Together"   *A-lone* together
"Sunshine on My Shoulder"   *Sun-shine* on my shoulder
"Somewhere, My Love"   *Some-where*, my love
"Put a Little Love in Your Heart"   *Think of* your fellow man

MAJOR THIRD — FOUR HALF STEPS

"You'll Never Walk Alone"	When you *walk through* a storm
"Help Me Make It Through the Night"	*Take the* ribbon from my hair
"Just the Way You Are"	*Don't go* changing
"Softly, as I Leave You"	*Soft-ly*

PERFECT FOURTH — FIVE HALF STEPS

"Here Comes the Bride"	*Here comes* the bride
"Look to the Rainbow"	*Look, look,* look to the rainbow
"Big Spender"	*Hey, big* spen-der
"Small World"	*Fun-ny,* you're a stranger who's …
"Chariots of Fire"	first two pitches

AUGMENTED FOURTH — SIX HALF STEPS

"Maria"	*Ma-ri-*a

PERFECT FIFTH — SEVEN HALF STEPS

"Stranger in Paradise"	Take *my hand*
"Love and Marriage"	*Love and* marriage
"Alfie"	What's it all about, *Al-fie*
"Georgie Girl"	*Hey there,* Georgie Girl

MINOR SIXTH — EIGHT HALF STEPS

"Bei Mir Bist Du Schoen"	*Bei mir* bist du schoen
"Weekend in New England"	*Last night* we said goodbye
"The Entertainer"	3rd to 4th pitches

MAJOR SIXTH — NINE HALF STEPS

"Jingle Bells"	*Dash-ing* through the snow
"NBC Chimes"	*NBC*
"Speak Low"	*Speak low* when you speak love
"Hey, Look Me Over"	*Hey, look* me over

MINOR SEVENTH — TEN HALF STEPS

"There's a Place for Us"	*There's a* place for us
"Heart"	*You've got* to have heart

MAJOR SEVENTH — ELEVEN HALF STEPS

"I Will Wait for You" If it takes for*ever, I* will wait for you

OCTAVE — TWELVE HALF STEPS

"Paper Moon" Say, *it's on*-ly a paper moon
"Over the Rainbow" *Some-where* over the rainbow
"When You Wish Upon a Star" *When you* wish upon a star

MAJOR NINTH — FOURTEEN HALF STEPS

"Through the Years" *Through the* years
"I Got It Bad (and That Ain't Good)" Nev-*er treats* me sweet and gentle

Going Downward

MINOR SECOND — ONE HALF STEP

"Just in Time" *Just in* time
"Enough is Enough" Enough *is e*-nough
"Spinning Wheel" *Ride a* painted pony
"Aquarius" This is the dawning of *the age* of Aquarius

MAJOR SECOND — TWO HALF STEPS

"Wishing" *Wish-ing* will make it s-o
"The Way We Were" *Mem-'ries* light the corner of my mind
"Honesty" *Hon-es*-ty, is such …
"Gloria" Glo-*ri-a*

MINOR THIRD — THREE HALF STEPS

"Bewitched, Bothered and Bewildered" *I'm wild* again
"Gonna Fly Now" (Theme from *Rocky*) Gonna *fly now*
"Don't Rain on My Parade" *Don't tell* me not to fly
"Honey" See the *tree how* big it's grown

MAJOR THIRD — FOUR HALF STEPS

"Song Sung Blue"   *Song sung* blue

PERFECT FOURTH — FIVE HALF STEPS

"Little Boy Lost"   Little *boy lost*
"Born Free"   *Born Free*
"Someday I'll Find You"   *Some-day* I'll find

PERFECT FIFTH — SEVEN HALF STEPS

"Copacabana"   At the *Co-pa*
"Feelings"   *Feel-ings*
"You Don't Bring Me Flowers"   You don't *bring me* flowers

MINOR SIXTH — EIGHT HALF STEPS

"You Don't Bring Me Flowers"   You don't bring me flowers *a-ny* more
"Love Story"   *Where do* I begin

MAJOR SIXTH — NINE HALF STEPS

"Moonlight Becomes You"   *Moon-light* becomes you
"Come to Me, Bend to Me"   *Come to* me, bend to me

MINOR SEVENTH — TEN HALF STEPS

"The Shadow of Your Smile"   The shadow of *your smile*

OCTAVE — TWELVE HALF STEPS

"Spring Will Be a Little Late"   *Spring will* be a little late this year

You may have noticed that certain intervals appear more frequently on the above chart and are commonly used, while others appear only rarely. Because they are more satisfying and easier to sing, seconds, thirds, fourths, fifths, and sixths, both ascending and descending, are common. The upward octave gives thrust to a melody, while the downward octave is beyond most people's range—difficult and undramatic.

The skip of a seventh (major or minor) upward or downward, while difficult, is most exciting. It is much used in concert songs but rarely employed in popular music. I believe it offers many untapped possibilities. But the skip of a ninth, while equally as exciting, is so hard to sing that I'd suggest you avoid it.

MOTIVES

Armed with some basics, almost anyone can put together a melody. You could arbitrarily say, "I'll start with a major sixth upward, followed by a perfect fifth downward, put the whole into 4/4 time, and see what happens." What you created would not be too bad, but it would not be a song; it would be a string of pitches.

To create anything more than a string of pitches, you must have an idea that "sings." It may come to you while walking in the park or when you're trying to fall asleep. It may be triggered by a phrase someone has said or something you read. It may come complete with words or be only a musical fragment. It is known to all songwriters as the most important element of the song. It is the musical motive. (Some call it the motif, but I find that word pretentious.)

Where does this germ of a musical idea come from? Those who can't write songs or are too lazy to try say it is God-given. Although I am unable to answer the question of origin, I can give you an idea of how many composers get started on their melodies.

Some get their musical kernels by fooling around with a group of pitches, not by being arbitrary, but by picking and repeating a certain string of pitches until they arrive at a series that takes their fancy. Others get started by humming a brief snatch of melody while strumming a chord background on the piano or guitar.

But for most professional songwriters, the title is the impetus for the musical motive.

Jim Webb says: "I choose the title before I begin writing the melody. Usually I first get some idea of the story or feeling I wish to convey, and then devote serious energy to the music."

Bob Barrett insists that "a good hook, often in the title, leads to a good tune and the lyrics will flow without effort." (One of his hits was titled "I Second That Emotion," the kind of hook-title discussed under *Gimmick Songs*.)

With Paul McCartney, it is the title again, and it doesn't have to have originated with him. McCartney: "I heard Spike Mulligan make this analogy with black and white notes on the piano; he said, 'You know it's a funny kind of thing—black notes, white notes, you need to play the two to make harmony, folks.'" This suggested the final title of "Ebony and Ivory." McCartney adds that he then began playing around with the key of E and found that when he had created a motive that satisfied him, he had used the black keys for the word *ebony* and the white keys for the word *ivory*. I suspect that the black-white execution of this motive required some forethought.

Paul Simon says that "Bridge over Troubled Water" was first suggested by a gospel singer's improvised line. "He said something to the effect that he will be somebody's bridge over deep water."

In the mid-eighties, Simon's primary method of composition was to play along with a recording of a song, following that composer's harmony. Paul Simon adds, "I started making chord substitutions, changing the harmony and then the melody. At a certain point I stopped and said, 'Well, this is no longer a Sam Cooke song, it's different, and I like it.'" Although this method seems like cheating, it is very common and respectable and one that all songwriters use on days when they are not feeling very inspired.

Jeff Barry has said that "the title of the song is as important as the name of any product, especially if it makes you want to hear what the song's about or can strike a responsive chord in the listener." He adds that he'll be sitting at a piano and "I'll think of a phrase, or someone will say something and I'll say 'Gee, there may be a song in that.'"

My advice to a songwriter is: Get the concept. Refine it into a song title. Set the title to music with as memorable a melody as you can find. Don't go on until you have polished the motive.

How to Turn the Title into a Musical Motive

Since music is so repetitive, your song risks its life on your apt setting of its title or hook. The best of titles cannot survive a draggy or, worse, dull setting. The more memorable your *first* phrase is, the more memorable the entire song. So spend time and *polish it*.

Richard Rodgers used to say that when he had the motive for "Bali Ha'i" (which came after a struggle), it was incredibly easy to write the song.

The three pitches that comprise that title have an inevitability. It is hard to say the words *Bali Ha'i* without a rising inflection in your voice. The big octave skip followed by the descending half tone is exotic and fitting for a song about a forbidden island, for the descending half tone is a "forbidden" note, because it goes out of the scale. The way the melody turns and goes in the other direction after the big skip is simply one of the rules of good melody writing.

Another example of an immediate grabber in setting of the opening words is the Gershwins' "A Foggy Day (in London Town)." George usually suggested the titles to Ira, who then went on to complete the lyric.

A fog-gy day in Lon - don town

These first three pitches give us a clue to the gloominess of the song. They help to establish the lonely mood of the protagonist. Although the words vary, the pitches remain static. Nothing's happening. The whole melody might have been written thus:

A foggy day in London town

At the end of the song, where the lyric proclaims, "Suddenly I saw *you* there and through foggy London Town the sun came shining ev'rywhere," the melody moves into eighth notes and skips all over the place with joy. George Gershwin, always sophisticated, was one of the first to flout convention and avoid the obvious. In setting the lyric at the spot "It had me low/ it had me down," he chose to have his melody *ascend* on the words "low" and "down."

Some - where   o - ver the rain - bow

This is another great motive. Coupled with its moving lyric, it suggests being released from a mundane, earthbound existence. The octave skip yearns and soars on the some-where syllables. Now the harmony of C7, after two heartrending minor chords, brings out the sun. Even though the lyricist, Yip Harburg, called the song "Over the Rainbow," the public always requests "Somewhere over the Rainbow," testifying to the importance of that octave jump in the motive. The leap over the rainbow seems to span several octaves, and we have to look again at the page to assure ourselves that it's only one.

A motive should suggest the feeling of the song. The Sondheim-Styne "Little Lamb" is a good example. The rising major sixth interval is a particularly gentle one, which befits a "little lamb." The Bernstein-Sondheim "Maria" uses an augmented fourth, a rare, elusive, and somewhat exotic interval suggesting the foreign character of the heroine, Maria. "Born Free" begins with the interval of the descending fourth, which has strength, openness, and honesty.

Single-Note Motives

A motive can be as long as eight or nine notes or as brief as one. The note may be repeated, but as long as the pitch doesn't change, it's classified as a single-note motive. Those that are composed of a single note must have some rhythmic interest or they will be insufferably dull.

"(ALL OF A SUDDEN) MY HEART SINGS" (MUSIC BY JAMBLIN, LYRIC BY HAROLD ROME, JAMBLIN, AND HERPIN)

All of a sud - den___ my heart sings

Although this song lacks great rhythmic variety, the ensuing rising scale line made it memorable and propelled it to the top of the charts.

"ONE-NOTE SAMBA" (MUSIC BY ANTONIO CARLOS JOBIM, LYRIC BY JOHNNY MERCER)

This is just a lit - tle sam - ba built up - on a sin - gle note___

The harmonic design, the samba beat (actually more of a bossa nova), but mostly the concept of returning to the same pitch made this song a hit.

"A MAN AND A WOMAN" (MUSIC BY FRANCIS LAI)

"A Man and a Woman" depends on its implied harmonies to make its one-pitched point. Besides having the asset of a splendid rhythm, this song has a fresh major-seventh interval relationship.

When using single-note motives, make sure you create interest by using interesting rhythm, implied harmony, and/or an interesting lyric. Of course, the combination of all three elements is best.

Two-Note Motives

Two-note motives are easier to use than those that remain fixed on a single pitch, but you must still be careful to avoid a boring ping-pong that frequently happens when bouncing from pitch to pitch as in the first example below.

"CAROLINA IN THE MORNING" (MUSIC AND LYRIC BY WALTER DONALDSON)

Noth-ing could be fin-erthan to   be in Car o - li-na in the morn - ing *(etc.)*

"S'WONDERFUL" (MUSIC BY GEORGE GERSHWIN, LYRIC BY IRA GERSHWIN)

Since a two-note motive turns out to be an interval, the composer should know which kind of interval creates which mood. Use the skips that suit your concept. The third as we see in the tunes above is jaunty and bouncy, while the interval of a rising second is full of hope. Perhaps that was what led Jule Styne to use it so movingly in "People" (lyric by Bob Merrill).

The same brightness (minus the hope) is apparent in "Dinah" (music by Harry Hest, lyric by Sam M. Lewis and Joe Young).

The interval of a major third downward can be most poignant especially when the composer keeps returning to the original note. Gershwin made it the motive of "Summertime," and Berlin used it in similar fashion for his saddest song, "Suppertime."

Perfect fourths as used in "Mame" and "Born Free" have strength, and sixths as used in "Love Story" and "Little Lamb" create tenderness. Remember when using two-note motives not to bounce boringly, and to select an interval that *suits* your concept.

Three-Note Motives

It has been said that the perfect motive length is three. After all, we began this book with "Three Blind Mice," one of the sixteenth century's big hits. But seriously, if we examine *this* century's greatest hits we'll find that most of their motives are built on three pitches. "Tea for Two," "The Man I Love," "Body and Soul," "Superstar," "Yesterday," "Through the Years," "I Love You," "Song Sung

Blue," "Maria," "Just in Time," "Spinning Wheel," and "Gloria" are merely a few of the triple-pitched winners. And there are two good reasons for this: Title length is ideally short and sweet, and the composer can start off on an upward interval and complete the motive with a downward one (or vice versa), which makes good balance. Sometimes, as in "The Man I Love," the first two pitches can bounce back and forth and land on the third.

I have illustrated a few remarkable three-note motives below.

"THE MAN I LOVE" (MUSIC BY GEORGE GERSHWIN, LYRIC BY IRA GERSHWIN)

"DON'T BLAME ME" (MUSIC BY JIMMY McHUGH, LYRIC BY DOROTHY FIELDS)

"SONG SUNG BLUE" (MUSIC AND LYRIC BY NEIL DIAMOND)

"TEA FOR TWO" (MUSIC BY VINCENT YOUMANS, LYRIC BY IRVING CAESAR)

As you can see from most of the motives, pitches may be repeated without destroying the feeling that you are listening to a three-note motive.

Motives of Four or More Notes

Motives of more than three pitches usually rely heavily on repetition or on scale line, and because they have more elongated lines, they are not usually as immediately memorable as short ones. Think how "People," once we have heard it, never leaves us, or how "I Want Muscles" drags its tune along with the words and becomes unforgettable. I have notated some longer motives below. All are beautiful, but are difficult for the listener to recall.

"IF HE WALKED INTO MY LIFE" (MUSIC AND LYRIC BY JERRY HERMAN)

Did he need a strong-er hand

"FASCINATION" (MUSIC BY T. D. MARCHETTI, LYRIC BY JEAN REYNOLDS DAVIS)

It was Fas-ci - na - tion I know

"FALLING IN LOVE WITH SOMEONE" (MUSIC BY VICTOR HERBERT, LYRIC BY RIDA JOHNSON YOUNG)

For I'm fall - ing in love with some - one

Where to Take the Motive

When you have composed what you consider an interesting motive, polished it, and arrived at an original lyric to match the accents of the melody, you should begin to explore the possibilities inherent in your motive. You might do the following:

1. *Repeat the motive exactly as you created it* (with a different or the same lyric).
2. *Repeat it exactly but on* higher *pitches.*
3. *Repeat it exactly but on* lower *pitches.*
4. *(If the motive is long enough) Repeat only a part of it.*
5. *Repeat it as before, but change the intervals slightly.*
6. *Put it aside for a few measures while you announce another motive, and then return to the original motive.*

Since all songwriters begin to chew their pencils after they've completed their motives, I feel it's worthy of the time it takes to investigate each of the different treatments of the motive. I shall use a simple, not very inspired motive that can be handled in any of the above ways. That will allow us to see the effect of each treatment.

You're all   I   want - ed

1. Repeating the motive exactly, we get

which is very dull. When you have a motive that does not have much interest in itself, it is rare that you can repeat it exactly. John Lennon and Paul McCartney repeated their motive three times exactly as first stated in "Lucy in the Sky with Diamonds," but what a motive it was. The placement, coming after a wordy verse in 3/4 time, also influenced its need to be repeated. It is usually better to change the harmony. A discussion of harmony and how it affects a motive begins on page 206.

Some well-known motives that *do not* change harmony are: "Weekend in New England," "Blowin' in the Wind," "Mr. Bojangles," "Day by Day," "Reunited," "Today," "A Man and a Woman," "Mack the Knife," and "The Rose." In most cases I believe they would be more interesting if they *did* change harmony.

Listen to the opening two phrases of "My Funny Valentine"; when you hear the bass descending, on the words "sweet comic Valentine," you will understand that the motive is much intensified by the use of altered harmony. In addition to "My Funny Valentine," "How Deep Is the Ocean," "It's All Right with Me," "Feelings," "If He Walked into My Life," "Until It's Time for You to Go," "The Man That Got Away," "Maybe This Time," and "I Can't Smile Without You," are some of the songs that repeat their first motives exactly *but change* the harmony.

2. Repeating the motive exactly, but on higher pitches, we get:

You're all   I   want - ed,   You're all   I   dreamed of...

Of course, the harmony would change as pitches rise. The melody could be moved up a tone or more, as in the following, which creates a more interesting line.

Some songs that employ the same motive moved higher are "Sing," "The Impossible Dream," "Mame," and "Brand New Key." Often, the motive is slightly changed, as in "Raindrops Keep Falling on My Head" or in "Hello, Dolly."

3. Repeating the motive exactly, but on lower pitches, we get:

This too is interesting and much better than repeating the motive where it stands. Sing the beginnings of "Don't It Make My Brown Eyes Blue," "MacArthur Park," "More," "Strangers in the Night," "Love on the Rocks," and "The Candy Man," and you will hear the effect of repeating the motive lower.

4. Repeating only part of a long motive is generally best done after several exact repetitions of the motive, as in "If He Walked into My Life" (Jerry Herman).

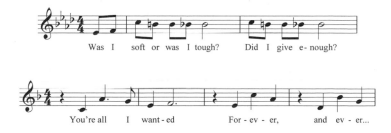

Our sample motive could be handled as above, but you can see that it is not as effective or as strong as total repetition.

5. Repeating, but changing the intervals.

This is always a way to create interest in a well-worn motive. It seems to work best when the motive has very definite intervals:

Some well-known songs that use this technique are "You Needed Me," "You Don't Bring Me Flowers," "Bewitched, Bothered and Bewildered," "A Ship Without a Sail," "Alone Again—Naturally," "Oliver," "Five Foot Two, Eyes of Blue."

6. Abandoning the motive (only to return to it later):

The verse of "Lucille" (Music and Lyric by Roger Bowling and Hal Bynam) uses a motive repeated exactly as before, but the chorus announces a motive and then abandons it. The words "you picked a fine time to leave me, Lucille," return again at the end of the chorus, but the MOTIVE does not. This is an extreme example, for usually songs insist on repeating their opening motive. Using the motive that we used before, we might arrive at:

Some of the greatest songs announce their motives and then abandon them. They may be long motives, where immediate repetition would be bothersome, or indelible ones that become imprinted in our memory as soon as they are announced. Songs like "Just the Way You Are," "The Best of Times," "Those Were the Days," "I Don't Know How to Love Him," "The First Time Ever I Saw Your Face," "Delta Dawn," "Don't Cry Out Loud," "The Way We Were," and many, many others use this technique.

How to Freshen a Worn Motive

By the time you have worked your motive through all the possibilities listed above, you may discover, as many songwriters do, that you have written a worn out series of pitches or, worse, an unoriginal one. What do you do now? Throw it away? Not at all! Freshen it. Below are several ways you might breathe new life into a motive that you, or your friends, find boring.

Example 1

How   dry   I   am

Could anything be more tired than those four pitches? I may have chosen an extreme example, the like of which you would never create, but even it can be disguised to make it more palatable.

Example 1. Upper appoggiatura

Add an upper appoggiatura (*appoggiatura* means a leaning note), one that does not belong to the prevailing harmony. It can be used above the important note as decoration (Example 1).

Example 2. Lower appoggiatura

Upper appoggiaturas sound best when they occur on a strong beat, because they stand out and are thus more interesting, but lower ones (Example 2) could occur anywhere. (The tune with the addition of the *upper* appoggiatura sounds like Jule Styne's "The Party's Over"; with the addition of the *lower* appoggiatura it resembles one by Richard Strauss.)

Example 3. Passing tones

Passing tones (pitches that pass from one important pitch to another) can decorate and disguise the "How Dry I Am." Jerry Herman added a jaunty rhythm to his passing tones to create "Open a New Window" in *Mame* (Example 3).

Example 4. Lower neighbors

Neighbors (decorations a half or whole tone below [Example 4] or above [Example 5] any chord tone) may be added to freshen a motive. Lower neighbors generally are a half tone below the principal tone; upper neighbors usually conform to the scale.

Example 5. Upper neighbors

Example 6. Repetitions

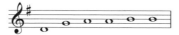

Repetitions: any member of a series may be repeated. Suddenly the banal "How Dry I Am" is transformed into an intense motive like "What Kind of Fool Am I?" Anthony Newley created interest in his song by having the repeated note fall on a strong beat.

Example 7. Changing the mode

Changing the mode: A common, almost laughable method of freshening a worn motive is to put what is major into minor and vice versa. I once heard "Jingle Bells" in minor, presented as "Russian Jingle Bells." I find these things boringly predictable, but audiences love them (Example 7). This kind of disguise is passable if you extend the motive (Example 8).

Example 8. Changing mode and lengthening

Example 9. Hurry through

Hurry through: If we use fairly quick rhythms on the motive so we are almost unaware it's there we can intensify what is to come. Cole Porter did just that in "Don't Fence Me In" (Example 9).

It would not be difficult to go on and find many examples of similar motives and tunes that use these same four pitches. ("You're My Sunshine," "Lush Life," and the "Merry Widow Waltz" ring readily to mind.) By now, you should be aware that composers frequently employ pitches already used by others. After all, we all work with the same twelve pitches. Remember, *never* throw away a good series of pitches. If you feel they lack personality, find a way to fix them. Beginning composers are often too insecure, feeling they have stolen someone else's motive. I always advise them to write it as they hear it and then to ask one or two friends whether they have heard it before. Usually the answer is no. If yes, change it by using one of the methods above. After all, none of the songs above would have been written had its composer said, "That's no good," or "Someone else has already written that," or "It sounds like 'How Dry I Am.'"

EXPANDING THE MOTIVE INTO A PHRASE

What is a phrase? In musical language, it is "the motive expanded and completed," a section usually four measures long. For practical purposes, consider that a slice of the song between natural breathing points is generally *half* of a section.

In Billy Joel's "Just the Way You Are," the motive sets on the lyric "Don't go changing," while the *phrase* length (4 bars) would be "Don't go changing, and try to please me." In "Home on the Range," the motive is "Oh, give me a home," while the phrase expands to "Oh, give me a home where the buffalo roam, and the deer and the antelope play." *Think of a phrase as a completed thought.*

"Somewhere, My Love" (Music by Maurice Jarre, Lyric by Paul Francis Webster) is an excellent illustration.

In extending your motive into a phrase, generally use fresh material. You may have repeated your motive enough by now, and your listeners are eager for a change. Do not, however, use anything that will disturb the flow of the melodic line. Don't change rhythms or mood. Some have said that the motive is like a question and the completion of the phrase gives the answer.

EXPANDING THE PHRASE INTO A PERIOD

What is called a period in concert music is usually referred to as a section in pop or jazz. A period is a complete segment that may repeat. Usually it consists of eight measures or bars. I prefer to use the term "period" because it is more definite.

Notice that this period, appropriately enough, ends with period. A period may be thought of as a segment completed by a mark of punctuation. (A comma can often be your clue to phrase length.)

Oh, give me a home where the buffalo roam,
Where the deer and the antelope play,
Where seldom is heard a discouraging word,
And the skies are not cloudy all day.

Returning to the above examples, "Just the Way You Are" divides itself, as do thousands of other songs, into four periods. This time, periods mark off the phrases, too, but the thought is only completed at the end of the fourth line.

Don't go changing and try to please me,
You never let me down before.
Don't imagine you're too familiar
And I don't see you anymore.

The examples above fill their eight-bar period, and then would begin again with repetition. In many of the songs of the thirties and forties the melody (and lyric) ended at the beginning of the seventh bar, necessitating a wait until the period *felt* complete. Harmonically, this time was filled in with a turnaround or turnback (see the chapter on harmony, page 201).

RANGE

Like hemlines, range, the vocal span of a song, has varied with each era. In the 1900s through the flapper period, range was wide, since most music was operetta-inspired. It was common for songs to encompass an octave and a half.

Franz Lehar, Rudolph Friml, Sigmund Romberg, and even Noel Coward and Jerome Kern created music to exhibit the operatic gifts of their heroes and heroines. Most of the performers on the musical stage had originally come from opera and reveled in the chance to display their high C's. All the women used "headtones," or what is now known as "legit" voice production (allowing air from the diaphragm to vibrate the vocal chords rather than creating sound by tightening the neck and chest muscles). "Legit" voice production creates a high, flutelike sound, often at the sacrifice of word comprehension.

The men were all tenors, sometimes trained in opera, and in the few cases where their voices were very small, they used a megaphone, as Rudy Vallee did, to project their sound. Most of the big stars were "Irish tenors," who used a falsetto sound. Baritones were not popular, for they usually played villains, another tradition borrowed from opera.

With the emergence of Berlin, Rodgers, and Gershwin as leading songwriters, most of the "artiness," operetta quality, and wide range disappeared. "Belt" or "chest" sound became the vocal quality songwriters sought in their interpreters. Ethel Merman and Judy Garland, two legendary belters, set the standards. Composers, and especially lyricists, now wanted the man in the street to be able to sing their work. They had to eliminate the phony poetic language and narrow the range of the melody. The span for a popular song now dwindled to an octave, an octave and two notes at the outside.

Unfortunately, composers still wrote their songs with high vocal ranges, putting the music well above the garden-variety singer, but clever accompanists were able to transpose the tunes to make them comfortable for the newly developed crooners. Sopranos disappeared from the airwaves and were relegated to the choruses of Broadway shows. Belters had a range from G below middle C to C or D 12 or 13 notes above, and torch singers had an even lower range. Beyond her low reedy tones, a torch singer had to have glamour and a sultry delivery. Then with the advent of electronic recording, fabulous microphones could pick up everything, and small, intimate, breathy voices came into vogue.

Throughout the fifties and well into the sixties, most songs stuck to the parameters laid down in pre-rock days—8 or 10 scale tones maximum. But the sexual revolution permitted men to sing falsetto without being labeled feminine. Urgent issues motivated singers to express what they "felt," often necessitating that they reach for a pitch beyond their range. The songwriter-performer, emerged and the public accepted their authenticity and no longer sought trained or beautiful voices.

Songwriters like Jim Webb and Burt Bacharach, with their exponents Richard Harris and Dionne Warwick, wrote songs with wide ranges. The public accepted what they wrote and bought their recordings. In a group, somebody could manage to hit the high and low notes. Soul, a fervid, inspired sound, used religious feeling to break the chains of narrow range.

It became more important to have a "best-selling record" than to have a best-selling song. No longer was it necessary for the man in the street to be able to sing the song; he merely had to buy it.

Yet for most songs written today, the rule of keeping within the range of a tenth still applies. That is because *longer ranges do not make a cohesive sound*. In writing a song, try not to feel imprisoned by the range, but use it to keep your song from sprawling. Step beyond the tenth if you wish. As a rule, I'd say you can anything that *you* can sing. (Barbra Streisand uses a wide range in "Evergreen," and Billy Joel an enormous one, almost two octaves, in "Innocent Man.")

Tessitura

Tessitura may sound like one of those unnecessary fancy words, but it is a very important musical term that refers to general range. We say a song has a high tessitura when it stays around the top pitches for longer than it does at the bottom.

Songs that remain for a long period at the top of their ranges will not only be boring but will be tiring for the singer. We rarely hear anyone but the composer sing Billy Joel's "Piano Man" because the tessitura of the chorus is so unrelievedly high that most singers have to strain for those top notes. Try to save your highest pitches for the song's climax. Once that point is reached, most well-made songs retreat from the top to explore a lower tessitura. This makes a more satisfying melody and a balanced song. It is wise to check the tessitura of your song once you have completed it to see that you don't keep punching out the same top (or bottom) pitches.

MELISMA

The dictionary defines melisma as the "unit of melody that is sung to one syllable." Today, we frequently use many melodic notes on one syllable, but the popular songs of the thirties and forties forbade it. Melisma, or melismatic passages, are popular throughout concert music. Singers like to show off their voices, and Mozart and Handel and Berlioz gave them the opportunity. Here is a passage from Mozart's *Magic Flute*:

Jazz musicians have always improvised and used melisma in their work, but it was not until the advent of soul that the "bent" note or "florid group of notes" reentered our musical language. In addition to written melisma, recording artists of all kinds sometimes improvise and add subtle melismatic notes.

"DON'T IT MAKE MY BROWN EYES BLUE" (MUSIC AND LYRIC BY RICHARD LEIGH)

SEQUENCE

It has been mentioned that among other activities, a motive can move up or down. A movement of pitches separated by the same interval relationship is called sequence. Sequence is one of the composer's most useful tools.

Beginners are often not aware of the power of sequence, but it helps build excitement, unity, and balance. Of course one can overdo, (three times is the maximum), but I find new composers generally are too reluctant to use sequence in their motives or phrases.

"THE IMPOSSIBLE DREAM" (MUSIC BY MITCH LEIGH, LYRIC BY JOE DARION)

"LOVER" (MUSIC BY RICHARD RODGERS, LYRIC BY LORENZ HART)

SOME RULES FOR MELODY WRITING

Noel Coward has often written about his only class in harmony, during which he was exposed to *rules*. "The teacher told me I must never use consecutive fifths, and when I pointed out that they had been used successfully by Debussy and Ravel, he said they were exceptions to the *rule*. I walked out of the class and that was the end of my harmonic training."

You too will find many exceptions to the rule, especially when you are looking for fresh melodic effects. So, all rules must be prefaced with *most times*.

1. AFTER A WIDE SKIP, TURN AND GO IN THE OPPOSITE DIRECTION.

"OVER THE RAINBOW" (MUSIC BY HAROLD ARLEN, LYRIC BY E. Y. HARBURG)   **"I'LL KISS YOU IN THE HEATHER" (MUSIC AND LYRIC BY NORA NORDIC)**

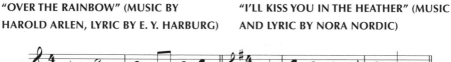

2. AFTER TWO SKIPS OF ANY SIZE IN THE SAME DIRECTION, TURN AND GO IN THE OPPOSITE DIRECTION.

"THERE IS A LAND" (MUSIC AND LYRIC BY STEPHEN CITRON)   **"GIVE MY REGARDS TO BROADWAY" (MUSIC AND LYRIC BY GEORGE M. COHAN)**

3. DON'T LET TWO OR MORE PHRASES SETTLE ON THE SAME PITCH. Songs repeatedly settling on the same pitches become tiresome. Any tone that keeps recurring will stand out and keep your song earthbound.

4. DON'T NOODLE. Melodies should have a direction, and if your line keeps playing around, above and below a particular pitch, it will sound namby-pamby or lack personality. Head for a certain spot; then once you arrive, go to another. This will give your music urgency.

WHAT YOUR SONG SHOULD INCLUDE

The A¹

This first section of a four-section song (the others being A², bridge, A³) must incorporate several things.

1. It must include your title. This can be at the outset, like in "Blue Moon," "I Didn't Know What Time It Was," and "Feelings," or at the end of the section, like in "The Man I Love," "Don't It Make My Brown Eyes Blue," and "Close to You."
2. The main melodic inspiration must be included. The hook can be a lyric idea that is best when coupled with the main melody.
3. This section should end on the seventh or eighth bar and be followed by a turnaround (see the chapter on harmony, page 201).

The A

This is the first section of a four-section song in what is usually considered theater form. The other sections are B A C.

1. It must include your title. This is more important than in the A¹ form because the *theme will not repeat* until you have finished the *next* (A) section. I generally like the title up front in this type of song, as in "Around the World," "People," "On a Clear Day," "I've Grown Accustomed to Her Face," and "You Don't Bring Me Flowers," although one could occasionally be subtle and bury the title, as in "Tenderly."
2. The main melodic motive must be included.
3. This section should *not* have too much pause. It is better to end your statement in the middle of the eighth bar.

The Bridge or Release

This is the third section of a four-section song. It gives your listener a chance to leave the main melody of the song, to return refreshed eight bars later. Concert musicians generally call it the bridge, while those schooled in the popular world call it the release. (Some have even jokingly referred to it as "relief.") Bridges are generally eight bars long. (Exceptions occur in songs that have overlong A sections; and occasionally composer', will telescope or shorten a bridge because the line is so intense.)

1. In composing your bridge, be aware of melodic contrast. If your A section is "skippy," make your bridge "scaley." Let the words contrast, too; if your song talks about the present, let your bridge project us into the future. If your song mentions how happy you are with your lover, let us know in the bridge what life was like before the lover. Jimmy McHugh and Dorothy Fields were both aware of the need for contrast in the bridge of their song "On the Sunny Side of the Street":

A¹	Grab your coat and get your hat
	Leave your worries on the doorstep
	Just direct your feet
	To the sunny side of the street.
A²	Can't you hear a pitter-pat
	And a happy tune is your step.
	Life can be so sweet
	On the sunny side of the street.
BRIDGE	I used to walk in the shade
	With those blues on parade
	But I'm not afraid,
	This rover crossed over.
A³	If I never have a cent
	I'll be rich as Rockefeller
	Gold dust at my feet,
	On the sunny side of the street.

Here, the bridge talks about former times and the "shady side of the street." The melody of the bridge uses many repeated notes — "I used to walk ... with those blues" — etc. where the melody of the A sections is largely skipping around. The contrast is not accidental. It helps to make a fine song memorable.

Another way to achieve melodic contrast is to try to invert your line. Richard Rodgers turned his melody upside down in "Bewitched."

A¹ MOTIVE   BRIDGE MOTIVE

(I'm)   wild a-gain   Lost my heart

2. Since the bridge will not be your song's selling point, don't feel you have to create an obvious melody. Composers often write for their peers in bridges. Hoagy Carmichael wrote simple, accessible tunes for his A sections, but often wrote freely in his bridges. Alec Wilder, a fine composer and author of *American Popular Song: The Great Innovators, 1900–1950*, writes this about Carmichael's "Skylark": "It starts on my favorite interval, the sixth, and it proceeds on its memorable, distinguished way ... until it arrives at one of the most extraordinary releases I've ever heard." I've written the melody below, but I must say that it needs harmony and a lyric to make sense.

"SKYLARK" (MUSIC BY HOAGY CARMICHAEL, LYRIC BY JOHNNY MERCER)

Other songs with intricate bridges are the same composer's "How Little We Know," and contemporary ones like "You've Got a Friend," "I Write the Songs," and "Bridge over Troubled Water."

3. Bridges usually contain one other element besides relief and freedom — they want to urge us back into the A³ section. To make us feel that we are "sitting on the edge of our chair," they must end on a feeling of expectancy. The questioning bridge of "The Way We Were" ends with some unanswered questions — "Would we? Could we?" — and the bridge of "I Won't Last a Day Without You" ends with "I can't really lose when you're near, when you're near ..." In each case we feel the need to return, in the former case because of the probing upward interval, in the latter because of the harmony (see page 212 for a discussion of the harmonization of bridges).

The A³

As mentioned above, the bridge must lead, even pull, into the final section, the A³. This should be like the A¹ and A², but it might reach for a higher pitch at the end. If your song begins with the title, it would be clever to change the lyric so the title occurs at the end.

"Once in a While" (Music by Michael Edwards, Lyric by Bud Green)

A¹   Once in a while,
      Will you try to give one little thought to me,
      Though someone else may be
      Nearer your heart.

A²   Once in a while
      Will you dream of the moments I shared with you,
      Moments before we two
      Drifted apart.

BRIDGE   In love's smoldering ember
          One spark may remain.
          If love still can remember
          That spark may burn again.

A³   I know that I'll
      Be contented with yesterday's memory
      Knowing you'll think of me
      Once in a while.

The B and C

Songs constructed in A¹, B, A², C form will, of course, not have bridges, but their B sections should have some of the pull and variety that most bridges display. Sing through "The Shadow of Your Smile," and observe the opposite direction taken at "Look into my eyes, my love..." "Mame" and "How Deep Is the Ocean" are further examples of ascending A sections and descending B sections. In this kind of show tune, the C section usually works its way up to a climax with the title at the end.

The Coda

Coda comes from the Latin word *cauda*, meaning tail. It is a section added to a song when the work lacks a final fillip. Harold Arlen often added this final section to his emotional songs to further wring our heartstrings. "Happiness Is Just a Thing Called Joe," "The Man That Got Away," and "Over the Rainbow" spring instantly to mind. "Me and Mrs. Jones," by Kenny Gamble, Leon Huff, and Cary Gilbert, does the same thing. My favorite coda was written by Cole Porter; it not only maintains the mood, but adds to the feeling of the song.

"Make It Another Old-Fashioned, Please"

VERSE	Since I went on the wagon, I'm
	Certain drink is a major crime.
	For when you lay off the liquor
	You feel so much slicker,
	Well, that is most of the time.
	But there are moments
	Sooner or later
	When it's tough, I got to say
	Not to say:
	Waiter,
CHORUS	Make it another old-fashioned, please,
A¹	Make another double old-fashioned, please,
B	Make it for one who's due
	To join the disillusioned crew
	Make it for one of love's new
	Refugees.
A²	Once, high in my castle, I reigned supreme
	And oh! what a castle, built on a heavenly dream.
C	Then quick as a lightning flash
	That castle began to crash
	So make it another old-fashioned, please.
CODA	Leave out the cherry,
	Leave out the orange,
	Leave out the bitters,
	Just make it a straight rye!

Other songs that use codas are "What I Did for Love," "Kiss Me Again," "Moonlight in Vermont," "I Got the Sun in the Morning," "Some Enchanted Evening," and "Bali Ha'i."

A final word about codas: Use melodic material that is similar to or extracted from the body of the song. The bridge is a good source, as in "Over the Rainbow" (Music by Harold Arlen, Lyric by E. Y. Harburg).

The Interlude (Trio)

Interludes are used in songs to give balance and roundness and to fill out the creative picture. The middle section of a minuet or scherzo was often written for three instruments, after which the first part played by the entire ensemble returned. The word *trio* referred to this section and was kept long after the custom of writing for three instruments in the middle of an orchestral work had been dropped. Today we generally call it the interlude, but you will find it referred to as trio in some old editions, especially of operettas or marches.

Contrary to a coda, which tries not to upset the applecart, a trio or interlude should be as *different from the song as possible*. Rodgers and Hart wrote a magnificently moving song in "Little Girl Blue," added a trio (unashamedly calling it that on the sheet copy) in 3/4 time (the song is in 4/4 time) then returned to reprise the chorus. They did the same thing (this time only reprising the A^3 section of the chorus) in "Ten Cents a Dance." In both cases, the added section tells us much about the heroine. In the well-known "I Wish You Love," the interlude (not so well known) talks about what it means to say goodbye. Here, the interlude works as a bridge and seems essential to the song.

In contemporary times the interlude has been rediscovered, as rap, a spoken rhythmic section that offers relief between choruses.

The Extension

Although an extension is more important as a harmonic device than as a melodic one, it should be mentioned here that it allows the composer to stretch out a melody *before* its conclusion, as distinguished from a coda, which may be added *after* the song is basically over. The melody can work up to an important pitch, announce that pitch over a chord that feels incomplete, and then go on to finish the song. There will generally be four extra bars when an extension is used. Beginning composers like to use extension after extension and sometimes add on a coda. Don't fall into the long-winded trap. The ending of "Hello, Young Lovers" (Music by Richard Rodgers, Lyric by Oscar Hammerstein II) uses extension beautifully.

END OF CHORUS   **EXTENSION**

Gershwin and Porter also loved extension, and one can find examples in "Nice Work If You Can Get It" and "They Can't Take That Away From Me" by the former and "It's De-lovely" and "In the Still of the Night" by the latter.

The Verse

Before 1950, a verse was a lead-in to the chorus, and if it composed by a good musician, it would have balance and unity. Rodgers and Hart's "Bewitched, Bothered and Bewildered," starts its verse with a downward skip and a step up; the chorus motive begins with an upward skip and a step up; while the bridge begins with a skip down and then a step down. Each of these motives is similar and yet different enough.

The contemporary verse, the lead-in section that prepares us for a chorus, is used in most of the songs written today, and because it is so varied, it is difficult to give you insight into its composition. But there are some things one can often rely on:

1. The verse should have a lower tessitura than the chorus.
2. The verse should use more words, often moving with more notes or pitches per bar ("Honesty," "Delta Dawn." "Honey," "Knock Three Times," "Ring Them Bells," Bojangles").
3. If the verse is static, the chorus should give a sense of movement ("Hello in There," "You Light Up My Life").
4. Above all—verse should not have as much melodic interest as the chorus. The chorus wants to be what your listener will remember.

The Fade

From the fifties onward, the advent of continuous air play, song running into song, created the fade. Commercial consideration, also helped, for it was easier to keep your audience from switching the radio dial if they were already into a new song before they realized it. The fade is easily accomplished—even on a "home recording"—by gradually turning down the recording volume level until it reaches zero.

All disco music used fade because disco clubs were equipped with two turntables, so that even in the rare cases where that music had a written-in ending, fade was preferable.

Fade has never been used in theater songs except for the well-worn device of having the first-act curtain descend during a fade while the music is still playing and having the second-act curtain rise as the volume increases and we resume the action.

6 CHORDS

MELODY, RHYTHM, and harmony are so intertwined in songwriting that it is difficult to discuss one without the other. Melodies are made up of intervals, and a collection of intervals will become harmony or chords. Chords create different effects depending on where they are located in the bar, and the roots of our discussion of rhythm lie in this. Rhythm is not as important to melodic construction as one might suppose, but is crucial to the finished song.

As I advise songwriting students who have thoroughly digested the foregoing section on melody, I would now set off the melody with chords, and then tackle the intricacies of rhythmic line.

But before plunging into the wonderful world of harmony, which I often liken to a painter's palette — the melody akin to the pen-and-ink outline of representational art, and the harmony to the colorful oils that make the completed canvas — I should mention that the discussion that follows is intended to be helpful only to songwriters. There will be no analysis of atonal music, counterpoint, chorale, or bitonal harmony, for they are the provinces of orchestrators or composers for the concert hall. Likewise, chords will be discussed not as entities in the manner of most treatises on harmony, but as tools that create mood, color, and emotional pull. For chords do not exist in a vacuum, but in relation to other chords that surround them and in relation to songs.

What is a chord? It is three or more pitches sounded simultaneously. Would that mean

EXAMPLE

are all chords? Yes, indeed, although most discussions and books on harmony only involve the first three examples, avoiding multi-pitched, wide spaced, and dissonant chords and those built on anything other than the interval of the third. Some texts call examples a, b, and c "consonant" and examples d, e, f, and g "dissonant," although I believe that is purely arbitrary as different standards of consonance and dissonance have prevailed throughout the centuries.

TRIADS

The triad is the building block, the A B C, of music. As its name implies, it has three *different* members. Its lowest pitch must be accompanied by two more pitches placed a major third or minor third above the name pitch or root. Once constructed, it can be inverted or spaced as freely as desired. There are four types of triads, each with different construction, sound, and function.

Major Triads

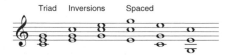

MAJOR TRIAD CONSTRUCTION = ROOT, MAJOR THIRD (4 half-steps), and MINOR THIRD (3 half steps)

The major triad is a tool you will use millions of times, so familiarize yourself with its bright strong basic sound. Practice constructing major triads everywhere on any keyboard or strumming them on the guitar. Learn to recognize its sound as you would a familiar voice. There are only twelve triads to be learned and each can be counted out according to the above formula. You should also be able to sing a major triad (the first three pitches of the "Blue Danube Waltz" or "On Top of Old Smokie"). Major triads have no pull; they are "arrival" chords.

Minor Triads

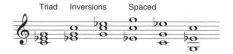

MINOR TRIAD CONSTRUCTION = ROOT, MINOR THIRD (3 half steps), and MAJOR THIRD (4 half steps)

The minor triad is used only slightly less than the major. Although most popular songs are in major keys, the minor sound is frequently desired. Strangely enough, the chords inherent in a major scale include as many minor triads as major triads. It might be a bit easier for you to recognize the sound of the minor triad than the major. There is a melancholy and heaviness about it. If you invert the C E♭ and G that comprise the C minor triad, making the G the lowest pitch, placing the C and E♭ above, and then change to a C major triad inverted to G, C, and E, you will certainly be able to hear the difference. The minor triad has no pull, like the major triad, it is an "arrival" chord. However, it arrives at a more intense, somewhat exotic, and often sadder place.

Diminished Triads

DIMINISHED TRIAD = ROOT, MINOR THIRD (3 half steps), and MINOR THIRD (3 half steps)

The diminished triad is rarely used in pop music. Because it feels lopsided, it is frequently replaced with the diminished seventh (see page 188), but it does have a melodramatic sound and has pull.

Augmented Triads

AUGMENTED TRIAD = ROOT, MAJOR THIRD (4 half steps), and MAJOR THIRD (4 half steps)

The augmented triad is not often used today. It has a strong pull, much stronger than the diminished triad. But many now consider the augmented triad dated, perhaps because it was the favorite turnback chord of operetta composers. It always appeared at the sixteenth bar, often on the word *dear* (itself an unnecessary syllable). Composers often describe it as "overripe" or "too sweet." However, there is some use to be made of this chord as part of a sequence of chords. (Don't confuse this with sequential melody.) Preceded by a major triad and followed by an added sixth chord (see page 190), the augmented creates tension, as in Kander and Ebb's intense song from *Cabaret*.

"MAYBE THIS TIME	I'LL BE LUCKY
C Major Triad	C Augmented

MAYBE THIS TIME HE'LL	STAY"
C Added Sixth	C (Dominant) Seventh

The same sequence appears in the opening bars of Stephen Sondheim's "Losing My Mind" from *Follies*.

Triad Abbreviations

Since the major triad is so often used, we indicate it with its letter alone. For example, C indicates a C major triad (C E G); F♯ indicates an F♯ major triad (F♯ A♯ C♯); B♭ indicates a B♭ major triad (B♭ D F).

The minor triad is abbreviated by adding a lowercase m after the letter name. (Be sure to use a lowercase m because the uppercase M stands for another chord in some systems.) Cm indicates C minor triad (C E♭ G); F♯m indicates F♯ minor triad (F♯ A C♯) and B♭m indicates B♭ minor triad (B♭ D♭ F).

Dim or DIM or ° indicates a diminished triad. For example, C° or C dim or C DIM all mean C diminished triad (C E♭ G♭). + or AUG or +5 indicates an augmented triad. For example, C + or C + 5 or C AUG indicates C augmented triad (C E G♯).

Scale-Tone Triads

To harmonize melodies, composers usually select chords composed of members of the scale in which they are writing. It would be useful to analyze which triads can be made from the notes of a scale. For the C scale:

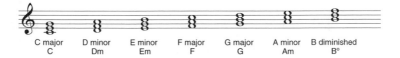

C major	D minor	E minor	F major	G major	A minor	B diminished
C	Dm	Em	F	G	Am	B°

You may have noticed that a major scale has three major triads and three minor triads and one diminished triad. Like all art, music is a combination of the light and dark.

THE NUMERICAL RELATIONSHIP

C, Dm, Em in the key of C is the same as G, Am, Bm in the key of G or A♭, B♭m, Cm in the key of A♭. Wouldn't it be simpler to call those chords I, II, and

III? That way of referring to chords has been used since the earliest times and is the principle upon which most harmony books are written. Usually the books go one step further by indicating whether the chord is major, minor, diminished, or augmented—its *quality*. In harmony books, I or C being major is expressed by a capitalized roman numeral; ii and iii being minor are indicated by lowercase. But composers of popular music do not bother with upper- and lowercase; it is assumed they know the qualities of the chords.

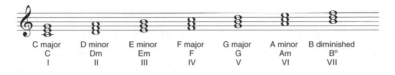

The numerical treatment would be limited to triads if there had not been jazz. Jazz composers have always sought richer chords, fuller and more intensely dissonant. They made the standard scale-tone chords into sevenths (4 notes), reserving the uppercase roman numeral for them and adding the letter T when their score called for an occasional triad. Compare the two charts below.

SCALE-TONE TRIADS (JAZZ)

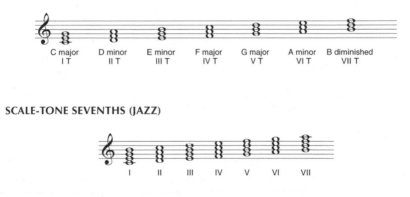

SCALE-TONE SEVENTHS (JAZZ)

SEVENTH CHORDS

A seventh chord is a triad with a fourth note placed a third above it. If you play through the scale-tone sevenths, you will hear that although each has the same number of notes, because of the distribution of half and whole steps on our keyboard, they do not all sound alike. Like the triads, they are varied, which makes them sound more colorful than had they been the same quality. They come in several varieties; you should understand the construct and use of each.

The Dominant Seventh

This chord got its name because originally it was only permitted to be used on the 5th tone of the scale, called the dominant. (The dominant note seems to dominate the scale.) The dominant seventh is still most often created on the 5th tone of the scale, but in contemporary times we have been able to build it anywhere. (Blues often uses a dominant seventh built on the IV or the I.)

Conservatory musicians refer to this chord by its full name, dominant seventh, but pop and jazz musicians call it "7," for the same reason that the word *major* is tacit. *It is constructed by superimposing a minor third (3 half steps) above a major triad.* (Some like to think of it as a major triad with the 7th found a full step below the octave.) It has great pull. Its root seems to want to go up a fourth (G to C; D to G, etc.) and its 7th wants to go down a half step (F to E; C to B, etc.).

The Major Seventh

This chord is so much used by songwriters today that it is hard to conceive that little more than a century ago it was considered avant-garde and extremely dissonant. Its outer members outline a major seventh interval, which even today may be strident to some ears, but its inner members soften the blow with the interval of a minor third. In a jazz system, the major seventh is found on the 1st and 4th degrees of the scale. Since most of our songs end on the I chord, the major seventh sound is softened by changing the I to a I with added 6th (see page 190).

The construction of the major seventh is simplicity itself. *It is constructed by superimposing a major third (4 half steps) above a major triad.* (Some like to think of it as a major triad with the 7th found a half step below the octave.) Except for its top pitch, which wants to go to the "do" of the key, the major seventh is not a pulling chord. It is abbreviated as Maj7, maj7, △, or M.

The Minor Seventh

With the minor seventh we complete the trinity of the most important seventh chords. The minor seventh occurs in the scale on the 2nd, 3rd, and 6th degrees. It has a dark pull and generally leads us to a dominant seventh. This in turn urges us to a bright major seventh, making a strong chain, perhaps the most iron-clad in all of music—the II, V, I of which more will be written later. *The minor seventh is constructed by superimposing a minor third above a* minor *triad.* (Some like to think of it as a minor triad with the 7th found a whole step below the octave.) Its abbreviation is m7, mi7, and sometimes – 7. I heartily disapprove of the last nomenclature because it can so easily be confused with lowering a different part of the chord.

The Altered Chords

One of my reasons for disliking the "minus sign" indication for minor is that it can so often be confused with the altered chords. Altered chords are dear to composers' hearts, for they are the chords we create ourselves. Some of them are in constant usage, while others turn up only rarely. Since they are altered from the pure scale, they have a great deal of pull. They are very easy to construct, for all one has to do is follow instructions—your own or the composer's. The abbreviations + and ♯ are synonymous, as are ♭ and – . In constructing, for example, a C7 + 5, merely create the C7 (C, E, G, B♭) and raise (+) the 5 (5th) G to G♯. The chart below should clarify.

EXAMPLE

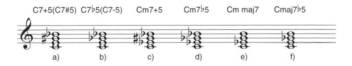

a) *The dominant seventh with raised 5th* (7 ↑ 5) is also known as the augmented seventh. It has great pull, certainly more than the augmented triad. It is more contemporary than the latter because some of the dated, sticky-sweet quality of the augmented triad is abated by adding the seventh.

b) *The dominant seventh with lowered 5th* (7♭5) is particularly intense. I often think of it as a "wake-up" chord, perhaps because so much morning music of Gershwin and Grofé in the thirties and forties used the upper and lower partials of this chord. It is also much favored in jazz. There is even an amusing tongue-twisting jazz composition called "A Flattened Fifth in a Fifth Floor Flat."

c) *The minor seventh with raised 5th* (m^7 + 5) is one of the "nonchords." Even though it could conceivably exist, we generally choose to spell it and write it as another chord. In this case it would be thought of as an A♭ triad with added 9th.

d) *The minor seventh with flatted 5th* (m^7♭5) is one of our most useful and lush chords. It is particularly used by Hollywood composers and is a favorite harmony of Frenchmen Michel Legrand and Charles Aznavour. It has pull, and will usually take you where a minor seventh will; the only difference is that there is an added sadness in the sound of the minor seventh with flatted 5th.

e) *The minor major seventh* (m maj^7) sounds like a contradiction in terms, but this chord is merely created by following directions. The chord has very little pull and has strong dissonance. It is an essential to jazz pianists, who often will juxtapose it against a minor sixth (see page 190) for dark dissonance.

f) *The major seventh with flatted 5th* (maj^7♭5) is another of the rarely used chords. It sometimes appears in contemporary blues, for the strongest blues lines are now lowering the 5th of the scale.

The Diminished Seventh

In the discussion of the diminished triad on page 183, I said that that triad was not much used. That statement is true, but its four-note version, the diminished seventh, *is* much used. It is an equidistant chord. Each member is three half steps above the other, and since there are only twelve different pitches in our musical system, there are only *three* series of pitches possible.

All others might contain the same pitches but would be inversions of the same chord. (The augmented triad is also an equidistant chord, there being four possible combinations of its three pitches.)

The sound of the diminished seventh is distinctive. In series, ascending, it was used in the silent movies because of its melodrama. In Bach's Fantasias he would announce a diminished seventh and, keeping the same bass note (called pedal point), move up a series of diminished sevenths to create a feeling of tension or null. Also, its equidistance destroys the feeling of the key, enabling us to rebuild in *another* key. This makes the diminished seventh invaluable in modulation. It is often used at the end of a bridge to return to the original key (see page 213).

The easiest way to construct it is to play the root, add another pitch 3 half steps above, another pitch 3 half steps above, and still another pitch 3 half steps above. The chord is abbreviated as dim 7 or °7 or usually just °.

Scale-Tone Sevenths in Series

Every composer should understand and memorize the seventh chords that can be made from the scale. We have discussed each of them separately. Here they are in series:

I and IV are major sevenths (maj7)
II, III, and VI are minor sevenths (m7)
V is a (dominant) seventh (7)
VII is the altered chord: minor seventh flat 5 (m7♭5)

I would suggest composers practice these chords *in all keys*, ascending and descending. Play I, II, III, IV, V, VI, VII, I (upper), VII, VI, V, IV, III, II, I, and in the following order: I, IV, VII, III, VI, II, V, I—the sequence used in so much music, popular and concert.

ALTERING SCALE-TONE CHORDS

The roman numeral system of naming chords can be used with equal ease to signify chords containing accidentals (pitches that are not members of the scale) as well as those whose roots are not members of the scale. To alter a chord from the way it appears in the series of scale-tone sevenths, mark the appropriate member with a sharp or flat.

To build chords on pitches that do not appear in the scale, place a flat or sharp before the scale number. These techniques will give you the ability to construct any kind of chord on any pitch, analyzing it in relationship to the scale.

INVERSIONS

Any of the above chords can be inverted. This is usually done so that the chords move smoothly to and from each other. The less motion in chord changes, the better. In a full sheet copy, these chords are written out, but modern composers write a "lead sheet" and to indicate an inversion they use a "/" followed by the bass note they desire. For example, G7/B or F♯m7/A or Cmaj7/E. Inverted chords make the music smoother.

ADDED SIXTH CHORDS

The chord of the "added sixth" is not really a chord, since chords are built by piling intervals of thirds on each other. The sixth, which is found a full tone above the fifth, would not conform to that construction principle. But the chord is much used. It gives dissonance to a major or minor triad. This is such a smooth dissonance that triads that omit the 6th sound pale in any pop or jazz context. Of course, the sixth is not used in folk, which eschews lushness, or rock, which seeks a stark, elemental sound.

In old editions, those published before pop composers ever dreamed of being conservatory educated, when the altered chords were well beyond the ken of most jazz musicians, the indication m6 (minor sixth) was used to indicate the above-mentioned altered chord. Performers were taught to put the "6th" in the bass. Thus the chord "Cm6" would have been performed with C, E♭, and G in the right hand, while the "A," the 6th, was placed in the bass. Today we would call those pitches (reading from the bass up) A, C, E♭, G the minor seventh ♭ five or Am7♭5, not the Cm6.

NINTH CHORDS

In the continuing series of chord expanding, lengthening, and expanding intensity by adding successive thirds, if we add the interval of a third to a seventh chord, we arrive at a ninth.

These chords, called E9 and F9, are constructed from a *dominant seventh*.

To create the ninth, merely add to the chord a fifth note, that is found a major third (4 half steps) above the *lowered* seventh. When we speak of a ninth chord, unless specifically mentioning it as a major ninth, we assume there is a *dominant seventh underneath*. The closeness of the members of the ninth chord make for a cluttered sound, so even if one could play all five members in one hand, it would not be desirable. It would be better to use the following distribution.

Adding the ninth will give your harmony color and intensity, and of course a good bit of dissonance. Remember that like the sixths, the addition of ninths is consistent with jazz but does not belong in soul, rock, or folk.

Ninth chords often have their 9th raised (indicated 9♯—preferably—or ♯9), in which case they create a blues sound. With the 9th lowered, they create a sentimental sound, rather reminiscent of Tchaikovsky. Study the preceding and following examples and play these ninths on every pitch.

ELEVENTH AND THIRTEENTH CHORDS

The more intense chords that follow the ninth are of course, the eleventh and thirteenth. These are not in the domain of song creation but of arranging, which is beyond the scope of this book. Let me say, however, that the eleventh is most often used as a suspension. The eleventh is the same as the fourth (yes, after 1, 3, 5, 7, since there will come the octave, the 9th could be considered as the 2nd, the 11th as the 4th and the 13th as the 6th of the scale). The suspension of the 11th or the 4th is common in much of popular music, most often moving down to the third of the key. Of course you'll omit the 3rd of the chord when you use the 11th or 4th.

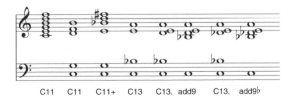

The thirteenth is an attractive chord that often is used in jazz. It looks like the added sixth chord, but is quite different in that it must have both the (lowered) 7th *and* the 6th. It is easy to remember, for 7 and 6 add up to 13.

Both the eleventh and thirteenth have tremendous pull and can be used in place of the ordinary dominant seventh at your discretion. I would suggest you practice them on all twelve pitches: C♯, D, D♯, E, etc.

7 SCALES

MAJOR SCALE

THE MAJOR SCALE, which was analyzed in the section on some basics, is certainly the most essential tool of all Western music. Its construction, which was merely touched upon in that section, has much to do with its success.

The location of its half steps are responsible for its utility and omnipresence. The half step located between its 3rd and 4th tones gives it variety at midpoint (3½ is the midpoint of 7) and the half step between 7 and 8 seems to lift the scale inevitably home.

Since most melody and harmony must be constructed on the pitches of this scale, I'd advise you to become familiar with all twelve of them. They will not be difficult to remember if you understand the principle of their creation rather than try to memorize them by rote. Visualize the members as being a full tone apart except between the *3rd and 4th members* and the *7th and 8th members*. The chart below should help:

C MAJOR SCALE

Any scale may be written with accidentals or with key signature. The construction is the same. I'd advise you to use the key signature if you intend to stay within the key for more than three or four bars.

E MAJOR SCALE (WITH ACCIDENTALS)

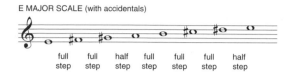

E MAJOR SCALE (with accidentals)

full step | full step | half step | full step | full step | full step | half step

E MAJOR SCALE (WITH KEY SIGNATURE)

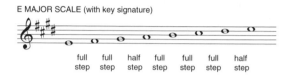

E MAJOR SCALE (with key signature)

full step | full step | half step | full step | full step | full step | half step

Beyond the major scale, there lies a whole world of others. Some will be useful to create color; others will be needed if you want an ethnic sound. All will be discussed in this section, but none of the remaining scales is more important than the minor.

Even if your song will be written in a major key, it will have, as we saw, many minor chords. Likewise, if your melody is based on a major scale, it will (if it's interesting) wander into the minor scale.

RELATIVE MINOR AND PARALLEL MINOR SCALES

Every major scale has two minor scales nearby. That means composers may work with a different set of pitches or chords after they have exhausted the possibilities their series of major-scale notes offers. The relative minor is built using the exact same pitches as the major, but this scale begins on the 6th tone of the major. The parallel minor uses the same pitches as the major, but flattens the 3rd, 6th and 7th tones. Study the chart below to see how these two scales (A minor and C minor) are associated to the major (C major).

C MAJOR SCALE

Relative Minor

A MINOR SCALE

Parallel Minor

C MINOR SCALE

Most textbooks of harmony consider the minor scales written above to be purely theoretical. Perhaps this was true before the great surge into folk music and folk-rock when they were rarely used in songwriting. The scales above (called pure minors) can originate minor triads on their first, fourth, and fifth degrees. This sound, sometimes called modal, is created by the use especially of the minor V chord. It is prominent in such songs as "Greensleeves," "Scarborough Fair," and "Love Is Blue."

HARMONIC MINOR SCALE AND MELODIC MINOR SCALE

The Pure Minor Scale has an *early* sound, which makes it far less useful than the Harmonic Minor. No one knows when the Pure Minor was altered to become the Harmonic Minor, but most musicologists agree that early in the eighteenth century composers began changing the V chord in works they composed on minor scales to create a brighter sound.

Changing the chord necessitated changing the scale. The new scale, the harmonic, has an interval of 1½ steps between its 6th and 7th pitches.

HARMONIC MINOR SCALE

Although we don't find that interval of 1½ steps difficult to sing today (actually it is amusing, with a mideastern sound), the musicians of the baroque era did. They created a whole new scale to avoid that troublesome skip. This second scale was called melodic, because of its easy melody line. It seems to reach a climax at the top and then, according to usage in classical times, it descends like the pure minor.

MELODIC MINOR SCALE

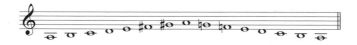

The rules of classical harmony intend composers to use the ascending form of the melodic minor scale when the melody is ascending and the descending form when the melody descends. Today's composers generally don't observe this but use whichever form they prefer.

The harmonic form, since it is fixed, is used to create the scale-tone triads and scale-tone sevenths.

SCALE-TONE TRIADS IN MINOR
AND SCALE-TONE SEVENTHS IN MINOR

SCALE-TONE TRIADS IN MINOR

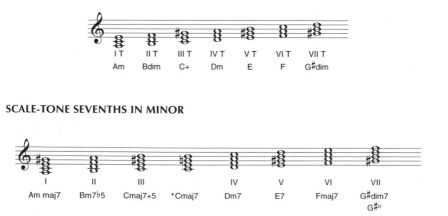

The scale-tone triads and scale-tone sevenths should be practiced in all keys. Use the same sequences suggested for major keys (I, II, III, IV, V, VI, VII, VIII, I, VII, VI, V, IV, III, II, I, *and especially* I, IV, VII, III, VI, II, V, I).

---

* The III *chord* is most often used as a major seventh, since it generally pulls to the VI chord. The use of the raised fifth in a major seventh chord, although academically correct, is awkward.

You will have observed that while the major key has many of the same kinds of chords, the minor key (because of the 1½ steps between its last two members) has *no two chords alike.*

Much of the music of Cole Porter, Michel Legrand, and Neil Diamond uses the minor key, especially the I, IV, VII, III, etc. sequence.

OTHER SCALES

Although major and minor scales are paramount in songwriting, many other scales could be useful to you when writing music of a particular ethnic character, when creating a sound effect, or when improvising. They are listed below. I have omitted many "composed scales," hoping you can create some that appeal to you.

Modal Scales

IONIAN (ALSO MAJOR OR FIRST MODE)

DORIAN (SECOND MODE)

PHRYGIAN (THIRD MODE)

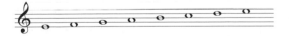

LYDIAN (FOURTH MODE)

MIXOLYDIAN (FIFTH MODE)

AEOLIAN (ALSO PURE MINOR, SIXTH MODE)

LOCRIAN (SEVENTH MODE)

Ethnic Scales

GYPSY

ARABIC

MOORISH

CHINESE

JEWISH

Color Scales

PENTATONIC

WHOLE TONE

or

DIMINISHED

CHROMATIC

8 HARMONY

BACK IN THE DISCUSSION of where inspiration comes from, I said that most songwriters get their ideas from the *concept*, which leads them to the *title* and thence to a *melodic motive*.

At that time it was never mentioned that harmony or a series of chords could be the inspiration over which a song might be created. But many professional songwriters work that way.

Gordon Lightfoot ("If You Could Read My Mind"; "Wreck of the Edmund Fitzgerald"; "Early Morning Blues") says, "The chord progression comes first."

Billy Preston ("That's the Way God Planned It"; "Nothing from Nothing") states: "Most of my ideas come through chord changes and then I work out a melody to go along with the chords. The melody is based on a chord structure."

Jim Seals and Dash Crofts ("Summer Breeze"; "We May Never Pass This Way Again") are at odds. Jim Seals says, "The melody line is based on the chord progression," while Dash Crofts maintains that "the concept gives the musical line."

The dictionary defines harmony as the "structure, functions and relationships of chords." Structure and function were analyzed in the section that introduced scale-tone triads and sevenths, but chord relationships — what follows what, where chords move — have not been discussed.

Perhaps it's easier to understand the convoluted principles of chord movement if you think of chords as pure oil colors, straight from the tube. You would no more make a painting all one color than write a song using only one harmony. (A few blues songs stay with a single harmony, but that is rare and, eventually, very dull.)

To carry the analogy further, if you were putting your colors on canvas, you would find that certain pigments lead smoothly from one shade to another while others clash. As a songwriter, you will generally seek out the smoothest relationships — but you should be able to employ the clashing or violent ones at will.

The smoothest relationship is always between the I and V chords (the I being the "home," "at peace" sound, the V being the "tension," "pulling" sound). If you can create these chords on any keyboard instrument (I in C = C, E, G and V in C or G^7 = G, B, D, F) or guitar (the easiest to create on that instrument are D and A^7) and you move back and forth between them, you will be listening to the strongest progression in Western music.

So that you will not get lost in the myriad of chords and progressions possible, work at first with only two chords. Sing other composers' songs over these chords (a list follows in the section "Two-Chord Harmony"), trying to hear where the chords change. Gradually add the other chords and common progressions, which appear in the remainder of this chapter. And then I would suggest trying to create simple tunes using *only* these two chords as your background harmony. If you can do this and have the patience to explore each chord fully as it is introduced into your harmonic palette, you will soon be able to handle the whole harmonic rainbow.

TWO-CHORD HARMONY

Some melodies are obvious in their melodic implication. The melody uses exclusively or almost exclusively members of the chord. In this case there is no implied harmony.

The harmony of "Skip to My Lou" follows definite rules. The first two bars use no pitches except those found in the IT or C triad, and the third and fourth bars use members of the V or G7 chord. (Yes, F and D also are pitches that belong to the Dm or II chord or the B dim or VII chord, but if you have only two chords to choose from and if the melody is straightforward, choose the I and V chords.) The next to last bar in simple and even complex music is almost invariably the V. The last chord is usually the I, making us feel the key and coming to rest.

If you can strum the guitar, you can get the same effect by singing the melody over a strum that follows this chart. (I have transposed up a tone to D, which is easier to play on the guitar.)

D OR Iᵀ   **A⁷ OR V**

Skip, skip, skip to my Lou, Skip, skip, skip to my Lou,

D OR Iᵀ   **A⁷ OR V**   **D OR Iᵀ**

Skip, skip, skip to my Lou, Skip to my Lou, my dar - lin'.

Much of our folk music is composed of tunes that need only these two harmonies to feel complete. I can think of "Down in the Valley," "Ach Du Lieber Augustin," "Did You Ever See a Lassie," "The Old Gray Mare," "He's Got the Whole World in His Hands," "Polly Wolly Doodle," "Clementine," "London Bridge," and "Ten Little Indians." Among popular songs one would assume that this simple harmony would be too naïve, but songs like "Deep in the Heart of Texas," "The Music Goes Round and Round," "Never on Sunday," "You'd Better Sit Down, Kids," "Give Peace a Chance," and even a relatively sophisticated lyric like "Honey" boil down basically to I and V chords.

Usually the chords stay put for a while, but sometimes they are hyperactive, as in "Three Blind Mice." In "Three Blind Mice," without the harmony being stated, we yearn for a chord change, especially at the next-to-last bar.

THREE BLIND MICE

TWO-CHORD HARMONY IN MINOR

The minor mode automatically has sophistication. Songs that in the major seem to belong in kindergarten sound quite mature in minor. Although "Josh'a

Fit the Battle of Jericho" uses only the I and V chords, it does not sound as naïve as "Skip to My Lou."

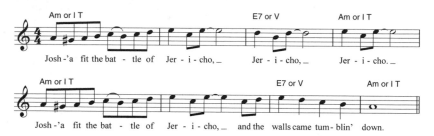

Even the verse of this spiritual can be sung using only the I and V chords:

IT
You may talk about your King of Gideon

IT
You may talk about your man of Saul

IT
But there's none like good old Joshua

V   **IT**
At the battle of Jericho

The A sections of "Yes, My Darling Daughter"; "Digga, Digga Doo"; and "Bei Mir Bist Du Schoen" use merely the I and V chords. (Of course when we come to the bridge, the pattern changes). If you are working with guitar, I'm sure you can hum some lovely melodies over Dm and A⁷ (I and V of Dm).

THREE-CHORD HARMONY

It has been said that folk singers know only three chords — I, V, and IV. Perhaps there was a grain of truth in that statement years ago, for it seemed that all "cowboys" strummed only those chords. These chords are often called *tonic* (after "tone" origin) *dominant* (see page 186), and *subdominant*, the subdominant being found *not a tone below the dominant, as one might suppose,* but fully a fifth below. These two chords setting off, or bodyguarding, the key, would be natural to embellish it. Think, then, of the I, V, and IV as outlined below:

V or dominant 7
I or tonic
IV or subdominant

In the key of C, the chords would be:

G⁷
C
F

If you think of the V and IV chords as bodyguards, it is easy to see why so many were satisfied with these three chords for so long. Literally thousands of folk songs use nothing else.

"On Top of Old Smokie"; "Clementine"; "Silent Night"; "Oh, Susannah"; "Red River Valley"; "Cielito Lindo"; "Battle Hymn of the Republic"; "Happy Birthday"; "Santa Lucia"; "For He's a Jolly Good Fellow"; "Yankee Doodle"; "The Glowworm"; "The Marines Hymn"; "Molly Malone"; "The Blue-Tailed Fly"; "You Are My Sunshine"; and "When the Saints Go Marching In" are some folk songs that use these three chords exclusively. And the list of pop songs is long indeed. The verse will often use I and V and the chorus will begin on the IV chord. Both "Candida" (by Toni Wine and Irwin Levine) and "Knock Three Times" (by Irwin Levine and L. Russell Brown) introduce the IV in their chorus. This pattern — IV, I, V, I — is found in many songs. "Spanish Harlem" (by Jerry Leiber and Phil Spector) uses only I, IV, I, V, I, but is far from naïve because its rhythm and lyric are especially original.

THREE-CHORD HARMONY IN MINOR

Three chords in minor seem less flexible, leading to less freedom than in major. They always seem to create an ethnic feel — Jewish, or Russian, or perhaps Italian. Songs like "Dark Eyes" ("O Tchichonya") and "Havah Nagila" are typical of the three-chord harmonizations, as well as some spirituals ("Go Down, Moses").

"GO DOWN, MOSES"

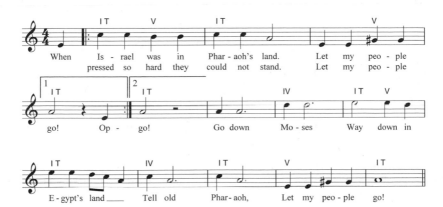

Notice the introduction of the IV chord in the chorus (on the highest pitch thus far — "D" on the word "Moses").

Perhaps I should mention here that like most arrangers and composers, I enjoy changing traditional harmonies (especially in something that originated anonymously). The use of the VI dominant, or F⁷ chord, on the third from the last bar gives the music poignancy and direction without violating the spirit of the piece.

CHANGING HARMONY FOR INTENSIFICATION

The basic three-chord harmonization can get mighty tiresome, especially for a sophisticated musician. As you become more aware of the power of chords to influence our emotions, I'm sure you will use them to color your line. Cole Porter compared saying goodbye to "the change from major to minor," and although it sounds like a cliché, there is sadness in a minor key. Changing unexpectedly to a series of minor chords will make your melody emotional; changing a dark minor harmonization into an unexpected major will bring out the sun. One of my favorite Scottish folk songs, "Annie Laurie," is traditionally harmonized merely with the I, V, and IV major chords. Notice how the addition of other chords belonging to the relative minor key embellishes the melody.

IMPERFECT CADENCE

Beyond the three-chord harmonization, if one were going to add another chord to the spectrum of harmony, it would be the II dominant 7 (in the key of C this

---

* This is actually the V of the relative minor (the V chord in A minor scale) and is very frequently used because it walks so nicely back to IV of the relative major. (E⁷ walks up a half step into F and we are back again on the track.)

would be D7, spelled D, F♯, A, C). This chord, pulling to the V chord, which as we mentioned earlier creates a strong urge to go home to I, can be an end in itself. Often you will need this feeling of expectancy, which will be resolved later. This expectant feeling has been compared to "question and answer." Textbooks refer to the combination of II dom to V or in the key of C, D⁷ to G⁷, as an imperfect cadence. I call the "middle feeling," because it usually occurs in the middle of a song.

Once you have sung a few songs with imperfect cadences, you will be able to understand and anticipate this feeling.

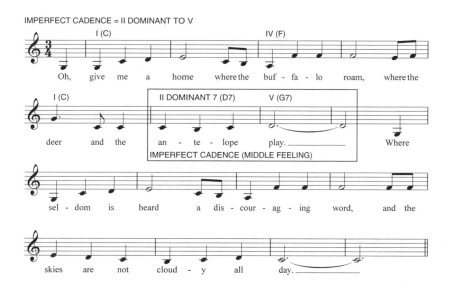

It is important for a composer to develop this question-and-answer sense. Without tension-release, yin-yang, music would have no urgency. Sing through "Jingle Bells," and see if you don't feel the urge to go on when you get to the word "sleigh":

I
Jingle bells, jingle bells,

I
Jingle all the way.

IV   I
Oh, what fun it is to ride in a

IMPERFECT CADENCE
MIDDLE FEELING
II DOMINANT 7 V
One-horse open sleigh …

Again, on the word "head" in "Show Me the Way to Go Home":

Show me the way to go home,
I'm tired and I wanna go to bed.
I had a little drink about an hour ago

And it | IMPERFECT CADENCE
MIDDLE FEELING
II DOM 7* (IIX)   V
went right to my head | ….

Some songs that use an imperfect cadence or middle feeling are "Show Me the Way to Go Home," "My Bonnie," "Dixie," "I've Been Workin' on the Railroad," "The Bowery," "In the Good Old Summertime," "Put On Your Old Gray Bonnet," "A Bicycle Built for Two," "Toora-Loora-Loora," "Give My Regards to Broadway," "I Guess I'll Have to Change My Plan," and "Hey, Look Me Over."

II V I

Popular songwriters have used the series of chords II V I so often that it has almost become a cliché. But the series is strong and can lead to so many places that there is still freshness in it.

Beginning with II, as it is found in the scale-tone sevenths, we observe that it is a minor chord and has a strong affinity to pull to the V. The 7th of the II pulls *downward* into the 3rd of the V, and the 3rd of the II pulls *upward* into the root of the V. Additionally, because of the circle of chords (see page 214) the root of the II pulls *upward* to the root of the V as well.

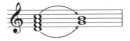

*The abbreviation "dom" for dominant is rarely used since it is too easily confused in manuscript with "dim" for diminished. Other and better ways of referring to this chord—D, F♯, A, C in the key of C—are II♯3, IIX7, or merely IIX. The X was created by jazz musicians, other symbols being △ for major seventh, ° for diminished seventh, and m for minor seventh.

The pull inherent in the II to V is equally strong if the chord is a II dominant 7 or II#3, but it doesn't suggest *the key* we are in as strongly as when the II is used in minor. Because II V I makes one *feel* the tonality so strongly, it has become a favorite device of composers wishing to modulate or change keys. The pull of II to V to I is shown in the example that follows.

Composers have a penchant for changing keys. As soon as they arrive at a key, they seem to want to leave it. I quote below a few examples of songs that modulate using II V I. Notice that they have no sooner arrived than they are off and running.

"LAURA" (MUSIC BY DAVID RAKSIN, LYRIC BY JOHNNY MERCER)

"LOLLYPOPS AND ROSES" (MUSIC AND LYRIC BY TONY VELONA)

"ONE-NOTE SAMBA" (MUSIC BY ANTONIO CARLOS JOBIM)

"JUST THE WAY YOU ARE" (MUSIC AND LYRIC BY BILLY JOEL)

I VI II V

No sequence of chords in all the popular repertoire has been used more often than I VI II V. In that order, they are pop songs personified. Whether heard on a piano from two preteenagers, one vamping or alternating hands while playing the "bottom part," the other plinking out a section of "Heart and Soul" or "Blue Moon," or arranged for big band or a disco beat, it is ubiquitous.

Each season several songs built on this series hit the top of the charts. Sometimes the sequence is slightly changed, but a small alteration does not affect its presence and comfortable-as-an-old-shoe feeling. The chords are so common they prompted a composer I know to remark that "when the recordings from our time are unearthed a thousand years hence, those people will wonder how our culture was able to spend a century listening to the same four chords."

Perhaps they are not worth a "century's worth of listening," but the four chords follow each other beautifully and the total sequence is extremely satisfying.

Starting with the I, it is easy to create interest by changing to VI. The VI being minor feels like a darkened version of the I and it pulls to the II (see page 214 for a discussion of the circle of chords). The II pulls to the V as we have seen, and the V urges us very strongly to go home to the I.

Once used, the I VI II V is sometimes then abandoned, but the total song still bears the imprint of this series of chords.

Some songs that use the sequence are discussed below.

- "Heart and Soul": This may be the one that started it all. As in most I VI II V songs, the first eight bars (and their repeat, of course) are built on the pattern. The Bridge uses another harmonic scheme.
- "Can't Help Lovin' Dat Man": Once the theme or motive is announced over the I VI II V, the composer departs from the pattern. (But many improvisers stick to it throughout the entire A section.)
- "The Way You Look Tonight": This is another melody that can be fitted against the I VI II V series. The VI in most instances, and sometimes even the II, may be altered to dominant to good effect.
- "Blue Moon": A very commercial song that fits neatly against the pattern.
- "My Heart Stood Still": This song uses the I VI II V but intensifies the second chord, changing from the VI to a diminished seventh. The second

time the pattern comes in changes the VI into an augmented. This is not uncommon. Composers often try to disguise the pattern. It is altogether to be commended; get your basic idea, polish and sophisticate it with all the technique at your command.

- "I Got Rhythm": This Gershwin classic uses I (full bar) II (half bar) V (half bar) instead of I VI II V for half a bar each. The result is practically the same, in fact most improvisers feel more comfortable adding the missing VI chord in the first bar. That way, one has a chord for each of the four pitches of the motive.
- "Ten Cents a Dance": This curious "theater song" was analyzed beginning on page 88. Like "My Heart Stood Still," also by Richard Rodgers & Lorenz Hart, it uses a diminished seventh instead of the VI chord. The verse, which talks about life at the dance hall, is pure I VI II V, and here the pattern takes on a gum-chewing sassy style.
- "Love Is The Sweetest Thing": This song uses the pattern throughout the A section but changes the II into II dominant or II♯3.
- "Try to Remember": Although this song has a Victorian feeling and was written with a pattern similar to "I Got Rhythm" (see above) it feels, and is most often performed, like a I VI II V. The beautiful bridge also feels as though it was written with the pattern in mind. The composer then used some intense major sevenths before returning to close the stanza.
- "Hey, There": The A^1 of this song begins with the pattern and then alters the quality of the chords to modulate in the A^2. This section uses the same sequences and one can see why the modulation was necessary. Three times an eight-bar section built on the same chord pattern would indeed have been too much had the composer remained in the same key.
- "I Can't Smile Without You": This interesting song uses the pattern for two bars before it moves to another chord. Thus, once through the I VI II V equals once through the first eight-bar section of the song.
- "More": This is another well-known ABAB-constructed song. The composer contrasts the I VI II V with a B section in the relative minor. (See page 221 for descending sequence in minor.) Both these strong elements and a "sensible" lyric contributed, I'm sure, to the song becoming a standard.
- "Don't It Make My Brown Eyes Blue": This song begins with the pattern and abandons it once it is stated to go into the relative minor. But the hook and motive have already been implanted in the listener's mind.

I could continue for pages giving examples of songs that use the I VI (or IV) II V. Other songs that use the pattern, or upon which the pattern may be *forced*, are "Blue Room"; "These Foolish Things (Remind Me of You)"; "Zing, Went the Strings of My Heart"; "Mean to Me"; "Love Is a Simple Thing"; "Don't Ever Leave Me"; "What Is There to Say"; "Breaking Up Is Hard to Do"; "The Diary"; "Footsteps"; "Go Away, Little Girl"; "I Believe in Music."

COMMERCIAL BRIDGE

If the I VI II V is the primary harmonic tool of songwriters looking to set their opening melodic idea, then the commercial bridge must be the most common series for bars 16–24. There are not nearly as many examples, because not all songs have bridges. Additionally, we do not always recognize the commercial bridge, for it is easy to disguise and make sound original.

The name commercial bridge originated in Tin Pan Alley. So many composers had to turn out so many songs for so many singers in so little time. Once they had created the hook or main melody they quickly completed the song using this series of chords:

	I dominant 7	IV triad	II dominant 7	V
(in C)	C⁷	F	D⁷	G⁷
	(2 bars)	(2 bars)	(2 bars)	(2 bars)

Perhaps the easiest way to understand the four chords of the commercial bridge is to observe how they work in B. G. De Sylva and Joseph Mayers's amusing song "If You Knew Susie (Like I Know Susie)."

C⁷
We went riding

F
She didn't balk.

D⁷
Back from Yonkers

G⁷
I'm the one who had to walk.

Other examples of a commercial bridge are found in "Easter Parade"; "Pennies from Heaven"; "That Old Gang of Mine"; "Are You Lonesome Tonight?"; "Something to Remember You By"; "Satin Doll"; "On the Sunny Side of the Street"; "When You're Smiling."

BRIDGES IN THE MINOR

Composers travel to minor keys for bridges almost as often as they write commercial bridges. The most common journey used to be to the *relative* minor (C to A minor), but some composers like to travel to the *parallel* (C to C minor), or to another minor key.

The Gershwins' "The Man I Love" moves beautifully into the relative minor, working its way back at conclusion into the major. Marvin Hamlisch's "What I Did for Love" does the same thing, and although almost half a century separates the two songs, both achieve the turning from sadness to bright hopefulness as they reach back for their A³'s.

It is often interesting to go to the key of the III, and songs as varied as "Let's Call the Whole Thing Off," "They Can't Take That Away from Me," (both by the Gershwins), "Fanny" (by Harold Rome), and "My Dad" (by Barry Mann and Cynthia Weil) use this harmonic change. Remember, when going to the minor for a section of your song, you *must get back to the original key*. This is generally achieved by going through a II-V or II dominant-V progression. Since 1960, composers have been intensifying the returning or "lead-in" chord by putting the V in the bass, and the II in the right hand, written Dm⁷/G (Right hand D, F, A, C; left hand G).

Many old continental songs used to change from the major into the parallel minor, and indeed this is an attractive change. Songs like "I Wish You Love," "April in Portugal," and "My Heart Belongs to Daddy" upset the major-minor relationship (the last is typically Cole Porter, who loved to switch back and forth from major to minor mode). "Ça C'est l'Amour," "Too Darn Hot," "Where Is the Life That Late I Led," "Easy to Love," and many more have this ambivalence.

BRIDGES THAT MODULATE TO FOREIGN KEYS

In our discussion of the melodic aspects of bridges, we mentioned that a bridge wants to be contrasting. What better way to create freshness than by choosing a totally new tonal center? Where does one go? Anywhere! II-V-I can pull you so many places. But some places are more common than others.

Going up a minor third and then a major third (or vice versa) is most common and natural (for example, from C to E♭, thence to G. From C to E, thence to G). The leaps are small enough to be easily sung, and the rising effect intensifies the song. Of course, arrival on the 5th of the key makes it so easy and natural to get back to the first section. You merely have to change the G *major* seventh into a G *dominant* seventh and there you are.

Study the harmonic subtlety of the bridge of "Blue Moon," by Rodgers and Hart (I have transposed it to C for comparison with other bridges).

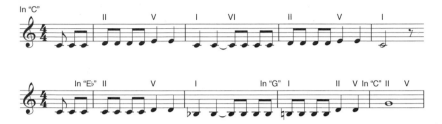

"Blue Moon" went from C to E♭ to G. "Happy Days Are Here Again" goes from C to E to G.

Other bridges that move by thirds are "Once in a While," "Lover," "The Song Is You," and "Moonlight in Vermont" (moves up a third and then up a half tone).

It is well known that bridges often go up a fourth (especially in country music), but sometimes they can go beyond that by taking their *second halves* up an additional half tone, as in Erroll Garner's "Misty," or up an additional third, as in Billy Joel's "Just the Way You Are."

THE CIRCLE OF CHORDS

This series is one of the most important in all of music. Put simply, it means the "pull" chords exert on each other. The circle is usually given in dominant sevenths and is a necessary tool for any composer because it suggests a natural progression of chords.

Like any circle, it can start anywhere. Like any tool, you can use as much or as little of it as you wish. Here are the chords. I have written them so that they progress *clockwise*:

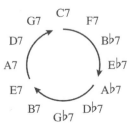

C⁷ progresses most logically to F⁷ (C, E, G, B♭ to F, A, C, E♭)
F⁷ progresses most logically to B♭7 (F, A, C, E♭ to B♭, D, F, A♭)
B♭⁷ progresses most logically to E♭⁷ (B♭, D, F, A♭ to E♭, G, B♭, D♭)
E♭⁷ progresses most logically to A♭⁷ (E♭, G, B♭, D♭, to A♭, C, E♭, G♭)
A♭⁷ progresses most logically to D♭⁷ (A♭, C, E♭, G♭ to D♭, F, A♭, C♭)
D♭⁷ progresses most logically to G♭⁷ (D♭, F, A♭ C♭, to G♭, B♭, D♭, F♭)
G♭⁷ progresses most logically to B⁷* (G♭, B♭, D♭, F♭ to B, D♯, F♯, A)
B⁷ progresses most logically to E⁷ (B, D♯, F♯, A to E, G♯, B, D)
E⁷ progresses most logically to A⁷ (E, G♯, B, D, to A, C♯, E, G)
A⁷ progresses most logically to D⁷ (A, C♯, E, G, to D, F♯, A, C)
D⁷ progresses most logically to G⁷ (D, F♯, A, C, to G, B, D, F)
G⁷ leads back to C⁷ (G, B, D, F to C, E, G, B♭)

It is not as hard to memorize the circle as it appears at first glance. The mnemonic device of spotting the word bead solves two-thirds of the circle. Think, C, F, BEAD, G, BEAD, G. (The first time BEAD occurs in "flats," the second time without flats).

Is the progression D⁷ to G⁷ a circular one? Yes, indeed. Is a simple song like "Jingle Bells," which uses these two chords in its middle, a "circular song?" No. Why?

Although these chords pull most logically to each other, we don't call a song circular unless it uses at least four of the circle chords in *succession*. "Five Foot Two, Eyes of Blue" is called circular because its bridge has the progression E⁷, A⁷, D⁷, G⁷.

The granddaddy of the circular song might be Pat Ballard's "Mister Sandman." In the quote below from its beginning, notice it goes down a half step from its opening I chord. Then it follows the circle faithfully until it arrives back home on C.

"MISTER SANDMAN" (MUSIC AND LYRIC BY PAT BALLARD)

* Most harmony books will call the circular progression from G♭ by the harmonic name of G♭ to C♭ (which indeed it is). Popular songwriters are more prone to simplify and avoid double flats and double sharps.

"Just in Time" (music by Jule Styne, lyric by Betty Comden and Adolph Green) is admired by musicians for its masterful use of the circle of chords.

Those two examples use circle technique in different ways. It is always puzzling to the beginning songwriter to know how far to go — how to jump in or to get out of the circle. I have written some rules below.

1. When entering the circle, jump to a dominant seventh built on any member of the scale you are in. The best members are III, VI, and VII. They would give you sequences like these:

$$C\text{-}E^7\text{-}A^7\text{-}D^7\text{-}G^7$$
$$C\text{-}B^7\text{-}E^7\text{-}A^7\text{-}D^7\text{-}G^7$$

Songs like "That Old Gang of Mine," "Five Foot Two, Eyes of Blue," and "Together" use this technique.

2. Begin your song out of the circle and head for home. This is the same principle as starting with the II V I, but here we carry it further. An old but still wonderful song, "Shine On, Harvest Moon," is a splendid example.

"SHINE ON, HARVEST MOON" (BY NORA BAYES AND JACK NORWORTH)

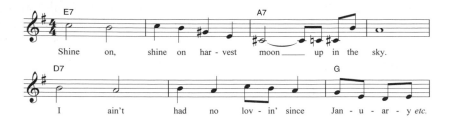

Other songs that use this technique of "starting out in left field" and then heading to their key are "Sweet Georgia Brown"; "Nice Work If You Can Get It"; and "The Best Thing for You."

3. Getting out: To stop the circle, you generally have to use a major or minor *triad*. What you want is a chord that does not have pull. Then you are free to go anywhere.

4. Fictitious use of the circle: We have mentioned before that the ear does not perceive large skips as well as it does short ones, and for that reason, it is possible to fool the ear with a skip of an augmented fourth up instead of a perfect fourth. This is frequently done to lead us back to the original key without going through all twelve circular chords.

Thus, in the key of C, F^7 to $B\flat^7$ to $E\flat^7$ to $A\flat^7$ to $D\flat^7$ should go next to $G\flat^7$; but a fictitious circular progression would substitute G^7 for the $G\flat^7$ and we would be led neatly back to C. "All the Things You Are" and "Autumn Leaves," among other songs, use just such a progression.

DIMINISHED CLICHÉ

Not unlike the popular I VI II V, but somewhat more dramatic, is the series of chords using a diminished seventh as its second member. Because these chords occur so often always in the same order, I refer to them as the diminished cliché.

	I	I DIMINISHED	II	V
In C	C E G (B)	C E♭ G♭ A	D F A C	G B D F

or

	I	#I DIMINISHED	II	V
In C	C E G (B)	C♯ E G B♭	D F A C	G B D F

These four chords work so strongly together that they make the strongest dissonance seem right. That, incidentally, is one of the most rewarding dividends of a strong harmonic line; it can make your melody sound logical even if the melody and harmony seem on first glance to be unrelated. Listen to the diminished cliché in an old song from World War I and I'm sure you'll observe how, though the series of chords seems to suggest the beginning of this century, it seems contemporary because the harmony fights and yet supports the melody.

"MY BUDDY" (MUSIC BY WALTER DONALDSON, LYRIC BY GUS KAHN)

Nights are long since you went a - way, I think a - bout you all thru the day. My

The diminished cliché is not a series that may be used again and again like the I VI II V. Thus, many songs that begin with it abandon it and go on to something else.

Some of the literally thousands of songs that use this cliché are "Time on My Hands"; "Witchcraft"; "Stormy Weather"; "I Can't Give You Anything but Love"; "My Heart Stood Still"; "Pennies from Heaven"; "Why Do I Love You"; "I'm Through with Love": "Beyond the Blue Horizon"; "You Made Me Love You"; "S'wonderful"; "Whispering"; "Penthouse Serenade"; "Maybe"; "Heart of My Heart"; "Among My Souvenirs"; and "Mame."

OLD-FASHIONED ENDING

The term is my own for a combination of clichés that, like the diminished cliché and commercial bridge, are basic training to songwriters. In former times, the last eight bars of a song had a standard series that everybody knew and headed for. The canny listener will notice the same harmony is used in songs that span half a century. From Irving Berlin's "Always" to Kander and Ebb's "New York, New York," the series is incredibly the same. This is not an isolated chord, but a whole series of seven chords filling eight bars of music (the I chord is generally held for two bars). Obviously, it is a series you should memorize.

				II*			
IVT	IVmT	IT	VI♯3	II♯3	V		IT
F, A C	F, A♭, C	C, E, G	A, C♯, E, G	D, F, A, C	G, B, D, F		C, E, G
				or			
				D, F♯, A, C			

What follows is only a partial list of songs that use these chords.

"April Showers"; "Who's Sorry Now"; "Gonna Sit Right Down and Write Myself a Letter"; "It's a Sin to Tell a Lie"; "All of Me"; "Up a Lazy River"; "I'll Never Smile Again"; "Ramona"; "You'll Never Know"; "When Irish Eyes Are Smiling"; "Don't Take Your Love from Me"; "One of Those Songs"; "New York, New York."

BASS LINES

As a chef is proud of his entrée or a diver beams when she executes a perfect double jackknife, so every composer and arranger relishes bass lines. Sure, everyone

---

*Composers (and arrangers) vary. Generally, the II suggests the thirties and beyond, while the II♯3 suggests the twenties.

wants to write a singing hit tune, but when we talk with our peers, we're proudest of the bottom line.

Some of the progressions discussed above lead naturally into rising or descending bass lines, and others that will be discussed in this section will move up or down by a half or a whole step.

Bass lines, whether ascending or descending, are especially effective when a melody is static. The Gershwins' "The Man I Love" has an emotionally moving melody appreciated by jazz musician and pop singer alike, but what makes it special is its descending bass line. Arrangers often "rearrange" a bass line to intensify it. Luther Henderson took Fats Waller's "Ain't Misbehavin'," with its ordinary I VI II V opening, and transformed it by using I, ♯I diminished, II, ♯II diminished, etc., which stepped up the music's energy.

Ascending

To ascend almost always is to brighten. Scott Joplin and the ragtimers were aware of that. They took the IV chord to a ♯IV diminished, thence to V so frequently that this almost became a cliché. Perhaps the best example of the rising urge is in "Oh, What a Beautiful Morning" (Music by Richard Rodgers, Lyric by Oscar Hammerstein II).

Don't forget that the diminished cliché using I, ♯I diminished, II, V can be an example of the ascending bass line. Here are some other useful ones:

I, II, III, IV
IV, ♯IV diminished, V
I, II, ♯II diminished, III

Ascending Through the Augmented

Merely raising the 5th of a chord is not strictly a rising *bass* line (in the change from I to I augmented, the bass does not move), but the sequence is so bright and feels like it's moving that I feel it should be discussed in this section.

The change may be from I to I+ to I⁶ (sometimes even going as far as adding I dominant and/or IV to IV+ to IV⁶). The I I+ I⁶ usually occurs at the beginning of

---

* I $^6_4$ = I triad with its 5th (G) in the bass.

a song and always makes me feel as though something is about to happen. The IV IV+ IV⁶ most often occurs near the climax and leads us into it.

Kander and Ebb expressed it with traditional intensity in "Maybe This Time," and Stephen Sondheim used it in one of his saddest songs, "Losing My Mind." In the latter, the brightness of the harmony actually helps intensify the tragedy, creating an effect like tears of joy at a "reunion scene," bearing out Tchaikovsky's musical quote "I save the major keys for my saddest melodies." But the best example of the augmented rising and pulling is in the melody Harold Arlen created for Johnny Mercer's "(You've Got to) Accentuate the Positive." Using the I I + I⁶ on the title words and darkening things on the words "eliminate the negative," where he turned major to *minor*, the whole song seems like "tone painting," a rare and much sought quality.

Other songs using this series of chords are "California, Here I Come"; "Of Thee I Sing"; "It's Delovely"; and "Don't Rain on My Parade."

The IV IV+ IV⁶ appears in "Who Can I Turn To" and "The Best of Times."

Descending

Perhaps because descending bass lines are quite romantic, composers seem to favor them over ascending ones. Of course, when a melody *ascends*, a descending bass line would be especially apt, creating what is known as contrary motion, the tension of two lines pulling in opposite directions. In the example below the tension is heightened by this motion.

Even when the melody is fixed and the motive repeats on the same pitches, as in "The Man I Love," "Do You Believe in Magic," "Until It's Time for You to Go," or "My Way," the descending bass involves our emotions and pulls like a rubber band against the anchored melody, creating tension.

The diminished cliché using I I diminished II V with the 3rd of the I chord in the bass, as illustrated below, is called oblique motion.

* I⁶₃ = I triad with 3rd (E) in the bass.
† I° is usually played with its 3rd (E♭) in the bass.

But the most frequent and contemporary bass descent in oblique motion is I; I with major 7 (in the bass); I with dominant 7 (in the bass) to VI. I've illustrated it below in F.

Descending in Minor

In minor keys, the descending line has so often been used as to become a cliché. The sequence is usually built on the I chord. In the key of A minor, it would become (lower pitches indicate bass notes):

Am	Am (or C+)	Am (or C)	Am (or D⁷)	Dm (or Dm⁷)	E⁷
A	G♯	G	F♯	F	E

This sequence was used successfully as the harmonic motive of "My Funny Valentine," "Feelings," "What Are You Doing the Rest of Your Life," "The Summer Knows," and in the final bars of Bobby Hebb's "Sunny." It was even buried in the "come to pappas" in "Embraceable You," but it is perhaps easiest to understand when seen in Marc Stephens's "Take My Love."

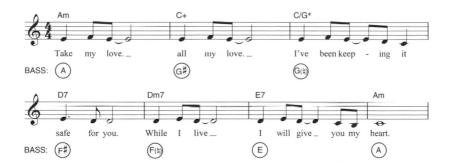

CHORD SUBSTITUTION

What do composers do to "dress up" a boring harmonic scheme? Sometimes, as we have seen, they toss away their original and create a bass line. If the original

---

* Bass notes other than roots are currently indicated immediately to the right of the slash mark; D⁷/ F♯ = D⁷ chord with F♯ in the bass.

is country, rock, or punk, this may not be desirable, but if the original is pop or jazz, theater or ballad, this is not only desirable but obligatory. So these changes should be in every composer's bag of tricks. You may use the intensifications listed below as long as the added notes don't create a dissonance with the melody.

Intensifying the Chords

- To any major triad — you may add the sixth, major seventh, or ninth. (C E G may become C E G A; C E G B; C E G B D)
- To most minor triads — you may add the sixth, minor seventh,* or ninth. (C E♭ G may become C E♭ G A; C E♭ G B♭; C E♭ G B♭ D)
- To any dominant seventh — you may add the raised fifth, or sixth in addition to the ninth or flat ninth. (C E G B♭ may become C E G♯ B♭; C B♭ E A; or C B♭ D E G♯; C B♭ D E A; or C B♭ D♭ E G♯; C B♭ D♭ E A)
- To any minor seventh — you may add the ninth or flat ninth. (C E♭ G B♭ may become C E♭ G B♭ D or C E♭ G B♭ D♭)

At this point I must caution you not to overdress the chords. Especially in rock and soul, use suspension rather than chord sophistication.

Suspension

Suspension means exactly that. A pitch is hanging in air, waiting to drop. It is clear to the ear that this suspended pitch needs to go to where it belongs, and therein lies the tension. Suspensions formerly always had to descend to their proper chord before a composer could go on, but now suspensions travel forward without resolution. But of course suspensions cannot *ascend*, resolved or not.

The most common suspension is the 4th. It is sometimes indicated on sheet music merely by the abbreviation "sus" (older editions will print "sus 4", and some editors call this the 11th). The 2-1 suspension was formerly indicated as "sus 9," but since it is so common these days, editors and composers no longer notate it on a lead sheet. That leaves only the 4-3, as indicated below.

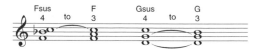

Anticipation

Sometimes the dominant seventh is present for such long periods that it sounds boringly naïve. Because of this, composers developed a habit of preceding all these

---

*You should not add the minor seventh when your triad is acting as a I chord.

V's with II's. There must be enough time (one or, better, two beats), and the chord must not clash with the melody. Put simply: *anticipation chords are minor sevenths that lead us to their dominants*. The simplest way to find one is to build a minor seventh on the 5th of the chord you wish to anticipate.

> the anticipation for G7 is D minor 7
> the anticipation for B7 is F♯ minor 7
> the anticipation for A♭7 is E♭ minor 7

Remember that anticipation chords must resolve to their dominant sevenths. You may double up — that is, use anticipation, resolution, anticipation, resolution — but don't leave the harmony hanging by omitting the resolution. Study the example below and notice how the anticipation creates urgency and interest.

WITHOUT ANTICIPATION

WITH ANTICIPATION

Scale-Tone Substitution

Anticipation is one of the ways of creating fresh color, but it can only help where a dominant seventh is concerned. What can we do for major and minor chords? There is no blanket rule, but because of their similarity, certain chords are often substituted for others.

I may be exchanged for VI
(C E G B is not unlike A C E G, for three pitches are identical)

I may be exchanged for III
(C E G B is not unlike E G B D, for three pitches are identical)

Using these chords in place of I can create freshness, but be aware that both of these chords are minor and used in place of I will create a quasi-religious sound.

II and IV are often exchanged

The old rock and roll substitutes IV for II, transforming the I VI II V pattern into I VI IV V. Of all chords, II and IV are most often exchanged.

V exchanged for ♭II dominant or ♭VII T

As we saw on page 222, V may be *anticipated*. It may also be exchanged for a ♭II dominant seventh, the raison d'être being that if V can move *circularly*, as in II V I, the I chord can be approached *chromatically* as well, using II ♭II I. The ♭II dominant seventh then becomes equal to the regular V. Here's how it works with a common "I love you" ending:

In country music, with its omnipresent V chords, Glenn Campbell and Jim Webb often use the ♭VII triad *before* the V chord. This works instead of an anticipation and gives an open prairie feeling.

Beginning composers are always tempted to use complicated, intense chords when a simpler one will do. So before I close this discussion of harmonic changes, let me caution you again not to overdress your melodies. Don't let them sink below the weight of their chords, and don't make your harmonic line so involved that it takes hours of rehearsal to perform.

TURNAROUNDS

What harmony is useful to pull around the corner for a repeat? What about an A¹, A², section, and how does one get from one to the other? There are many progressions. A few of them are listed below. They can be transposed to keys more comfortable for the guitar, and although they take two bars as written here, they may be telescoped into one bar by using quarter notes. Called turnarounds, turnabouts (in England), and turnbacks, they may serve equally well at the close. All you have to do is add some attractive form of the I chord. (I with added 6 and 9 is interesting.)

The turnarounds below follow my personal order of preference, best first, but I'd suggest you learn them all.

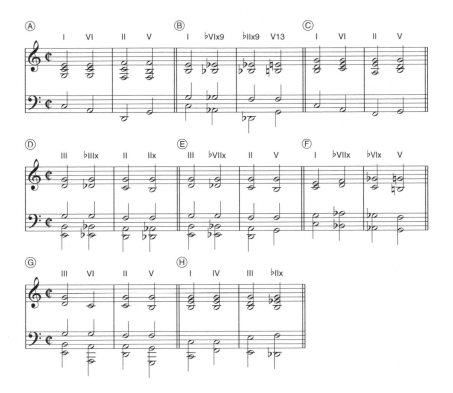

EVASION

Time was when every song had a long introduction. These days no one has that much patience to delay getting started, but singers still like to stretch things out at the end. You will often hear them heading for the last pitch and, instead of hitting it, evading it. This can send them into an added phrase before concluding. The most common evasions are listed below.

Example A is a simple ending. Examples B through E evade the last note every time it is about to occur and tag on a final phrase.

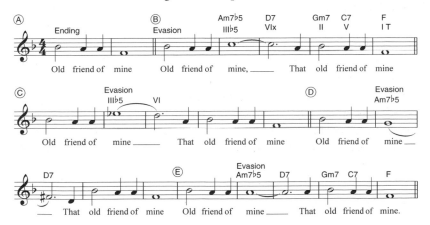

BLUES MELODY AND HARMONY

Blues melody is so inextricably wedded to its harmony that it was impossible to analyze in the melodic section of this book. It will be discussed on the following pages. However, before embarking on it, I'd advise a review of the lyric principles of blues, beginning on page 26.

From the earliest, blues has followed a rigid harmonic line. The twelve satisfying bars are usually divided and harmonized as follows:

Melody line		Improvisation	
I T	I T	I Dominant Seventh	

Melody line		Improvisation	
IV Dominant Seventh		I T	

Melody line		End	
V	V or IV Dominant Seventh	I (Turnaround)	V

It is possible to have many different harmonic sequences (sometimes beginning with minor, substituting the IV chord on the second bar), but what *makes* blues harmony is the presence of the IV dominant seventh in the fifth bar. *This must not be altered* or the blues sound will be lost.

It is quite typical of blues to have each melodic phrase occupy only two and a half of the four allotted bars. This provides the improviser with breathing space and a chance to collect new ideas. If the improviser is a vocalist, this gives him or her a chance to think up new rhymes. When the improvisor is quite "laid back" and knows what phrase comes next, this breathing space may be filled with wild flights of vocal and instrumental improvisation.

In creating their line, blues vocalists tried to copy other instrumentalists, especially those playing trumpet or clarinet. They attempted to get somewhere between the major and minor key, the black and white.

They "worried" the line and created the "blue" note, coming not from the color of the key, but from the squashed feeling. Keyboard players tried to emulate other instrumentalists, who could bend their pitches. They often played E♭ and E together, releasing the former. In concert circles this is known as a "grace note"; popular musicians call it a "crushed" note.

Because of the minor I and the minor IV and the frequent flat 5th, the blues line and the blues scale became the sinuous line shown below.

9 RHYTHM

WHAT IS RHYTHM? What do we mean when we say someone has it? Usually that they sing or dance with a strong sense of awareness of the pulsation in the music. When we say a song is rhythmic, we often mean it has rapid tempo and strong pulsations.

The word *rhythm* is probably the most misunderstood in the composer's lexicon, because it hinges on an understanding of beat, tempo, pulse, and meter.

BEAT

Beat or pulse is a unit of measurement. The number of beats in the bar depends upon the time signature. Well, not exactly, for the beats came first and the time signature was created to explain this natural phenomenon, just as singing came first and notation explained what was sung.

But for our purposes let's assume the time signature gives us the clue. We must also consider the speed (tempo).

When we see a time signature of 4/4, we assume there are going to be four beats per bar. That is true when the music moves moderately, but if the song is very slow, a wise conductor will indicate eight beats with his stick. If the song moves rapidly, it is generally conducted in "two," meaning there will be two beats per bar. (Composers frequently use the sign C, which they call "cut time"; concert musicians using the same sign for the same purpose call it "alla breve").

Although we all know that waltzes are in 3/4 time, it is only the *valse lent*, or slow waltz, that has three beats, or oom-pah-pah. Most waltzes are conducted, sung, and danced in *one*. Leonard Bernstein says that the waltz, like all music, takes its clue from our human heartbeat, that there is no such thing as triple rhythm, and I agree. Actually, a fast waltz comes out *strong* two three, weak two three; *strong* two three, weak two three, which eventually boils down to STRONG la la, Weak la la or ONE / Two. Beat, then, is the basic unit of the music, the bricks of the building that you will eventually put together to make up your song.

TEMPO

Tempo refers to the speed of the beat. Before the Renaissance, tempo was set by the leader, the composer having no say in the matter, but with the advent of modern times, Italy and then the rest of the world began using terms such as *largo*, *adagio*, *allegro* and *presto* to indicate how fast or slow they wanted the beat to be. This opened music to individual interpretation, a much sought after commodity in concert music. A symphony conducted by Dorati might last forty-five minutes while the same score led by a more expansive contemporary conductor like Muti might be a full five minutes longer; this shows how much tempo can vary in the concert hall. But in the jazz world, a performance of, say "Round Midnight" by Thelonious Monk or by Horace Silver (assuming they improvised the same *number* of choruses) would take approximately the same time.

Concert music depends on fluctuations in tempo to hit its emotional points, but this would never work for popular music, which had its origins in the dance hall.

Fortunately for us, Maezel invented the metronome in 1816. Beethoven was the first to use this wonderful contraption that keyed to the clock ($\downarrow$ = M.M. 60 indicates 60 quarter notes per minute). Now we have an accurate tempo measure at our disposal, which we can use for laying down tracks in a recording studio or helping us with overdubbing.

Some songwriters use the M.M. markings at the beginning of their efforts, but most prefer to be a little less rigid and write "moderato," "maestoso," "calypso tempo," or even pretentious things like "tempo di blues." I'd advise "moderately" instead of "moderato"; "with a lilt" instead of "giocoso"; and "stately" instead of "maestoso."

Tempo, then, means how *fast the beats go by*. If they speed, say, $\downarrow$ = 120, this is called "up-tempo," a phrase well known to all popular musicians. Incidentally, I've never heard anyone ask for "down-tempo."

METER

Although the notes above may *look* alike, they don't *sound* alike. There is a built-in accent on the first of each bar. This happens because it is almost impossible to say a series of divisible pitches or drumbeats without placing some sort of weight somewhere. We want to divide them, to group them, and to place an accent on the first of the group. In the example above, the meter is 4/4. It indicates where the accent comes.

We discussed the common meters of three (triple) and four (duple) in the basics section of this book, but there are also meters of 5, 6, 7, and others.

A meter of five can be comprised of *one* two three four five, *one* two three four five, but more often it has a secondary accent, sounding like ONE two three *four* five, ONE two three *four* five or ONE two *three* four five, ONE two *three* four five. The best known example is Paul Desmond's "Take Five," which swings naturally in this most unnatural meter. It uses 3 + 2 and totally succeeds in concept as well. ("Take five" is the common phrase for the smoking break in a jazz rehearsal).

"TAKE FIVE" (MUSIC BY PAUL DESMOND)

A meter of six is usually done as ONE two three, *four* five six, ONE two three, *four* five six, which as you can see would be felt and performed in two. This is the stock-in-trade of the Irish jig or the highland fling. Scottish music generally used "alla zoppa," meaning "in a limping manner," but was usually written in 6/8 meter.

Six-eight meter can be wonderfully exciting when used to create a Latin sound. Treated

$$\frac{6}{8} \quad \text{etc.}$$

as Leonard Bernstein did in "America" (from *West Side Story*), it seems to be throwing us constantly "off kilter." If you can clap it out, you'll see the possibilities of 6/8. What about 4 + 2; 4 + 2: then 3 + 3? or any other you can come up with?

"AMERICA" (MUSIC BY LEONARD BERNSTEIN, LYRIC BY STEPHEN SONDHEIM)

Meters more compound than six are rare in popular music. Sometimes dance arrangers will use seven (when used, it is generally 4 + 3), and there are composers who write 9/8 and 12/8 frequently. These meters merely make it easier to read what we feel. Nine-eight is most often felt *one* two three, *four* five six, *seven* eight nine, which boils down to three beats, and 12/8 is almost always felt as *one* two three *four* five six *seven* eight nine *ten* eleven twelve, which adds up to four beats per bar.

Contemporary concert musicians, especially Stravinsky, have been known to create much interest in their work by changing meter frequently. They can switch from 2/4 to 11/8 to 4/4 and so forth with the greatest of ease. I believe this is because concert musicians are accustomed to placing the accent almost invariably on the first of the bar. Pop and jazz musicians are used to "offbeats," backbeats, and syncopation (see page 235). They do not adjust the meter, but by accenting unexpected pitches, inserting rests where one expects sound, and especially by moving the accent to different parts of the bar, they vary the beat.

RHYTHM

Now we can put the terms together. Rhythm could be defined as *the way a bar (or series of bars) is filled* with *sound*. Will it be four simple quarter notes or a combination of eighth notes, triplets, and sixteenth notes? Will we have silence where we are ready for a strong downbeat?

Time is a most important element in music, and one might also define rhythm as the *distribution* of *sound over time.*

In order to understand the subtle effects of rhythm, you will have to know more subdivisions of a basic beat than were touched upon in the section on basics. Imagine then that the length of one line, comprising four quarter notes, takes four seconds. I have printed eighth notes, triplets, sixteenth notes, and thirty-second notes. (Even sixty-fourth notes are possible and are used in concert music, although I have not entered them here.)

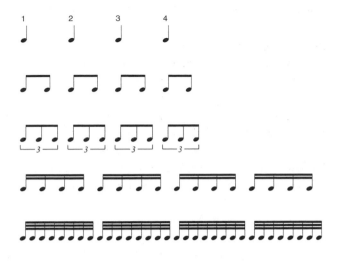

The straight triplet is a useful tool. It divides the beat into three parts. It is related to the "quarter-note triplet," which is written so:

and the "sextuplet," which looks like this:

Remember when counting meter to fill the bar. Perhaps the following story will illustrate how non-musicians, especially dancers, have a different way of filling the bar.

One of my first commissions as a young composer was from a well-known dancer. She entered my barren studio one January day and said she had been listening to me improvise while walking down the hall, and could I write the music for a dance she had choreographed. She wanted it exactly three and a half minutes long, "vitally exciting, and in three."

Since I was not familiar with "dancer's time," I wrote what I considered a vitally exciting dance that lasted exactly three and a half minutes. Of course the time signature was 3/4. When I played it for her the next week, she said, "You have the spirit of what I want, but I asked for a dance in *three*." "But, it is in three," I protested.

"Three!" she said. "One, two, *threeeee*."

I could see that she was holding the three for an extra count.

I said not a word, but went back and rewrote my dance into 4/4, with a heavy accent on the third beat. She performed it with her dancers, teaching them the steps while calling out, "One, two. THREEEEEEE!, One, two THREEEEE." Anyone who can shout "TURN TWO, THREE FOUR LEAP, KICK FIVE SIX STEP SLIDE SEVEN EIGHT" has to be incomprehensible to someone with a sense of the regularity of meter.

Dancers are not the only ones whose performance, while metered, can appear to be arbitrary. If you go to a music store and look at the *printed* sheet copy of a song, you will *see* the most complicated rhythms written. However, if you examine the work of Billy Joel, Jim Webb, John Kander, and the "old" masters like Arlen, Berlin, Gershwin — those who know how to write down music — you will rarely find subdivisions of the beat beyond the sixteenth note. The reason so much sheet music appears so "complicated" is because the music has been transcribed for those who do not know how to notate by someone in a publishing house. Somebody listened to the recording and wrote down exactly what he or she heard.

To make a record successful it is necessary that the beat be free, and this freedom is difficult to read. So I'd suggest that when you have recorded your own melody, learn how to transcribe it yourself. It is a tight line to walk; keeping the rhythm alive without becoming too complicated.

HOW RHYTHM FILLS THE MUSIC

The rhythm should be inherent in the pitches and written *into* the line. Examine rhythms that are memorable, in songs like "The Best Is Yet to Come," "Gonna Fly Now," and "Knock Three Times." Looking at the rhythmic motive, it is obvious that the distribution of the beat, not the melodic construction of these songs, propelled them into the hit category.

"GONNA FLY NOW" (MUSIC BY BILL CONTI, LYRIC BY CAROL CONNORS AND AYN ROBBINS)

"THE BEST IS YET TO COME" (MUSIC BY CY COLEMAN, LYRIC BY CAROLYN LEIGH)

"KNOCK THREE TIMES" (MUSIC AND LYRIC BY IRWIN LEVINE AND L. RUSSELL BROWN)

SYNCOPATION

Syncopation relies on our built-in childhood urge for singsong regularity; by placing an accent on a part of the bar that is *not* regularly important, it upsets our sense of order and thus intrigues us.

is very regular, but by misplacing accents to

we feel out of kilter, even more so when we do

or

The last is sometimes called by the fancy name of anticipatory syncopation. Indeed it is that, but I feel it best to generalize that anything that does not occur *on* the beat is syncopation.

We have come to expect syncopation as part of every melodic line. Certainly it is omnipresent in jazz, soul, blues, and pop. Heavy metal and acid rock use less as, of course, do hymns and the simplest folk tunes.

If you hear your great-aunt Matilda play a popular ballad and wonder why it sounds so "unpopular," it is probably because she has read the notes as written and omitted the "understood" syncopation that a professional would give it. "Don't Blame Me" (music by Jimmy McHugh, lyric by Dorothy Fields) for example, is written thus

Don't   blame   me

but sung and played thus:

Don't blame _   me ____

One final note on syncopation. Be aware that syncopation is *off* beat and to have its effect it must be contrasted with *on* beat. A series of off beats will eventually sound regular; the ear soon forgets where the strong pulses are. This rhythm

is not as exciting as this.

RHYTHMS OF POPULAR MUSIC

Over the years popular music has been cast in familiar rhythms, which in turn spawned dances. Some of these rhythms are listed below. The simplest ones are complete in one-half or one bar. The more complex ones need two. I don't know of any *recurring* rhythm that has more than two different bars. The ear cannot hold on to a longer series.*

March

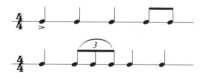

---

*Similarly, it has been said, the ear cannot handle more than two melodies at once. Three or more separate vocal or instrumental counterpoints are satisfying only to the mind and the eye.

The straight beat of the march is generally kept for a long period. In interludes, however, it is usually very syncopated, but when the beat returns, it is straight again so the other instruments and lines can do an obligato (counter melody above).

Fox-trot

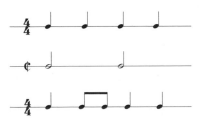

This dance, popular during the twenties and thirties, was in straight 4/4 time. It was often in cut time, and sometimes it included an accent on the weaker third beat, which became known as the backbeat.

Modified Fox-trot

A hesitation on the second beat became the most frequent variation of the fox-trot.

Shuffle

A jazz rhythm that came about in the twenties. It was later transformed into boogie-woogie.

Boogie

As noted above, boogie had its origins in the shuffle. Boogie became known as "eight to the bar" (8 eighth-notes in each measure). Boogie uses the blues chord progression (see page 226) and often has a walking bass.

Ragtime

Ragtime began as a piano style and was most popular from the end of the nineteenth century until World War I. It was generally written in 2/4 (sometimes 4/4). The left hand performed a strong oom-pah beat that became known as stride while the right hand played syncopated melodies derived from banjo or guitar arpeggios. After the seventies movie *The Sting*, which used Scott Joplin's rags, there was a tremendous revival of interest in this rhythm.

Cakewalk

A dance with strongly accented syncopation. It began as a contest in high stepping while keeping an erect bearing. The couple who were able to do this with the most verve were awarded a cake.

Polka

Polka is a dance of Polish origin with its accent on the first of the bar. It is in fast duple meter — usually in 2/4, but possibly in 4/4 or ¢. "Shall We Dance," "Beer Barrel Polka," and "I Love Louisa" are prime examples.

Alley Cat

A group dance with a triplet up-beat, usually done with all participants facing the leader, similar to a dancing class. This is sometimes called the "hully-gully."

Gavotte

An elegant dance of French origin in fairly quick time. Usually in 4/4, it frequently begins with a pick-up on the third (sometimes fourth) beat of the bar. It was used with ironic lyrics as the "Ascot Gavotte" in Lerner and Loewe's *My Fair Lady*.

Minuet (Menuet)

A French dance in moderate tempo. The minuet was very popular in the seventeenth and eighteenth centuries. Some classical scholars say it was the precursor of the waltz because of its strong accent on the first beat of the bar.

Waltz

Although written in 3/4 meter, the true waltz has only one beat per bar (see page 229). The waltz came into prominence in late nineteenth-century Germany and Austria. It reached its zenith of popularity when written by the Strauss family in the 1860s.

Waltzes rarely change harmony in mid-bar, for this would slow down the pulse and thrust of the music. Jerome Kern turned the waltz into an American product and a vehicle for Astaire and Rogers in the movies. "The Waltz in Swingtime" and "I Dream Too Much" are good examples.

Boston Waltz

Richard Rodgers contributed his own syncopated ideas to the American waltz and transformed the European sound into the Boston waltz ("Lover" and "The Most Beautiful Girl in the World"). The accented third beat is held over the bar, creating an accent on the second beat of the succeeding bar. Although the waltz is much used in theater music (Stephen Sondheim wrote *A Little Night Music* totally in multiples of the 3/4 pulse), it is rarely used in pop or rock.

Country Waltz

But the waltz has become one of the staples of country music. Its naïve, homey beat imparts a kind of honesty to the song, especially when accompanied with a fiddle and a straight oom-pah-pah on the snare drum.

Jazz Waltz

Although jazz is generally played in duple meter, the jazz waltz is dear to the hearts of most jazz artists. Sometimes with a rest on the first beat of the bar or sometimes closer to the beat of the shuffle (page 237), it has remarkable freshness. Jazz pianists especially seem to enjoy transforming "My Favorite Things," or "Who Will Buy" into 3/4 improvisations. Sometimes they write their own, like "Waltz for Debby" or "I'm All Smiles."

Gospel Waltz

Although in slower tempo than the jazz waltz, the gospel waltz is another attempt to update the old-fashioned waltz. The lyric will of course be inspirational, and the beat will be closer to country. The gospel waltz almost invariably has three quarter notes with three distinct beats. "What the World Needs Now Is Love" and "You Light Up My Life" are prime examples.

Charleston

TANGO

CHARLESTON

It has been said the Charleston grew out of the tango (see page 244), that the dance was merely a tango with the last two beats omitted, but the accent so frequently on the last beat of the bar makes me doubt that. In any case, the Charleston was the most popular dance craze of the twenties and even today refuses to be forgotten. It certainly led us directly into jazz rhythm with a strong accent on the fourth eighth-note in the bar.

Jazz Rhythms

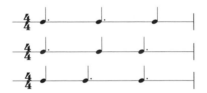

Eight eighth-notes in the bar can be divided in so many ways. Concert musicians often use 2 + 2 + 2 + 2, but jazz musicians generally prefer a less "square" division. 3 + 3 + 2 is a favorite combination, but there are many other possibilities, too many more to notate here. Once a rhythmic combination has been selected, it should be maintained for a sizable section of the song, because it is very hard to change from one jazz beat to the other.

Jig (Gigue)

The regular 6/8 duple meter of the jig is described on page 231. 6/8 is the same as 2/4 in that there are two pulses to the bar. 6/8 is somewhat easier to read. Examples are "The Irish Washerwoman" and "Open a New Window."

9/8

As mentioned earlier, 9/8 *can be* the same as 3/4. However, with the accents placed irregularly, it can turn into a rollicking jazz rhythm. I'm sure you can find your own way to subdivide 9 pulses rather than the usual 3 + 3 + 3.

12/8

12/8, likewise, can be the same as 4/4. The bolero often uses this rhythm. ("The Impossible Dream" is sometimes performed in 9/8, sometimes in 12/8; the former more youthful and electric, the latter more grandiose.)

Country

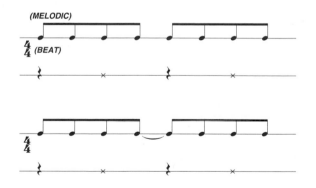

Country music is deceptive. It sounds pure and easy. But there are two things always going on. The melodic line is usually in straight eighth notes while the drum beat falls on two and four. This heavy accentuation of two and four is called a backbeat. Sometimes the melodic line is syncopated, as in the second example.

Disco

Disco, which became suddenly passé in the eighties, relied heavily on a straight 4 beat. Mixed into this regular and somewhat tiresome pulse were straight eighth notes, sometimes syncopated. The rhythms above are typical.

Tango (Habanera)

The habanera was imported from Cuba through Spain into the United States. Generally written in 2/4 time, it has a strong accent on the first of the bar. Some well-known ones are the one from *Carmen*; "La Cumparsita"; and "Love, What Are You Doing to My Heart."

Tango (Argentine)

The Argentine tango became very popular in Europe and the United States around 1910 and is generally written in 4/4. It often has an up beat or a few lead-in notes. Again, the accent is very strong on the first beat of the bar. "Hernando's Hideaway"; "Jalousie"; "Kiss of Fire"; and "Magic Is the Moonlight" are examples.

Bolero

The true bolero is in 3/4 time. But the triplets have given the bolero such a recognizable sound that music that is written in 4/4 is often "boleroized." Ravel's famous *Bolero* became a best-selling record after Bo Derek admitted in the movie *10* that she enjoyed fornicating to its throbbing rhythm. Indeed the piece caused a riot at its premiere fifty years earlier. Other boleros are "Temptation": "Silencio"; and "Mi Corazon."

Merengue

The merengue is a dance that originated in the Dominican Republic. The dancer kept one leg straight while leading with the other, creating the "limping step." Supposedly, this dance was invented in order not to embarrass a Dominican general who returned from the wars with a wounded knee. The story may be as bogus as the one concerning the reasons the Spanish court speaks lisping Castillian (because an effete king did), but the dance and its misplaced accent are fascinating. Some titles are "Bim Bam Boom"; "La Pachanga"; and "Con Permiso."

Cha-Cha

The cha-cha was most popular around 1960. Society, which had been dancing the rumba and samba for a long time, had to go back to dancing school to learn this one. The cha-cha then became the dance of the "tired businessman," who demanded well-known "tunes" above his Latin beat. It spawned things like the "Tea for Two Cha-Cha"; "Blue Moon Cha-Cha"; "Never on Sunday Cha-Cha"; and "Dansero."

Conga

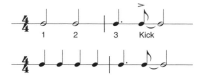

The conga is a two-bar rhythmic dance that fits the words *one, two, three, kick,* and its attendant dance was as simple as that. The second bar uses a syncopation on the *kick.* Dancers formed a conga line, each holding the one before by the midriff. It was popularized by Carmen Miranda and Desi Arnaz. The most memorable conga was called, appropriately, "One Two Three Kick!"

Guaracha

The guaracha is a popular Cuban dance somewhat faster than the 4/4 bolero. "Quisas" ("Perhaps") is the best-known example.

Rumba

The rumba is the quintessential Latin dance and the most enduring of all Latin rhythms. It uses 8 eighths in the bar, accenting them 3 + 3 + 2, similar to jazz. Xavier Cugat popularized the rumba in America in the early 1930s, although it had been widely popular abroad before that. As with most any pulse, it is not the melody that creates the dance. Popular rumbas had such different tunes as "The Carioca"; "Wish You Were Here"; "Say Si-Si"; and "The Walter Winchell Rumba."

Beguine

The beguine is said to have originated in the French Islands of the Caribbean (even though Cole Porter, its most eminent practitioner, states he first heard it in Tahiti). Although it's a background beat, it does have a somewhat melodic line that begins on the second eighth-note of the bar. What makes the beguine rhythm unique is that nothing happens on the (first part of the) second beat of each bar. The bass is generally one of the two examples as above.

Mambo

It's easy to see why the mambo craze developed in the 1950s. This joyous beat is infectious, and the dance is an easy hip-swinging affair not unlike the later twist. Tito Puente was the mambo's best-known advocate. He recorded over 100 mambo albums, relinquishing his crown at last to Perez Prado, who added his own 4th-beat "grunt." As far as the dances go, the mambo and cha-cha are interchangeable.

Samba

The samba is a fast Brazilian dance in duple meter. It uses a rising bass. The samba is an important part of the bossa nova. Besides "One-Note Samba," there are "Brazil"; "Tico-Tico"; "Chico-Chico"; and "Cae-Cae."

Bossa Nova

Bossa nova means "new beat," and even though this beat was new many decades ago, it has never lost its "newness" to these ears. Brazil's eminent composers Jobim and Bonfa did much to make this sophisticated rhythmic excursion popular in the United States. The bossa nova must use two bars, the first similar to the samba and the second like a jazz rhythm. Some of my favorites are "Quiet Nights"; "Desafinado"; "Wave"; "Eso Beso"; and "The Girl from Ipanema."

Paso Doble

One cannot create a complete Latin compendium without an example of the music that recalls bullfights. The Paso Doble (twostep) is in fast triple meter. It often has an up beat. The most famous one is "El Relicario."

Reggae

JAMAICAN

COMMERCIAL

Reggae, a strong Jamaican beat that seemed to sweep American popular music in the mid-eighties, takes two strong forms. They both imply an anticipation of the third beat of the bar. The truly Jamaican form adds a cha-cha beat in the bass; the American version (the one you are most likely to hear on recordings) includes a persistent backbeat on the fourth beat of every measure.

Bo Diddley

Bo Diddley, rhythm and blues guitarist of the late fifties, created a rhythm much used by the Rolling Stones. (It was used on Buddy Holly's "Not Fade Away," which uses only the E and A triads.) Blues effects are often used in conjunction with this beat (lowering the 3rd and 5th of the chord).

Punk Rock

Since punk rock is an attempt to return to simplicity, its rhythms are generally straight 4 or eight-to-the-bar, always with an accent or backbeat on 2 and 4.

AFTER THE SONG IS COMPLETED

GETTING A SONG ON PAPER

On page 8 I discussed the music paper and pencils I prefer, and on page 143 I began a rundown of ways to get the pitches, rhythms, and lyrics of your song on a page. It might be advisable to review those sections now before preparing to make a first sheet copy.

Lead Sheets

The term *lead sheet* is not derived from the word *bandleader*, as is commonly thought, but from the "lead," or melody line. A lead sheet displays all the elements of the song while leaving the creative style up to the individual performer. Melody, harmony, rhythm, and lyric are set forth (older lead sheets include diagrams of guitar frets for fledgling guitarists, sometimes omitting the chord names entirely), but the performer is given no advice about style. He or she must decide to arpeggiate the bass or use blocked chords; whether to invert chords or use them in root position; to perform in open or stride; to play one chorus or eight; what turnaround to use; which bass line; and finally whether to put a rhythmic beguine behind the singer or a country rock beat. All decisions are up to the artists.

Writing a lead sheet is quicker than writing a full sheet two-stave copy (see page 255), or three-stave copy (see page 254), and it keeps the song loose. It is also the way most professionals notate their music, and if you want to consider yourself a songwriter, I would suggest you master the technique of writing your own lead sheet.

A collection of lead sheets is called a fakebook. Fakebooks used to be illegal, for they were printed clandestinely and the songwriters and publishers received not a penny in royalties. There was a great demand for them, legal or not, because band musicians, solo pianists, or singers could not carry around the reams of music necessary to play a gig. Legal fakebooks are sold in music stores now, the royalties going to the proper parties.

Assume you have created the words and music to "Sometimes I Feel Like a Motherless Child" and have notated the melody:

When you have added the lyric, below the melody line, and the harmony, above the melody line, your lead sheet should look like this:

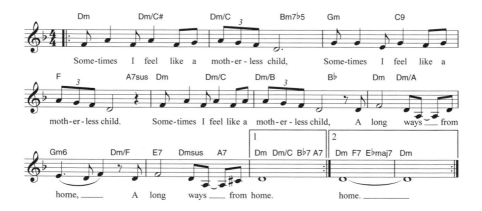

When Preparing a Lead Sheet

1. If you do not have one of the computer music writing systems, I suggest you get a music writing book and write in pencil. Songwriters use the eraser end of the pencil more often than they do the lead one. Most of us prefer a mechanical pencil with soft lead. (Use .07 or .05 mm so that the tip of your pencil doesn't blunt and your pitches don't spread over into adjoining lines or spaces.)

2. *Don't crowd.* Amateurs are prone to crowd as many notes as possible onto a page. Don't. The music swims, and the performer gets lost.

3. Place chords exactly where they belong:

4. Don't be ambiguous on chord symbols; don't use shorthand. Of course, Roman-numeral relationships should be understood and kept in your head, but they are never entered on a lead sheet.

ACCEPTABLE SYMBOLS	UNACCEPTABLE SYMBOLS
major triad = (nothing)	
minor triad = m	− ; mi; ♭
diminished triad = m♭5	0; dim; dim T
augmented triad = +	aug; ♯5
major seventh = maj7	M; Ma;
minor seventh = m7	mi; mi 7; −
dominant seventh = 7	Dom 7
augmented seventh = 7 + 5	7♯5; Aug 7; aug 7
diminished seventh = °	Dim 7; °7
minor seventh, lowered 5th = m7♭5	°; °7; ½ dim 7

5. Observe proper spacing. Give a half note, for example, more room on the line than a quarter note.

6. Fit the pitches *clearly* onto lines or spaces. Make notes round, and don't let them spread out.

7. On normal manuscript paper, write on *every other* staff.
8. Use hyphens to separate syllables of the lyric.
9. Use upper- and lowercase on lyric lines as if the lyric were a poem.
10. When you encounter the entire and exact title in the lyric, set it in uppercase.
11. Check over the work for accuracy. It's costly to repair typos or to stop a recording session to change a mistaken chord or pitch. I also look at lyric and melody backward so my eye will spot errors.

Three-Stave Arrangements

If you can notate in both treble and bass clefs (if you can't, see the *Yellow Pages* of your phone directory under musical arrangers to find someone who can do it for you) and you know exactly what you want the back-up accompaniment to your song to be, a three-stave arrangement is better than a lead sheet. Of course it does take more time to notate, and it should not be attempted until you have a completed lead sheet from which to work.

The three-stave arrangement follows an unbroken line of composition that stretches from opera through operetta and lieder into Broadway musicals (in which it is called a piano score). The three staves are: 1) vocal line; 2) piano treble clef; and 3) piano bass clef. Editors may add chord names above the vocal line as in a lead sheet. This is never done in a full show score, but always in an album of selected sheet music.

The melodic line may be incorporated into the accompanying piano part or omitted. In the forties and fifties, it was always included, but then as composers and performers became more self-sufficient, songwriters like Joni Mitchell, Randy Newman, and Jimmy Webb began letting the accompaniment go its way, different from the vocal line. The background then became a way to help the composer get the concept across.

A three-stave arrangement of "Sometimes I Feel Like a Motherless Child" is printed below. Examine it, noticing that the piano part supports, adds color to, and does not intrude upon the vocal line.

Things to Remember About Three-Stave Arrangements

1. Choose a comfortable singing key. If you have a high soprano or a very low baritone, write out a lead sheet for yourself but put your melody line somewhere in the middle of the treble clef.
2. Don't make your accompaniment so difficult that it overshadows the melodic line, or so intense that our ears are tuned to it rather than the premier line of the song.
3. The accompaniment should *move* when the melody stops.
4. The accompaniment may go above the melodic line occasionally but should mostly stay below it.
5. Write the melody line exactly as you would for a lead sheet, using a two-stave piano part below. Then add your chord "explanation" above the melody (vocal) line. (English scores put the chords below the bass clef.) You may erase your chord explanation to create an "art song."

Two-Stave Arrangements

Most commercial arrangers are now incorporating the melodic line into a simple two-stave arrangement. It is much easier to follow, but I have always disliked it. I feel it duplicates the singer's line, and because of that, it seems more difficult to omit the "lead" line and improvise freely.

Professional pianists and professional singers prefer a three-stave arrangement to a two-stave one because each does not have to step into the other's domain, but amateurs usually hate it. They like to have the melody included in the line of the instrumental part. They are often insecure, especially when the line is difficult.

A typical two-stave arrangement of "Sometimes I Feel Like a Motherless Child" is printed below.

Things to Remember About Two-Stave Arrangements

1. The lyric is written between the staves, the chords are listed above.
2. Keep the melody uppermost at all times.
3. Keep the arrangement simple. Remember this is a commercial effort, not an artistic one.
4. Don't let your bass wander into the treble or vice versa, for the notes will be hard to read.

Arrangements for a Group

Arranging for more than singer and solo accompanist is beyond the realm of songwriting. It wanders into the art of song arranging and as such is out of the scope of this book. There are many good books that deal exclusively with arranging for a small group to full orchestration, and they are listed in the Bibliography.

Professional Copies

When you have written down your song or captured it using music-notation software, whether lead sheet, piano score, or two-stave arrangement, you will want to make a professional-looking copy of your song so you can have it copyrighted. You can buy music writing books at any large music supply store. If you are unable to notate your score, the Library of Congress now accepts recordings as proof of authorship. You can also register your copyright online at www.copyright.gov.

Once you have an original that is clear, accurate, uncrowded, deeply black, with notes large enough, and lyric *printed* in, you may have it reproduced. But if your manuscript looks sloppy or if you are unsure of rhythms or harmony, seek the services of a professional copyist in the former case and a professional arranger in the latter.

The fee (in urban centers) for copying is about $50 per page, about $250 for a normal-length song. Don't fool with students or amateurs, who may be a bit cheaper but in the end usually turn out shoddy work, little better than you might do. You will find a list of copyists and arrangers in the *Yellow Pages* of large cities. Don't hesitate to ask to see their work.

If you haven't used a notation program and have created your work on paper, and once the arrangement satisfies you, it can be reproduced in one of three ways:

1. Photocopying is the most common: As music paper is larger than the standard 8½ x 11, most recently manufactured photocopy machines can handle this, or if you wish, they can reduce your manuscript to the 8½ x

11 size. New machines print on any kind of stock. I prefer double thick semi-cardboard sheets that don't flutter or flop onto the keys. I find beige stock easier on the eyes. If you write yours with black felt-tip pen or electro-sensitive pencil, you will get a sharp image. Caution: Avoid blue ink. It does not reproduce.

2. The diazo whiteprint process: Until the advent of the duplicating store on every corner, this process was the simplest and the least expensive. The technique gets its name from a paper with a special diazo chemical coating. It is called whiteprint, to distinguish it from another common diazo process, blueprint.

   When a transparent master copy of a work is placed in contact with the paper and exposed to an intense ultraviolet light, then developed with ammonia fumes, the resulting copies come out black on white.

   Transparent masters are necessary, and you may buy sheets printed with any number of staves from many companies. Get the best, most transparent paper with the highest rag content. Copy your song on the *unprinted* side of the onionskin (writing on the unprinted side makes it easier for you to erase without destroying the staves printed other side).

   Check your work by holding the paper up to the light. When making the transparent master, the density of the writing is crucial. Dense black or india ink is best. Pencils with electro-sensing lead will reproduce well, but be careful to prevent smudging the soft lead. Felt-tip or ballpoint will not make good copies as the pigment is not dense enough to block out the intense light of the diazo process machine.

   Whiteprint copies can easily be bound in a number of ways. The simplest is "accordion fold," which is perfect for orchestra parts. In this method, copies are printed on one side of a sheet four pages long. Works longer than four pages are taped together with a special tape. Long scores can be bound rather inexpensively with spiral plastic spindles and cardboard covers.

   The diazo had other drawbacks as well. It was harder to write on the onionskin than regular paper. The "skins" had to be stored carefully; a new copy had a strong ammonia smell; unless well made and clearly written, the repro could come out gray. Worst of all, when exposed to sunlight, after a while the page turned brown and the music was almost illegible.

3. Photo offset: This is the most economical technique to use when 200 or more copies are needed. The work to be reproduced is photographed, and a plate is made from the negative. The plate is then mounted on a rotary press, inked, and the image is "offset" onto a rubber blanket. The copies are clear and sharp. But since most of us don't need 200 copies of a song right off the bat, photo offset is generally impractical.

   Of course, if you've created your work with a notation program, you can simply print it out on a laser printer.

GETTING YOUR SONG RECORDED

Earlier I suggested you invest in a tape recording device that could be kept running, to ensure that the ideas you created when improvising would not be lost. That was for your own sake. But when you have completed your song and wish to record it, another set of values applies.

Home Demos

Every songwriter is aware of the importance of a demo recording that is professionally made, but many songwriters and books on songwriting overlook the value of making their own demo.

In judging a songwriting contest recently, I heard a country singer interpret her song to her sensitive guitar accompaniment on a home demo. Her song won a prize and outshone many large orchestral demos and rock epics with back-up singers. If the song is good, its excellence will shine through the simplest performance, and a lousy song will be lousy (sometimes lousier) when magnified by a hundred-piece ensemble or a costly twenty-four track demo with a crew of back-up singers.

Most young rock groups make their own home demos on digital multitrack equipment, because the recorded sound is as important as the song, sometimes more. For most songwriters, a medium-priced recorder will do. Again, you can find what works best for you by visiting your local music store and consulting with a digital recording sales expert. Most good music stores have one or more salespeople that know this area of equipment. I believe that the less you are involved with the peripheral, technical things, the more important will the words and music of the song become to you, and a songwriter should write songs. Still, home digital recording is so prevalent today that many songwriters find themselves very proficient with digital home recording, which allows them to make a pretty good-sounding demo. But if possible, I advise songwriters to leave the recording to the people who do *that* best, the recording studios.

Studio Recording

After home recording your song, spend a few days replaying and listening to it. Play it for friends and get their reactions. Be honest. Perhaps some part of the song will always make you wince, something that could be changed. Remember Alan and Marilyn Bergman's advice — "Songs are not written, they're rewritten!" Make your song as good as it can possibly be, then get it under copyright, and if you believe it has a chance in the professional market, consider having a professional demo made.

The cost of the demo may be met by a producer who has heard your home recording and believes in it or, more often, by you, the composer-lyricist. If you collaborate, the cost of the demo should be split squarely down the middle; any other arrangement eventually lead to the dissolution of the partnership.

Listed in the *Yellow Pages*, even in middle-sized towns, you will find a heading recording service—sound and video. Some of these advertisers state the kinds of equipment they use and others tell the number of tracks they can record. Call any that appeal to you. If you are recording a show or theater piece, multitracking is not important to you, but if it's rock, you should try for the studio with the most professionally live sound. As do copyists and arrangers, studios will quote prices over the phone and, if you go in, will let you hear examples of their work.

Remember that studio time is billed per hour and that rehearsal time, engineer's time, and mixing costs are *not* included. They could add considerably to your final cost. Studio costs in New York City in mid-2007 ran from $100 an hour for a small three-flight walk-up to about $1,000 for a large multiboothed studio equipped with the latest sound equipment and the finest acoustic and electronic instruments.

Once you have recorded your song, you should be there at the mixing session so that you can approve dynamics, reverb, and which track will predominate.

You may want to overdub, or add another voice to the existing track to create harmony, which is one of the most common techniques in country recording. If your voice is strong enough, you might want to do the vocals yourself. I always feel there is something special about composer-lyricists who record their own material, an authenticity not present when someone else records. But if your voice is not appealing or your diction is bad, it might be better to have someone else record for you. This could be a friend whose style you admire or, lacking that, a session musician. These people (whose fees run about $150 per hour) can sing and play in many styles and keys, with or without earphones, against a track or live. Although their fees seem high, they usually end up saving you more money because they are so experienced that they seem not to waste precious studio time. Every studio has session people on call.

When booking studio time, allow about an hour per song. If the song is very complicated, you may need considerably more, but don't be spendthrift. When it's you, the songwriter, who is paying for the time, ask the studio head to approximate how much you will owe. You may be shocked by the answer. If you have a producer, remember that what he lays out for the recording will eventually be deducted from your royalties.

As mentioned before, a multitracked recording, which allows each musician to play along with any other or all tracks, will give you more freedom and definition. If something dissatisfies you, that track may be deleted and another punched in. It might be wise to have your song recorded by both male and female singers, which will double the market for your song. But a multitracked recording, or even a simple recording played through studio speakers, may give you an inflated opinion of your song. The ultra-high fidelity and gigantic speakers in most professional studios can make even a garden-variety singer sound like Barbra Streisand, so I always ask to hear the completed demo played through a "lo-fi" speaker (which every studio has). This will eliminate the booming bass notes and bring the vocal line more forward. It will give you a true picture of how the demo will sound when played through the speakers of those for whom your song is intended.

When you have completed the recording (and after you have paid the bill), the studio will offer you the option of taking it home and storing it or leaving it in the studio. Keep it in the studio, for then if you need a disc or mp3 of a single song or the entire group you may have recorded, you merely have to call them on the phone and they'll prepare one.

The digital recording you have completed in the studio will be your closest approximation of a live performance. All burned CDs should be copied directly from the digital recorder. When working in a studio, I generally ask the studio to make copies, and I find the cost reasonable. Some electronic companies have put out dual CD burners. These can also be used, but the quality will not be as good as burning directly from the digital recorder.

When ordering copies from a studio (or making them yourself) it is best not to put more than three songs on the recording that you intend to use as a demo. You will be presenting this to record producers, A & R people, and music publishers, who can get an idea of your style and talent from your recording. If you put too many songs on the recording, they may end up sounding alike. Besides, people in the record industry rarely listen to the entire demo. Keep a consistent style among the three songs. If you write heavy metal and rock, don't demo them on the same recording, because they will be aimed at different markets.

COPYRIGHT

Copyright means just what it says. It is your *right* under a country's laws to own and protect your *copy*, your creation. You can restrain anyone from using the copyrighted material knowingly or unknowingly. If they continue to do so and if you can prove they had access to your material, you may sue and collect the money they have earned by riding on your coattails in addition to damages.

The United States' copyright laws were formerly out of step with the rest of the world, but sweeping changes in 1978 allowed our copyright laws to conform. No longer is one protected for twenty-eight years, renewable for another twenty-eight. Before, there were too many sad stories about songwriters who forgot to renew their copyrights, allowing their song to lapse into the public domain. These works were quickly pounced upon by unscrupulous vultures, who copyrighted them under their own names. I know songwriters who have outlived their copyrights, never again to write a hit.

Fortunately, all that has changed. Essentially, the new copyright laws (enacted in 1990) provide for your work to be protected for seventy years after the author's death, or ninety-five years from creation. That means if you are a youthful songwriter, let's imagine twenty years old in 2008, you have created a song this year and sent a copy to the U.S. Copyright Office in Washington, D.C. Assuming you live to be eighty-five, your words and music will be protected until almost the middle of the next century—the year 2143. If you are an older songwriter, let's say fifty, (and you also live to be eighty-five) and you want to copyright a song you wrote last year, your rights under the law protect you until 2112. Additionally, if you are an older songwriter and you wish to copyright, the law protects your song for ninety-five years from its copyright registration. Assuming you wrote that song twenty years ago, it is protected until 2089.

For works originally created before January 1, 1978, but not published or registered by that date, the law provides that they have been automatically brought under the statute and are now given federal copyright protection. The duration of copyright in these works is generally computed in the same way as for works created on or after January 1, 1978—life-plus-seventy-years or ninety-five years after copyright registration.

Very few cases of copyright infringement are recorded and the ones that make the headlines are generally instituted by well-known songwriters, who have the money to prosecute. Occasionally, a simple melody copyrighted long ago will be similar (by chance, I believe) to a hit. The old-time songwriter will sue, and the case will be settled out of court to avoid a nuisance-value suit, which could lead to a restraining order and cut the song's popularity.

How to Copyright a Song

Formerly, it was common practice to write down your song, date the copy, and have the paper notarized or at least witnessed and then to send a copy of your song to yourself by registered mail. This proved that the package was stamped in the post office on a certain day. If you then heard your song performed, you could whip out the unopened letter in front of a judge to show that your creation had predated the one you heard. The many complications of this chintzy method should be obvious, but amateur songwriters still use it. You have to store at least two copies of this registered letter; and what happens in flood or fire or if you lose it? It has always seemed simpler to me to let the Library of Congress keep the records.

You may copyright a song, a lyric, a musical composition, a musical show, or a suite. Here's how to go about it.

1. Write for form PA to the Library of Congress, Copyright Office, Publications Section, 101 Independence Avenue, SE, Washington, D.C. 20559-6000. Ask for 20 copies, and they will send you extras so you can always have some on hand. If you are in a great hurry, call them at (202) 707-3000 or

(202) 707-5959 and they'll send out the forms. If you are in a greater hurry, you can apply online at www.copyright.gov, or get forms from ASCAP or BMI at their online websites.

2. Fill out the form, and enclose the song(s). Thrifty songwriters sometimes group a few songs together under the title of SUITE and save the $45 fee that each separate song would entail. The protection is as strong as if they had copyrighted the songs individually. Call the collection something like "October Suite" or "Autumn Love Songs" so you will know what is included.

3. When sending a lead sheet, write "Music and Lyrics by————" under the title on the first page and "© John Doe month/year" on the bottom of the first page of the lead sheet (many amateurs invalidate their copyright by putting the notice at the end of the piece instead).

4. Send the lead sheet, CD, or mp3, and the form along with the $45 fee to the Library of Congress, Copyright Office, Publications Section, 101 Independence Avenue, SE, Washington, D.C. 20559-6000. You can copyright a song merely with CD or recording, but most songwriters include a lead sheet if one is available. The law says "recording" and I suppose a CD is a recording, but I sleep easier when I send along a lead sheet too.

Instructions for Filling Out Copyright Form PA

Space 1: Title

Title of this work. This is what you will be copyrighting. It may be a single song title like "My Lonely Nights" or "Remember." The title cannot have been used before with or without your knowledge. You may save money, if you like, by combining a group of songs into a "suite," such as "Winter Suite" or "October Songs."

Previous or alternative titles. If you have already copyrighted a song and have rewritten it, you will want to recopyright the new version. For example, had you written a song called "Lucy" and rewrote it to be called "Lucky," you would write on this line "Lucy" as the previous title.

Nature of this work. Usually "lyrics" or "music," or if it's a complete song, write "music and lyrics"; if it's a show, write "musical play." If it's a total score, write what it is (opera, ballet, symphony, etc.).

Space 2: Author(s)

This section has room for listing three collaborators. If more than three collaborated on a work, you will have to request Continuation Sheets from the Library of Congress. Generally the top (a) section or the (a) and (b) sections are used.

Name of author. Write your full name, including a middle name if you have one. This will make identification easier.

Dates of birth and death. List your true birthdate. Don't lie about your age. No one in the Library of Congress will publish it, and falsifying your age can damage the validity of your copyright. The date of death will be necessary only if you have written this work with a deceased collaborator.

Work for hire. If you are employed by a publishing house that will hold copyright on what you produce, check the box marked "yes." Most unaffiliated songwriters will check the box marked "no."

Author's nationality or domicile. The country of which you are a citizen or a legal resident. If you are a legal or illegal alien, you may still copyright your song; merely print the name of that country on this line.

Was this author's contribution to the work… You may want to remain anonymous (and if so check the "yes" box) or you may want to copyright the work under a pseudonym (and if so check that "yes" box). I can see no advantage to remaining anonymous, but there might be any number of reasons why you'd want to use a pseudonym, especially if you are employed by a house that takes all your output.

Nature of authorship. Generally, this will be "lyrics" or "music" or, if you have written both words and music, "lyrics and music." The (b) and (c) sections are for each collaborator.

Space 3

Year in which creation of this work was completed. Since your copyright will protect your work until seventy years after your death, this information is not necessary to protect it. It will be necessary, however, if there is any infringement dispute or if somebody comes out with a work similar to the one you have under copyright.

Date and nation of first publication. If the work has been published before, perhaps with other lyrics, or if it has acquired a new melody, write when and where it has been previously published. This clause is especially important for translated songs.

Space 4

Copyright claimant. This will be your name (unless you are employed by a publishing house that has the rights to all you produce). Be sure to print your name *and* address.

Transfer. If the claimant is not you, the author, write here how the claimant obtained the copyright: "by assignment" if you sold or gave away your rights to the song; "by contract" if you are employed by a publishing house; "by will" if you inherited the copyright from someone else. Do not write in the corner box.

Space 5: Previous Registration

Has registration for this work already been made? These questions are intended to find out if an earlier registration has been made for this work and, if so, whether there is any basis of a new registration. As a rule, only one basic copyright registration can be made for the same version of a particular work. You would check the "no" box unless you've previously registered this work.

A published version of a previously unpublished work. You might want to reregister the work if this is its first publication.

First application submitted by author or other copyright holder. If you have reacquired a work that you had formerly sold or given to another, check this box.

Changed version of a work. If the work has been changed and you are now seeking registration to incorporate, then check this box. Give the earlier registration number.

Space 6: Derivative Work or Compilation

Preexisting material. If this is a changed version or if this work incorporates one or more works that have already been published or have come from the public domain, you must list that in this section. If you have for example written new lyrics to "Three Blind Mice" or have changed the tune substantially and wish to copyright your version, you must insert "Three Blind Mice" in this section.

Material added. Give a brief summary here of what you have added to the work. If you have written of three blind rats as a parable of warmongers, say so in this section. If your melody has taken off in the direction of bop, write "bop version" in this space.

Space 7: Deposit Account

Publishers who use the copyright service may maintain a deposit account to facilitate paying their bills and to avoid sending in the fee with each form. The fee is $45 and it should be included with this application. A check or money order payable to Register of Copyrights is acceptable. Do not send cash.

Correspondence. Write your name and address here (including daytime and evening phone numbers). The Library of Congress will contact you if there are questions about your form.

Space 8: Certification

If you have collaborated on a work, only one of the collaborators must check the box "author." If you have given the rights to an agent or another copyright claimant, he or she must check the appropriate box. On the line below, print your name and the date. Write (do not print) your name on the line with the pointing finger.

Space 9: Address for Return of Certificate

Print or type your name, street number, apartment number, city, state, and zip code. Make sure this is clear, because your certificate will be registered and returned to you in a window envelope.

BE SURE YOU ENCLOSE YOUR LEAD SHEET OR CD AND YOUR CHECK FOR $45. Check over the form to see you have not left any blank spaces.

Mail to: Register of Copyrights, Library of Congress, Washington, D.C. 20559.

What You Cannot Copyright

1. Titles, even long ones, are not covered by copyright. I know at least eight songs called "I Love You." Perhaps this is because titles are so general (even when they are specific, like "What Are You Doing the Rest of Your Life?") it would be limiting free creation to put them under our copyright laws.

2. Material that is beyond copyright and already in the public domain, not only by Chopin and Tchaikovsky but by any creator who has been dead for seventy years. If you want to write new words to the Tchaikovsky piano concerto that made a lot of money in the forties as "Tonight We Love," it is yours for the taking. Just be sure you go back to the *original*, avoiding any changes in the melody that may have been made when it was transformed into "Tonight We Love." Classical composers have always written new *melodies* to old lyrics. Debussy and Fauré each published his setting of the same poem, each well aware of the other's effort.

   But remember, *you may not infringe on the copyright of another's melody* without written permission. If you have a sudden inspiration for lyrics to "Hey, Look Me Over" for an advertising jingle, you or your ad agency must get the original copyright owner's approval. Someone has to pay for it.

   If you come across an old melody in the public domain you may use it, but don't be disappointed if someone else releases a recording of it before you. Most songwriters prefer to write their own rather than risk being scooped by someone who has stolen from the same well.

How Much Can You Quote?

The law is vague. Different judges have different interpretations, but most agree that *seven bars essentially the same is plagiarism*. In some recent cases it was proposed that record production has advanced to an art, and a performer could sue if he felt another was copying his sound.

LANGUAGE OF THE MUSIC INDUSTRY

acetate   An individually cut record. Acetates are generally cut from tape masters and are limited to a single copy. These are no longer in common use; masters are now created directly from the original digital recording. Multi-copies are called "pressed records."

administration   Handling by a publisher or recording company of all the financial, copyright, and contractual work necessary in the production of a song or a full catalog of songs.

advance   Monies paid by the publisher or record company to the artist before the song is released. These sums are to be deducted from future royalties.

advance man   A publicist who precedes an artist in the area where the artist plans to give a concert. The advance man arranges newspaper interviews and radio appearances for the forthcoming appearance.

A & R   Artists and Repertoire. The A & R person is responsible for new talent, selecting the songs that talent performs, and developing that talent. This job generally precedes the one of record production.

angel   An investor in a play or musical. Angels should be prepared to lose their investments if the theater work fails; if it succeeds, they may recoup many times their investment.

artist   The name given any singer, instrumentalist, indeed any performer whose contribution is essential to the success of a recording.

"A" side   The more important song on a traditional 45-rpm record; the one the record company is promoting. Nowadays, individual songs are no longer promoted on 45s; instead they are e-mailed in an mp3 format directly to radio stations or made available at the record company's website to download. Many artists market their own recordings in this same manner, bypassing record companies altogether.

assignment   Transferral of a copyright from one publishing house to another.

"axe"   A guitar, and by extension, any instrument—including piano, brass, or wind.

bof   A record-business acronym for the "best of"; an album made up of the artist's previous hits.

booking agent   The direct link between the artist or the artist's manager and the user of the talent. Managers generally call booking agents to find work for their artists; the booking agent contacts clubs, stations, and other places where the artist may appear. Booking agents deal with live performances only.

"B" side   The second side of a traditional 45-rpm record, the one with less potential. "B" sides were rarely best-sellers, but there were many examples of "B" side records making it big, such as Elvis Presley's "Don't Be Cruel," which was the "B" side to "Hound Dog"; both songs hit #1 on the charts.

bullet   A notation that indicates an especially fast selling record, one climbing quickly to the top of the charts.

catalog   The total collection of songs that a music publisher has under option, songs to which he has been assigned the copyright.

chart   A song written in musical shorthand listing chord letter names, only with their division into bars.

charts   The listings in various magazines and trade papers of the fastest-selling records in the country. Charts are created from surveys in sample areas and are divided into listings of country, pop, soul, gospel, and jazz. *Cashbox, Record World, Billboard,* and *Variety* each conduct their own polls. *The New York Times* runs a listing every Friday of the ten best-selling singles and albums.

clearance   Permission obtained by a radio or TV station to use copyright material. This is usually obtained through one of the "clearance societies," like ASCAP or BMI.

click track   A track used in multitrack recording that enables the conductor or orchestrator to hear a predetermined beat. Click tracks are used to eliminate human fallibility and to create an unvarying, metronomic beat. They are easily eliminated from the final recording.

clinker   A wrong note.

combo   An abbreviation for "combination," meaning a small group of musicians—frequently on piano, guitar, and string bass.

commercial   Salable, having mass appeal. Commercial songs are distinguished from show songs by having a hook and much repetition.

contact man   Originally a "song plugger," and now a record promoter, but this job has always been to bring the song to the awareness of artists and public.

cool   Relaxed, calm, in control.

corny   Clichéd, banal, obvious.

cover recording   A recording by an artist other than the one who originally recorded the song. Cover versions generally do less well than the originals but are a way of making extra dollars on an especially popular hit.

crossover   A song intended for one market that becomes successful in another. A song intended for the jazz market, for example, may cross over and rise to the top of the soul charts.

cut   A record; to record; a selection from an album, as in "the third cut on side A"; to eliminate.

cut in   To allow someone to share in the profits from a song.

date   An appointment to record.

distributor   A company that handles the dissemination of a record company's product and sees that the merchandise is distributed to jobbers and retail outlets.

dub   A trial copy made from a master tape.

easy listening   A category of popular music that features gentle, constrained, mostly low-decibel songs. Sometimes called MOR, or "middle of the road."

echo effect   An effect now produced by digital delay that creates an exoticism and atmosphere much prized in rock recordings.

engineer   The person who operates the studio equipment during a recording session.

fakebook   A collection of lead sheets formerly pirated and used without the copyright holder's permission. Fakebooks are now printed legally and are available at large music stores.

falsetto   A high-pitched male voice simulating a female sound. Groups featuring the falsetto prominently include the Ink Spots, the Orioles, the Four Seasons, and the Bee Gees.

folio   A collection of songs.

football   Slang term used by back-up singers for their part, which is generally slow-moving whole notes that resemble footballs.

Form PA   The copyright form necessary to be registered by a songwriter for his or her protection. Form PA is available on request from the Copyright Office, Library of Congress, Washington, D.C. 20559.

freeze   To hold a song for eventual recording.

funk   Blues, rock, or jazz that has a "dirty" or sexual quality.

gig   A date to perform or record.

gliss   An abbreviation of *glissando*, a rapid sliding of the voice or of the fingers over the keys of the piano.

gold album   Certified by the Recording Industry of America as having sold 500,000 copies.

gold single   Certified by the Recording Industry of America as having sold 1,000,000 copies.

Grammy Awards   The awards presented annually by the National Academy of Recording Arts and Sciences. The Grammy was originally intended as an award to honor excellence in all phases of the recording industry.

groovy   A slang term for having an appealing rhythmic quality, feeling relaxed.

hit   A fast-selling record. Hit status generally means achieving a place in the top 40 on the charts.

hold   To keep a "demo" for further evaluation.

hootenanny   A gathering of folk singers that originally featured singing, dancing, and a bit of food. Recently it has come to mean an informal concert of country music where the public is invited to participate.

jam session   A convocation for making music (generally jazz) by a group of performers. Jam sessions are often spontaneous performances that take place before or after a regular "gig" and for which the performers receive no compensation.

jingle   A musical commercial with or without lyrics. Jingles are generally brief. Most do not exceed fifteen or twenty seconds.

label   A recording company.

laid back   A relaxed, understated style.

leader tape   Traditionally, the white tape used to precede a demo or used to separate one selection from another. With the advent of digital recording, this is usually represented on the digital recording device's LED with a different color representing the "white tape" before it changes to another color representing the start of the actual recording.

license   A permit; to permit use of a song.

lick   In jazz, an improvisation, usually brief and instrumental.

liner notes   Credits given to artists, engineers, arrangers, and producers that are listed in the booklet accompanying the recording.

lip-synch   A technique much used at outdoor events and in TV in which an artist merely mouths the words to a prerecorded recording.

LP   A long-playing record. LPs revolve at 33⅓ rpm (revolutions per minute). Traditionally, this is the favorite recording speed for albums. It is to be distinguished from popular singles, which are recorded at 45 rpms and recordings made before the LP era, which whirled at a dizzying 78 rpms. LPs and 45s are mostly used by live DJs only. There is also a growing number of serious audiophile listeners that prefer the sound of vinyl that analog recording delivered on LPs. So it is no longer rare to see an LP section in a commercial record store, but still the majority of recordings are released on traditional CD or via mp3 downloads from the Internet.

master   The finished recording of a song. Demos can be pressed from the master and records can be pressed and distributed to stores. Masters completed in commercial recording studios are generally stored there. Additional demos can be run off when needed merely by telephoning the studio.

mechanical right   The right of the creator or creators of a song to profit by its mechanical reproduction. (If the creators have assigned copyright, this right is then transferred.)

mechanical royalties   Monies coming from record companies to the publishers for sales of recordings.

mix   The blending (usually by the sound engineer) of several tracks to get the desired part highlighted.

mixing session   A meeting, usually of the engineer and the composer and lyricist, where the desired sound is created.

MOR   "Middle of the Road." A genre of songs in relaxed tempo with a smooth and very prominent melody. Sometimes known as "easy listening."

Moviola   A machine that projects film on a small screen so that elapsed time and projection frames may be counted. For film composers, the Moviola has largely been replaced by digital equipment and software.

Muzak   A company known for supplying lush instrumental arrangements of standards in gentle, relaxed tempos, meant to be heard in such places as elevators, department stores, restaurants, and banks. The name became a derogatory term for bland and spineless music. However, the Muzak company mostly moved away from this kind of music in 1997, and now it uses mainly "original artists" as the sources for its repertoire.

out take   A recording rejected (but not erased) that has not been used because of a fluff in the performance or faulty engineering. Out takes are generally filed away with the "takes," in case the producers change their mind at the mixing session.

overdub   The addition of instruments and/or voices to a preexisting work. Singers, especially in country music, frequently overdub by singing harmony against themselves. Sometimes a large choral sound is created through overdub.

payola   The illegal payment of monies to a disc jockey or recording program host for "pushing" a preselected recording. Record companies and record producers are frequently guilty of this reprehensible action.

performance royalties   Money earned from the use of copyright material on radio, TV, in concerts, etc.

performing right   A copyright holder's right under the law to approve of any public performance of his or her work.

pirating   Unauthorized copying and sale of recordings.

platinum album   Certified by the Recording Industry Association of America that the album has sold 1,000,000 units.

platinum single   Certified by the Recording Industry Association of America that the single has sold 2,000,000 units.

playback   At a recording session, listening to what has been recorded to correct balance and performance.

plug   A mention of an artist's upcoming concert or of a song. Artists sometimes appear on TV to plug their latest albums.

plugola   An illegal payment to jockeys or record-show hosts for the mention of their products on the air.

producer   The person who oversees all aspects of a recording from the selection of talent to the repertoire to the recording, overdubbing, and mixing.

production number   For theater music, a number that will involve the entire company and usually have lavish sets or costumes. Musical comedies usually have three or four production numbers in their two-hour span.

professional manager   An employee in a publishing house who is responsible for placing the songs in his company's catalog with artists who will record them.

program director   The radio station supervisor who determines which songs receive performances.

race records   A genre of recordings made by black artists for black audiences. These were mostly blues that later were called rhythm and blues and were the precursors of rock and roll.

reverb   The electronic production of echo, variable and controllable. Reverb can be used to cover up faulty vocal production.

SASE   A self-addressed stamped envelope. This should always be included when sending unsolicited material to a publisher or recording company.

self-contained artist   An artist who both writes and performs his or her own material.

session   A meeting, most often to make a recording, sometimes a rehearsal.

showcase   A club that specializes in presenting new talent.

single   Traditionally, the single refers to the "A" side of a 45. This was the side that record companies released in hopes of having a success. Today the single is released in the format of a traditional CD or a downloadable mp3.

song plugger   One who auditions songs for prospective performers. Song plugging is not practiced these days, having been replaced by the contact man and the demo.

song shark   Someone who deals dishonestly with songwriters. Song sharks often present neophytes with contracts that while barely legal, are totally unfavorable to the composer and lyricist.

spec   Short for *speculation*. Any work done by a writer or performer without pay. Sometimes this is done in hopes that a deal may be consummated at a later date.

split publishing   Dividing publishing rights between two or more publishers.

staff writer   A writer (of music or lyrics) hired by a publishing house and given a weekly salary (usually against royalties). All material written then becomes optionable by the parent house before it is offered to any other publisher.

standard   A song that has a long life and continues to be popular for several years. Of the thousands of songs that are published yearly only a handful become standards.

studio   A place to record songs; space to work out theater or recording material.

subpublisher   The firm that prints a composition and handles its contracts in an area beyond that of the original publisher. The subpublisher frequently handles the foreign rights.

sweetening   Adding "sweet" instruments, often the brass and strings, to an existing vocal or rhythmic track.

synchronization   Adding music to a film with an awareness of how the song fits into the mouth movements or the action on the screen.

take   A recording which, when listened to, gains the approval of those involved; an attempt to make such a recording.

timber or timbre   The quality of tone. Differences in timbre are what separates for example, an A blown on the clarinet from the same pitch struck on the piano or scraped on the violin.

Top 40   The list published in trade magazines and journals of the best-selling recordings. These are sometimes performed on radio or TV.

Top 100   The list of best-selling singles generally divided into particular markets.

trades   The musical industry publications: *Billboard, Cashbox, Record World, Variety,* etc.

UNIONS, AGENCIES, AND ORGANIZATIONS

AF of M   American Federation of Musicians. A union for instrumentalists, arrangers, copyists, and orchestrators. The AF of M is the strongest musical union in the United States, and anyone performing in any major city at a reputable theater, concert, or club would be wise to join. Addresses of local chapters will be found in telephone books of major cities or may be had by contacting the main office, Local 802, 261 West 52nd St., New York, NY.

AFTRA   American Federation of Television and Radio Artists. A union for singers, actors, announcers, narrators, jingles performers, and sound-effect artists. Anyone working in these or related fields is advised to join. Addresses of local chapters will be found in telephone books of major cities or may be had by writing to the main office, 1350 Avenue of the Americas, New York, NY.

AGAC   The American Guild of Authors and Composers (40 West 57th St., New York, NY 10019, or 6430 West Sunset Boulevard, Hollywood, CA 90028) was originally called the SPA—Songwriters' Protective Association. It is a voluntary organization run by and for songwriters, created to defend them in their dealings with publishers. Membership in AGAC can provide the songwriter with a standard royalty contract, collaboration service, a royalty collection service and, for a percentage of royalties, an estate collection service.

ASCAP   The American Society of Composers, Authors and Publishers (One Lincoln Plaza, New York, NY 10023, or 6430 Sunset Boulevard, Hollywood, CA 90028, or 700 17th Avenue South, Nashville, TN 37203). The most prestigious and oldest performing-rights society in the world. ASCAP monitors air, television, clubs, concerts, publications, etc. and logs the performances of its members. Then it pays them quarterly the royalties it has collected for them. Participating members must have had at least one published or recorded work, associate members need not. In March 2008, ASCAP charged a one-time $25 application fee for membership and no yearly dues.

BMI   Broadcast Music, Incorporated (40 West 57th Street, New York, NY 10019; or 6255 Sunset Boulevard, Suite 1527, Los Angeles, CA 90060; or 10 Music Square East, Nashville, TN 37203. BMI has offices in Chicago, Vancouver, Miami, San Francisco, Montreal, and Toronto as well). A performing-rights society that has the largest membership in the world. BMI was formed in 1940 for the new and young songwriters, who were unprotected by performing rights societies up to that time. It rose to prominence when ASCAP withdrew its music and authors from the airwaves in a dispute over higher royalties. BMI then began with a whole galaxy of songwriters, whose membership it has continued to hold. BMI's services are basically the same as those of ASCAP except that the former organization has no membership fee. Songwriters may join if they have a work that has been recorded, published, or is "likely to be performed." Both organizations conduct workshops for semi-professional songwriters eager to improve their craft.

CLGA   The Composers and Lyricists Guild of America (270 Madison Avenue, New York, NY 10016, or 6565 Sunset Boulevard, Hollywood, CA 90028). The CLGA is a union that represents composers and lyricists who write for motion pictures, film scores, background music, and music for TV. This organization handles contracts between film or TV producers and production companies and the artists. Membership is available only to those who have had at least one assignment to write for TV or cinema.

CMA   The Country Music Association (7 Music Circle North, Nashville, TN 37203). The CMA is an organization devoted to the promotion of country music through records, TV, and live shows. Membership is open to anyone who has had two songs published, recorded, and released.

GMA   The Gospel Music Association (3S Music Square West, Nashville, TN 37203). An organization for the dissemination of gospel music. The GMA gives awards annually to creators and performers in all aspects of gospel. Trade membership is available only to those who earn a portion of their living by writing gospel music or working for a company involved in gospel music. Associate membership is available to anyone who supports or is interested in this music.

Harry Fox Agency   110 East 59th Street, New York, NY 10022. The oldest and largest agency for the collection of mechanical rights—that is, the creator's fee for use of the song on recordings, audio and video, and background-music purposes. Publishers, not songwriters, belong to this organization, which collects a percentage from all mechanical use of the song. The publisher then pays the songwriter according to contract.

NARAS   The National Academy of Recording Arts and Sciences (4444 Riverside Drive, Burbank, CA 91505). An organization of people who contribute creatively to the making of records. Active members vote for winners of the Grammy Awards.

NSAI   Nashville Songwriters Association International (25 Music Square West, Nashville, TN 37203). A non-profit organization formed to advance the profession of songwriting. Membership is open to all songwriters, published or unpublished.

performing right   The right granted by copyright law, which states that "one may not publicly perform a copyrighted musical work without the owner's permission."

performing rights organizations   (sometimes referred to as clearance agencies) These are agencies whose goal is to collect monies for the performances of its members' copyright material. These organizations—ASCAP, BMI, and SESAC—monitor over 7,000 radio stations, 700 television stations, 30,000 hotels and nightclubs, ballparks, cabarets, buildings, lobbies, bandstands, cafes, airlines, and any place where music may be publicly played. These music users must obtain the right to broadcast or play on their premises any music licensed by that performing-rights organization. It is, of course, totally to the advantage of the songwriter to join one of these organizations, for it would be impossible for songwriters to monitor and see who is infringing on the popularity of their songs.

SESAC   The Society of European Stage Authors and Composers (10 Columbus Circle, New York, NY 10019; 11 Music Circle South, Nashville, TN 37203). As its name implies, SESAC formerly specialized only in the market outside the United States and Canada; however, with the advent of broadcasting, its catalogue grew to include gospel and country music. Now it represents creators in every field. SESAC is the only performing rights organization to represent both publishers and songwriters in performance as well as mechanical rights.

Union scale   Minimum payment to members of the AF of M, AFTRA. and SAG for performance, arranging, or copying of a work.

AFTERWORD

If you have written songs with the aid of this book, you should have traveled from concept to title to hook passing by way of a rhythmically interesting motive, which led you to construct a phrase and then a section. Later, you will have increased or decreased the span of your melody and sought fresh rhymes, bringing the song to climax and conclusion. Having accomplished all that, you are still not finished. Now you will have harmonized the whole and recorded or notated it, then copyrighted, and "demoed" it. It will now be a completed song, an entity.

If you lost your way in some of the chapters, read them again, ask another songwriter to explain, or investigate some of the other songwriting books listed in the Bibliography. Don't be ashamed to seek as much help as you can. What is paramount is that you be able to finish your songs.

To finish the song is the professional way. So many beginners can play or show you an idea or concept, maybe even a fragment of melody that has great promise, but they can't bring it to fruition.

I have always made a rule for myself that I have no more than two works in progress simultaneously, usually one up-tempo and one ballad to fit my happy or depressed mood of the day. Any concept that comes into my mind is quickly notated or recorded and filed to be picked up when one of my works in progress has been completed.

Completion is important, yet each of us worries about inspiration.

No book can inspire you, but the foregoing principles can help you. Actually, I have found that as you write many songs, inspiration creeps in without your awareness. Good luck.

APPENDIX

BLUEGRASS

Bluegrass is a form of American music that is derived from Irish, English, and Scottish roots. Its distinctive style developed during the early 1940s when, because of war rationing and the need for the chemicals that went into the old 78 rpm recordings, record production was nearly stopped. At that time, this self-entertaining genre developed.

Because, in its earliest days, it originally used acoustic instruments and simple folk-like melodies, it was often confused with country music. But there was a world of difference between the native, nasal sound of bluegrass, which sometimes employed instruments (washboards, mouth-harps, and harmonicas) no longer widely used in mainstream bluegrass, and country music (which, at the time, was known as country and western).

Bluegrass's origin can be traced to one band. Bill Monroe was the leader of the band, the Blue Grass Boys, which was formed in 1939. By 1945, Earl Scruggs joined the band playing the banjo with a three-finger roll originally developed by Snuffy Jenkins. At that time, singer/guitarist Lester Flatt, fiddler Chubby Wise, and bassist Howard Watts created the definitive sound and instrumental configuration that remains a model today. By 1947, other bands had sprung up: Carl Story and His Rambling Mountaineers, Mac Martin and the Dixie Travelers, etc.

The songs they created were mostly simple, using a naïve harmonic language of I, IV, and V, and the method of presentation was similar to that of jazz. One instrument played the melody while the others provided the harmonic backing, or, to use a jazz term, "comped." Then each of the other instruments took the solo spot while the others provided the background. In its purest sense, in the beginning, the instruments themselves were not amplified, although there may have been microphones on stage to bring the subtle sounds to the audience.

What is known as the second generation, which moved the genre into the 1960s, made bluegrass much more popular throughout the country, and by the time we reached the 1980s, common usage demanded that some of the instruments, especially the bass guitar, be amplified. As the eighties came to an end, non-traditional chord patterns (I, III, VI, II, V, or I, V, IV) became more acceptable. The Johnson Mountain Boys were one of the decade's most widely touring popular groups, and they played strictly traditional bluegrass.

For writing bluegrass songs, a student of the genre can do no better than to listen to the recordings of Alison Krauss. She is a vocalist/fiddler whose first album was released when she was just sixteen. Krauss and her band, Union Station, were major contributors to the soundtrack of *O Brother, Where Art Thou?* As a solo artist, collaborator, and producer, on her own and with Union Station, Krauss has won over twenty Grammys. Proving the current viability of bluegrass, as of the time this book goes to press she holds seventh place in the all-time winners circle for the Grammy Awards.

GANGSTA RAP (see also page 286)

The first gangsta rap song I ever heard was called "N'y Va Pas, Manuel," and concerned a young man whose mother warns him, in the first chorus, not to associate with the rough kids of the neighborhood. He does not listen, and in the second chorus, his wife gives him the same precaution. Finally, in the third chorus, after he tells her that he is going to pull off his last job and give up crime for good, he is caught and killed.

I mention the song here, because it is, I feel, the antithesis of what I generally thought of as gangsta rap.

This genre, which tries to be as tough as nails, relies on the pulsing beat of the drum or a drum machine and is an offshoot of straight hip-hop, beginning in the mid-1980s. In the argot of the streets and of songdom, phrases beginning with the same or similar consonants will run together. (See page 286 for a fuller explanation.) Thus, we have the hip-hop genre known as gangsta rap. (Not gangster rap!) It can be credited to EmCee Schoolly D, who was the first to use "gangsta" images in his songs. In 1985 he wrote "P.S.K." ("Park Side Killers"), a song in which he describes putting a pistol against another rapper's head.

Two years later, Ice-T, the first to use the language of the streets with words like *ho* and *nigga,* released "Six in the Morning," a song about the arrival of the police at an early hour, and this brutal genre was strongly launched. His later albums, *Rhyme Pays* (1987), *Power* (1988), and *Just Watch What You Say* (1989) all contain strong political commentary and street language, and they walk the line between glorifying the gangsta lifestyle and criticizing it as a "bound-to-lose" situation.

But the message of the genre became much more violent as we moved into the 1990s. It espoused breaking the law and not cooperating with the police. Later in that decade, gangsta rap and hip-hop in general, which had always been outside the popular-song mainstream, became part of it, and more successful commercially. When The Notorious B.I.G. released *Ready to Die* (1994) and *Life After Death* (1997), the sound was suddenly lighter and more singable—even though the themes of the songs were still drug dealing, guns, and street thugs.

By now, in 2008, gangsta rap has seen a decline, and sales of records have fallen steadily in the past few years. The relentless aggression and the ridicule of women as untrustworthy sex objects have contributed to the genre's unpopularity. Events such as the 9/11 calamity, the Columbine High School massacre, and the Virginia Tech shootings have in some ways made gangsta rap inappropriate to the times. Although many songwriters view it as a form of entertainment, and others see the genre as a form of catharsis, it has to be written with great subtlety in order not to be viewed as an offensive form of entertainment.

HEAVY METAL

With roots stemming from blues rock or psychedelic rock, heavy metal (or simply metal), so popular in the middle-to-late twentieth century, in 2008 continues to take shape in new incarnations. Although not as broadly popular as it was in the 80s, progressive metal, extreme metal, and other mixed forms have taken hold among both fans of traditional heavy metal and younger new fans to these new versions of the genre. But as we describe the traditional form of heavy metal, the chief characteristic of songs is their loudness, machismo, and theatricality.

Metal's distinguishing qualities are to be found in the rhythm section, mostly with the major presence and prominence of pulsing bass guitar patterns and driving drums.

As the genre faded in the 1990s, a new wave of heavy metal bands emerged with a mixture of genres called "nu-metal." These bands, such as Korn, Papa Roach, and Limp Bizkit, incorporated elements ranging from hip-hop to death metal. Nu-metal, which was introduced at Ozzie Osborne's Ozzfest in 1996, brought about a resurgence in heavy metal itself, which gained prominence through MTV. In 1997, Korn released *Life is Peachy*, the first nu-metal album to reach the top ten, and followed it, two years later with *Follow the Leader*, which hit the top of the charts. But by 2005, the nu-metal movement was waning, as traditional metal fans did not embrace this style, and as mentioned above newer forms have taken its place.

Metal continues to be popular in the United States, but not in numbers like the eighties and nineties. And it seems to have a bigger following in Europe, especially Germany and Scandinavia. This is evidenced by the number of open-air festivals held around the continent in spring and summer.

Thus it seems that any impetus for a revival of metal will come not from the United States but from abroad. Wolfmother, an Australian band who call themselves "retro-metal," went to #5 on the *Billboard* chart with their first album. Roadstar, an English group, and Northern Ireland's The Answer also had respectable chart showings.

For songwriters who are enamored with the heavy metal sound, I recommend they think about embracing the rock-steady sound and adding elements of hip-hop to their songs to make the genre viable to today's audiences.

HIP-HOP

Hip-hop had its origins in the 1970s in the boroughs of the Bronx and Queens in New York City. It was an expression predominantly of Latinos and African-

Americans. The term is supposed to have been originated by Keith Cowboy as a joke on the army drill sergeant ordering a march by calling out a persistent and repetitive rhythm: "Hup-two-three-four." Cowboy, who was a scat singer, it is said, was making fun of a friend who had just joined the U.S. Army by transmogrifying the sergeant's command into "hip-hop-hip-hop." When Cowboy used the rhythmic term as part of his act on stage, because of its delightful rhythm, others soon copied it. The opening of the song "Rapper's Delight," by the Sugarhill Gang, is a good example.

Although the terms "rap" and "hip-hop" are often used synonymously, one must understand that rapping is just one component of the hip-hop movement. The others are break dancing, emceeing (more commonly called DJing), and graffiti art.

It is unfortunate that hip-hop, which began as a lighthearted joke, once it was established turned in the next twenty years to scatological rhymes, often demeaning to authority, women, and gay and lesbian lifestyles. Their examples are too full of profanity to be entered here, but let it suffice to say that I consider the subjects jejune and immature.

But I have to add that although the genre and its "music" has very little relevance for me personally, in all fairness to the true artists of hip-hop, the movement has much to recommend it. Beyond the few artists like Ludacris, 50 Cent, Snoop Dogg, and others who are willing to spout cartoon violence and perpetuate some of America's racial and sexual stereotypes, there are some true artists at work. One must note that hip-hop's influence on the graphic arts, theater, film, dance and especially on modern poetry—all well beyond the scope of this book—is considerable.

That the genre has become "respectable" is evident in the recent PBS documentary created by Brian Hurt, "Beyond Beats and Rhymes," which tried to be enlightening and did not hide the fact that hip-hop music can be homophobic and sexist. According to music critic Jeff Chang, American popular culture is to blame. Mr. Chang contends that it has "trafficked in racist and sexist images for centuries and provides all sorts of incentives for young men of color to act out a hard-core masculinity."

Hip-Hop in the Twenty-first Century

In recent years, however, perhaps because of public outcry against pornography, or maybe because they just tired of the dirty words, hip-hop became more acceptable. It even became somewhat family fare with the release of Eminem's album *The Marshall Mathers LP*, which sold over nine million copies, and Nelly's debut album, *Country Grammar*, which has sold almost as well. Deeply entrenched in our culture by now, we can consider hip-hop a major part of the recording industry in the United States and abroad. It was not until the breakthrough success of the hard-edged 50 Cent that hard-core hip-hop returned to the *Billboard* charts.

My belief is that too many of the hip-hop artists are taking advantage of the relaxed morality of the times and allowing themselves too much liberty, and that as soon as the smut loses its power to shock the genre will be as dead as the two-step of the 1920s. Treating women as mere sexual objects and lack of respect for the law are the two current main themes for hip-hop.

How to Go About Creating a Hip-Hop Song

1. *Set up a constant rhythm,* using a drumbeat or a recording of a drumbeat. (Alternatively, play a hip-hop recording in the background and record your creation over it.)
2. *Decide on your concept.* Make sure it is a contemporary subject. Remember, this is a genre that implies revolt, and though much hip-hop demeans gay and lesbian lifestyles, there is room for songs that *promote* these lifestyles. You might want to demean or laud political or business leaders, or complain about taxes, medical fees, or inflation. War and its senselessness, human insensitivity, and greed are all fine subjects for hip-hop.
3. *Create a short motive* (see page 155) that bears repetition.
4. *Sing this over the rhythm,* using dummy lyrics (see page 5) if necessary. This is the most important part of the song. Make sure the meter of your lyric is anything but 3/4 (see page 138), which is a meter that creates an old-fashioned sound. Iambic rhythm is good. Keep your lines long as you improvise so you can get used to putting a rhyme at the end of each line. Lines will usually rhyme as AA or BB. ABAB is far more difficult and almost impossible to improvise.

Here are two excerpts from hip-hop rap songs written by students in some of my workshops:

"Fatties keep the money rollin' into they banks,
Stuff it in they safes and never say thanks.
Me, I call it lucky that I still have my stash,
Shove it in my pocket up along with my cash…"
    Randy Solowitz (used by permission)

"Livin' is my bizness, meanin' this is *my* life
Never need a woman and for sure not a wife.
Me and my partner are just doin' fine.
Gonna stay that way till the end of the line."
    John Meghan (used by permission)

MUSIC-NOTATION SOFTWARE

According to many serious songwriters, particularly those of the older generation, the computer is both the boon and the bane of the craft. It is so easy to sit at a computer, toy with a MIDI input device such as a digital keyboard, play in a tune, and have the computer print it out, making a hard copy of the song or, if desired, have the computer burn a CD or create an mp3 of the song. But this is, in my estimation, not songwriting.

Composers Jerry Herman, Charles Strouse, Mike Stoller and many others, like myself, prefer to work out a song in private at the keyboard (or with guitar backing), and then when it is finally polished and satisfies us as creative artists, then we can turn to a notation software tool or (as some of the composers listed above do) to another person to make a lead sheet or other arrangement that documents the song.

Why, you might ask, go through all the trouble of learning notation and studying scales, key signatures, and modes, when a music notation program will do the job for you?

In my classes and workshops I have always found that those songwriters who spent the time to learn how to craft a melody, understood harmony and rhythm, and really worked to create their best, most original work ended up writing the best songs.

I do propose that once the song is created and polished, and only then, one should avoid much of the dreary task of notation by using one of the two major music software writing systems, Finale or Sibelius. Their pros and cons follow.

Both Finale (which is available from MakeMusic, Inc.) and Sibelius (part of Digidesign, the audio division of Avid Technology, Inc.) are similarly priced for the complete version, which allows you to make a group arrangement or a full orchestral rendition of your song. They both make many different versions. I recommend that you visit both of the company's websites (www.finalemusic.com and www.sibelius.com) for further information and to determine which version my be right for you. Then visit your local music store or go online to purchase the right product that meets your needs. I do encourage fledgling songwriters to try one of the less-than-full versions of either program as a way to get into using notation software cost-effectively. You can always upgrade to the full version as your needs for notation and scoring music grow.

Essentially, either program can notate and digitally record a performance through MIDI. (MIDI is Musical Instrument Digital Interface.) Even the cheapest digital keyboards have it, but it is always good to check when buying the USB cable. The MIDI end of the cable connects to your keyboard, and the USB end connects to your computer.

All of the methods for note entry are well described in the manual that comes with the software.

The software will title your song, put the pitches on the staff, add the words below and add the chords above. (It can even add guitar diagrams if you choose.)

There are various small drawbacks to both software programs, but as you use it, you will find ways around any problem you may encounter.

As long as you are a registered user, both companies have help and support via toll-free numbers as well as at their websites. Their technicians are patient, helpful, and knowledgeable, eager to answer even what may strike you as the dumbest questions.

Although I use and recommend Finale, I must add that some of my serious composer friends, Luther Henderson and Thomas Shepard among them, working with larger orchestral forces preferred Finale's competitor, Sibelius. I have not tried Sibelius yet, but must add that for the purpose of this book, getting the song written and recorded, Finale is fine.

PUBLIC DOMAIN SONGS (see also page 77)

Music and lyrics published in 1922 or earlier are in the public domain in the United States. Since no one can claim ownership of a song in the public domain, these songs may be used by anyone. For proof that a song is in the public domain, you will need the sheet music *with a copy of a printed date of 1922 or earlier on it*. Or you can find information about public domain songs at the Library of Congress's website, www.copyright.gov, and at commercial sites.

But even though a public domain version of the song exists, some versions of the song may still be under copyright. The Elvis Presley estate has copyrighted its version of "Aura Lee," an old Civil War–era song that, with a new lyric, became Presley's big hit "Love Me Tender." If you were to compose, perform, or publish your own song to the same tune—say you called it "Cindy Lou"—make sure you have a copy of the original "Aura Lee" *with the copyright date on it*.

When you use music or lyrics in the public domain, you have no guarantee that another composer may not be taking that same melody and publishing their version, calling what you titled "Cindy Lou," for example, "Mary-Ann." Still, even though another musician may scoop you on it, writing new lyrics to a familiar tune can sometimes turn out to be a moneymaking project.

PUNK ROCK

Punk rock, which originated in the United States and England during the 1960s and 1970s, was musically speaking a simple version of rock and roll. It would have nothing to do with the idols of the recent past—Elvis, the Rolling Stones, and the Beatles—trying to get as far away from them as possible. The Sex Pistols said it all in their slogan: "No Future."

Perhaps the prime mover of the movement was Malcolm McLaren who ran a shop called "Let It Rock" on London's fashionable Kings Road; at the same time, while traveling to New York, he briefly managed a group called the New York Dolls (known in shorthand simply as the Dolls). In 1975, after the Dolls' popularity waned, McLaren changed his London shop's name to "Sex" and began featuring leather and rubber fetish wear. This was an idea whose time was right, and it brought all the punks to the shop. Then McLaren took over management of the group that met regularly at his shop, christening them the Sex Pistols. Their name alone, referring to male genitalia, although within the law, is anti-mainstream. Then he changed the band's lead vocalist/guitarist, dropping Steve Jones and bringing in John Lydon. McLaren even changed Lydon's name to Johnny Rotten (which is the British slang term for a leaky condom).

Punk rock bands usually employ one or two electric guitars, an electric bass, and a drum set. Punk rock bands tried to emulate the bare-bones arrangements, usually based on three chords (I, V, and IV), that were commonly known as garage rock. Because the instrumentalists had so little training, they made something positive of their lack of technique. Their vocals often sound nasal and are shouted instead of sung.

The songs themselves are usually shorter than the regular rock and roll cut, lasting some 2½ minutes, and are almost invariably in 4/4 time written in traditional verse-chorus form.

Punk rock lyrics are usually a comment on social or political issues, often with a heavy dose of irony. One of the biggest successes, "God Save the Queen" by the Clash, is a coruscating complaint against monarchy. "Right to Work" by Chelsea and "Career Opportunities" by the Clash, both of which were big hits, dealt with unemployment, boredom, and a lack of career opportunities.

Punk rock lyrics can be pretentious, juvenile, or self-pitying. Sometimes, although they may use artificial rhymes, they may have a naïve honesty. And some true emotions can still be found in punk rock lyrics. Yet sometimes they can get directly to the point. They often go over-the-top, so that the singer is often groveling.

RAP

One thinks of rap as the street music of the 1990s and beyond, but it has been a viable source of entertainment, albeit under different names, for over a century. In the 1890s at French cabarets, the program always included a poet, a (male) "diseur," or (female) "diseuse" (the title comes from the verb "dire," meaning to say). These entertainers spoke lines in a hypnotic rhythm that usually rhymed at each line's end. The content, like today's rap could be political, amorous, storytelling, revolutionary, scabrous, or, especially during the nonsensical "dada era," meaningless.

The backgrounds against which these recitations (one cannot call them songs) of the popular poets were spoken would often be a mood-setting piano accompaniment sometimes with a rhythmical background, sometimes a cappella. Most often they contained some kind of message, as today's rap songs often do. In time, the cabaret's messages disappeared in favor of pure entertainment. This, of course, led to today's versions of the cabaret song: narrative songs like "Ring Them Bells" or love songs like "Speak Low," as well as many country songs that tell a story.

Broadway, which had emerged through revue and spectacle into musical theater, did not entirely eschew rap, for some of the most memorable musicals used it. I'm thinking of Meredith Willson's *Music Man*, which is set in a 1912 time frame. Its first song is a salesman's pitch, spoken in time with the rhythm of the train on which several "drummers" are traveling. We are introduced to full-fledged rap—although in 1957, when the show premiered, it was called "patter." "Trouble in River City," a tour de force of litanies outlining the evils of pool, drinking, and sex, is the first theatrical rap song.

Then there were rap songs that had to be created because not every theatrical personality can sing. Yul Brynner, who starred in *The King and I*, growled most of his solos most effectively and Rex Harrison is said to have invented a unique song/speech style for *My Fair Lady*. (Actually, the style, known as *sprechstimme*, originated in the German expressionist era.) This style was copied by others, notably Richard Burton in *Camelot*.

The "masters of ceremonies" who created today's rap style could not have been aware of the genre's theatrical origins. Beginning in the 1970s in New York's Bronx and Harlem and using street language, they might create a stream-of-consciousness poem against a rock or reggae beat. Before long, these emcees (deejays on the radio or at house parties) started what they called "rapping" over the purely instrumental parts of the song. They had variety and most of the lyrics made sense, even if the rhymes were not perfect or often forced.

Soon, a group called the Sugarhill Gang took a pop song and turned it into something called "Rapper's Delight." Before long, rock's most popular group, Acrosmith cut a rap version of their hit "Walk This Way" with rap group Run-D.M.C. The song had many sexual innuendoes, but it was a gigantic hit, lasting ten weeks on the *Billboard* charts.

Although respected critics of pop and rap, like Kelefa Sanneh of *The New York Times*, can praise rappers like Chamillionaire for addressing "current events," I find much of the product juvenile and naïve (although I do appreciate that his songs do not use dirty words). Still, lines like

Terror alert, victory I stay dropping that bombness
Rosie O'Donnell and Donald Trump stay arguing about nonsense

Would they treat me as good as Hugh Hef' if I had a mansion full of blonde
  chicks?
If adultery was a felony then Clinton would be a convict.

are so far from rhyming that they are ludicrous. Also, the news of the day is
interrupted in the third line with personal envy, making it hard enough to get back
to the main subject of the song. One of the cardinal rules of good songwriting
(and even good rap) is to stick to your subject—don't wander.

REGGAE (see also page 248)

The reggae music genre, which began in the late 1960s in Jamaica and reached
the height of its popularity in the United States in the 1980s, is certainly an
outgrowth of ska. (See page 289 for the entry on ska.)

Although *Webster's Dictionary* says the origin of the word *reggae* is unknown,
scholars of Jamaican music avow that the term was first used by the ska band
called Toots and the Maytals, who had a hit in 1968 with "Do the Reggay." *The
Oxford English Dictionary* lists the term as having possibly been derived from *rege-
rege*, a Jamaican-English term meaning to quarrel. One theory is that the term
may have come from the word *stregge*, the Jamaican word for prostitute.

But whatever its origin, there is no denying that reggae music has a strong
propelling beat, perfect for energetic dancing.

If you study the rhythmic basis of reggae as explained on page 248, you will
see that its essential rhythm has a "chop" on the fourth beat of the measure. This
creates the impetus to propel the beat forward into the next bar.

Reggae is often associated with the Rastafarian movement, popular in the
1970s and '80s. This movement influenced many of the black musicians of the
times and invigorated their music with new energy. As far as subjects for lyrics
go, one has great freedom, but most popular are faith, love, sexuality, and broad
social issues.

An example of the subtlety one may achieve in social issues is Delroy Williams's
powerful song, "Three Men in a Truck."

No shackles 'round dem feet, but dem no free,
No handcuff 'round dem hand, but dem no free.
By de expression on dem face,
Let I know dey are in no shape,
Yet dey take dem to do the work of Babylon, yey, now.

SKA

Ska is a musical genre that originated in Jamaica in the late 1950s. It was the precursor of rock-steady and reggae. (For a discussion of reggae rhythms, see page 248.)

No one seems to know for sure how the name came about, but most music historians believe that the term *ska* originated with the Jamaican bass guitarist Cluet Johnson, who always greeted his friends saying, "How are you, skavoovie?" in imitation of the American hipsters of the era. Thus, any musician was a skavoovie, or ska. It is also possible that the offbeat scratching of guitar style that Ernest Ranglin used sounded to others as "ska, ska, ska."

The music combined the Caribbean calypso with lively American jazz and rhythm and blues. It is characterized by a walking bass line, an accented guitar part and piano rhythms on the second and fourth beats of the measure, and in some cases, jazz horn riffs.

Except for its offbeat rhythm and danceability, there was nothing especially interesting about the early ska recordings and the genre needed a shot in the arm. It was then that Jackie Mittoo, pianist of the ska band the Skatelites, suggested that his drummer, Lloyd Knibbs, slow down the beat, and what resulted was reggae. This spelled the downfall of ska at least for a decade.

But by the 1970s, the genre was given a new infusion. It became better than ever when it took on the influences of the early punk rock and accordingly had incorporated uncompromising lyrics and aggressive guitar chords. In the next decade the genre waned, as most of the practitioners moved away into various forms of rock or punk rock.

GLOSSARY

AABA   A common song form in which the first theme (usually eight bars) is repeated and followed by a contrasting theme. This second statement is followed by a return to the first theme. All the A's must be essentially the same; however, their endings may vary.

A¹ A² bridge A³   A preferred way of referring to the AABA form.

AABB rhyme   An analysis of rhyme wherein the first two lines rhyme and the last two rhyme.

ABAB   An analysis of rhyme in which alternate lines rhyme.

accidental   1) A musical symbol indicating a sharp, double sharp, flat, double flat, or natural preceding any note. An accidental applies to all subsequent repetitions of that note in the same bar, unless cancelled by another accidental. 2) A note thus altered.

acid rock   A form of rock that originated on the West Coast in 1965. The music sought to reproduce the mind-expanding experiences that LSD, a hallucinogenic drug, produced on the senses. To approximate this psychedelic state, the music employed feedback, Middle Eastern instruments, modal scales, languid melodies, and an absence of chord changes. The lyrical concept advertised the acid experience as transcendental, mind-liberating, and promoting self-awareness. Its best-known practitioners were the Byrds, the Doors, the Mothers of Invention, Jefferson Airplane, the Grateful Dead, Sly and the Family Stone, and Pink Floyd. Although the philosophy and style faded in the late sixties, many of the trappings have remained as part of all hard rock.

Aeolian   Referring to the sixth mode (on the keyboard, the Aeolian mode encompasses the white notes from A to A). This is also called the "pure" minor scale, which was in common usage until the fifteenth century.

afterbeat   See *backbeat*.

alla breve   A term used in concert music that refers to 4/4 time played so quickly that there are only two counts to the bar. Popular musicians call this "cut time."

alliteration   The use of the same letter for poetic effect. "Dancing in the Dark," "The Moon of Manikoura," or "No, No, Nanette" are examples.

answer song   A song, usually rhythm and blues, that tries to recap the success of an earlier effort. An answer song is often written by the same team as the original. The answer to "Tell Laura I Love Her" was "Tell Tommy I Miss Him"; the answer to "He'll Have to Go" was "He'll Have to Stay." Neither did as well as the original.

appoggiatura   From the Italian word meaning "to lean." A decorative note that leans into the next note, usually moving from above. In concert music, this is called a grace note. Jazz improvisers have always added appoggiaturas to their lines. It was almost Billie Holliday's signature to add an appoggiatura before the last note of every song.

arpeggio From the Italian word for harp, *arpa*. An arpeggio is a chord whose members are played individually. On an acoustic piano they are usually arranged in this order: root, 5th, 10th, 7th.

augmented 1) Raising the pitch a half tone. 2) A triad with its 5th raised a half tone.

backbeat In traditional music, the stress is on the downbeat or first of the bar. Most traditional popular music, being in 4/4, is accented 1̇ 2 3̇ 4. Rock and roll and rhythm and blues, however, accent the backbeats or afterbeats on 2 and 4 thus: 1 2̇ 3 4̇.

back-up group A term for the singers who accompany a star or lead singer. They generally sing responses to the star, echoes, or long-held notes.

ballad 1) A story song, often with many verses and a long, rather heavy narrative. Ballads usually lack a chorus. "Ode to Billy Joe" and "The Ballad of Sweeney Todd" are examples. 2) Any song dealing with love or romance, usually in slow tempo.

bar 1) A line separating a musical composition into segments. In 3/4 time, the bar line occurs every three quarter notes; in 4/4 time, it occurs after every four quarter-notes. 2) The metrical period, a synonym for measure.

barbershop A style of singing that harks back to the dawn of the twentieth century. The harmony is close, the chords are most often closely spaced dominant sevenths.

Baroque A lavish ornamental architectural style popular in the seventeenth and eighteenth centuries. The term has been borrowed by musicians to describe music of the same period or music with ornamentation. Baroque rock was developed in the late sixties by Procul Harum ("A Whiter Shade of Pale") and Jimmy Webb, who used the harpsichord sound in "MacArthur Park."

bass line The movement of the lowest instrument of a group or, if referring to a solo effort, of the lowest chord members. Musicians frequently strive harder for arresting bass lines than they do for their melodies. Amateurs often miswrite it "base line."

beat The unit of measurement of music. The number of beats in a bar depends on the time signature and the speed of movement.

beguine A sensual, languid dance said to be of Tahitian origin. Its accent is on the second eighth-note in the bar.

belting 1) Using the chest voice rather than letting air pass over the diaphragm to create what is known as a "head sound." 2) A style of singing that developed in the early thirties that was in contrast to the crooners. Belters include shouters like Sophie Tucker, Judy Garland, Ethel Merman, Georgia Gibbs, and Teresa Brewer.

bluegrass Country music, Dixieland style. Usually done in fast, cut-time meter, this music uses banjo, mandolin, fiddle, and guitar. Most prominent exponents of this style are Bill Monroe, Earl Scruggs, Lester Flatt, the Lovin' Spoonful, the Dillards, and the Byrds.

blue note The flattened 3rd, 5th, 6th, or 7th which, when used in conjunction with a major harmony, creates a distinctly biting and melancholy sound typical of the blues.

blues A form of musical expression that deals with feeling and self. The blues may be divided into four categories: 1) classic 12-bar blues based on a predetermined harmonic pattern using a series of 3-line stanzas wherein the first two lines are identical; 2) delta blues, which kept the 12-bar form but added instruments like the harmonica or guitar, and an answer to the singer's line; 3) urban or Chicago blues, which brought in the piano and clarinet as accompanying instruments; 4) rhythm and blues, which emerged in the 1940s and added a big band to the blues as well as a "jumping" sound and black emotion and excitement. Rhythm and blues flourished from 1945 to 1960. It later developed into rock and roll.

bolero A Spanish dance originally in 3/4 time but now often extended to 4/4 time. It has a characteristic triplet on its second eighth-note.

boogie-woogie (boogie) An 8-eighth-notes-to-the-bar piano style with a recurring left hand pattern that is derived from the blues chord structure. Boogie invaded the mainstream of American popular music in 1939 and its influence has never left. Famous exponents are Hazel Scott, Count Basie, Fats Domino, and Jerry Lee Lewis.

bossa nova Literally "new beat," this gentle jazz style was imported from Brazil in the early sixties. Joao Gilberto, Luis Bonfa, and Antonio Carlos Jobim are its best-known exponents.

bridge The B section of a traditionally constructed song, one that is constructed in AABA form. After the A section has been twice stated, the bridge, a contrasting section, is introduced. This is also known as the "release" or "channel."

C & W Country and western, or merely (preferred) country.

canon A polyphonic composition in which one part is imitated by one or more other parts entering subsequently in such a way that the successive statements of the melody overlap. The only difference between a canon and a round is that a round is generally sung with voices entering at the octave or unison, while a canon may have voices entering at any interval. (The fifth is a frequent choice.) Famous canons, all rounds, are "Three Blind Mice"; "Panis Angelicus"; and "Fugue for Tinhorns."

cha-cha   An Afro-Cuban rhythm akin to the bolero.

channel   Jazz synonym for "bridge" or "release."

chest voice   See *belting*.

chord   Three or more tones sounded simultaneously that create a desired sound.

chorus   1) Since 1950, or in folk music, the section of a song that returns with unvarying melody and lyric, as contrasted to verse. 2) Before 1950, the entire 32-bar section comprising four smaller 8-bar sections. A single record (78 rpms) comprised three choruses in rapid tempo; and one and a half choruses in slow tempo.

chromaticism   The use of accidental tones falling outside the prevailing key signature.

chromatic scale   A scale proceeding entirely by half tones.

circle of chords   The natural progression of dominant sevenths to tonics or the pull of V to I. The pull of the G^7 to C and C^7 to F, continuing until the return to the original chord. This series of twelve ensuing chords is generally written in circular fashion.

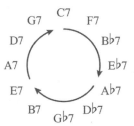

coda   A concert term synonymous with "tag." A closing segment designed to give the song more impact. Usually four or eight bars long.

collaboration   Writing a song with one or more partners. Separate credits may be given each collaborator for lyrics or music, or as is currently more common practice, all the creators are listed together after "music and lyrics by." This practice eliminates any royalty ambiguity and ensures a smoother working relationship.

commercial bridge   In an A^1, A^2, bridge, A^3 form song, the bridge is often constructed according to formula. A common bar division uses eight, the I dominant seventh, IV triad, II dominant seventh, and V dominant seventh for two bars each. In the key of C, this would translate to C^7, F, D^7, G^7.

composer   One who creates the music. The term can apply equally well to a jingle, popular or rock song, show tune, opera, concerto, or symphony creator.

compound intervals   Intervals that are larger than an octave.

concept   The basic idea behind the song. This can generally be stated in nonmusical terms.

conga   A dance popular in the 1940s whose rhythm was generally made of four eighth-notes followed by two quarter notes. There was a heavy accent on the 4th beat of the bar.

contrary motion   The movement of a bass line against a melody in opposite direction; that is, when the melody ascends, the bass descends, and vice versa. Contrary motion is a much-desired harmonic device.

copyright   1) The right of an individual to have his or her work protected from plagiarism. 2) To copyright means to obtain that protection by filing the proper forms, paying the proper fee, and registering that song with the Copyright Office.

copyright infringement   Using someone's copyright material. If it was unknowingly, the copyright holder may obtain a restraining order, which will stop dissemination of the illegal material. If knowingly, the copyright holder may also sue for damages.

copyright notice   The listing on the bottom of the first sheet of music. It must contain the following information: the symbol of copyright—either © or the word *copyright* or the abbreviation *Copr.*; the year of the copyright registration, *not application*; the copyright holder's name. If the copyright has been transferred to another holder, the notice should also state that fact and list "copyright transferred to ——," followed by the date of transferral.

copyright office   Actually, the Library of Congress in Washington, D.C. (20559). This is the place where all copyrights are kept.

country   The concepts deal with adult emotions, the pulse is most often 3/4, the lyrics, though regionally rhymed, are comprehensible, and the singers are sweet-voiced if female or sandpaper-rugged if male. All this made country music the most important export of the music industry in the United States in 1985.

cut time   See *alla breve*.

cycle of chords   See *circle of chords*.

demo   A demonstration recording made to audition a song or singer or both.

descriptive song   A song whose lyric describes a person or a place.

diatonic   The Western (as contrasted to the Oriental) system of constructing a scale of eight tones with its tonic repeated. This system allows no deviation from the arrangement of whole and half within the octave. Diatonic is for all practical purposes the opposite of "chromatic."

diazo process   A method of reproducing music that involves transparent master sheets. Diazo is mostly no longer in use for large scores, orchestral parts, symphonic music, and long show scores, having been superseded by the creation of scores using music software and large-format laser printers, which is simpler and more economical.

dictation   The art of writing down music from aural performance. Dictation can be developed to the ability to write down harmony and even contrapuntal music.

diminished   1) To lower by a half step. 2) A minor chord whose 5th has been lowered and whose 7th has been doubly lowered.

diminished cliché   The author's term for a frequently used series of chords comprising the I, I diminished, II, and V or I, #I diminished, II, and V.

disco   A musical style that flourished in the U.S. from 1975 to 1981 in which the music was made for nonstop dancing. Recordings were frequently double long and had a heavy four-to-the-bar beat. The lyrics generally used concepts of sex, revenge, and survival, and most of them consisted of repeating lines again and again. Best-known practitioners were Donna Summer, the Bee Gees, Gloria Gaynor, and Peaches and Herb. The disco craze began to wane in 1979 and by 1981 had almost totally disappeared.

dissonance   A jarring sound. This musical term must remain ambiguous since any sound is judged by each ear. The intervals of the minor second and the major seventh are still considered dissonant by many musicians.

dominant   The 5th tone of a major scale.

dominant seventh   A chord comprised of four tones. They are superimposed major third, minor third, and minor third. This chord formerly permitted only on the 5th note of the scale is constructed and used on any diatonic or chromatic member in contemporary usage.

Dorian   Referring to the second mode (on the keyboard, the Dorian mode encompasses the white notes from D to D). The Dorian mode is equally useful for creating Elizabethan music and baroque rock.

dot   A symbol which when written after a note indicates a prolongation of the note by a half. The double dot indicates prolongation of the note by 3/4.

$\textstyle\unicode{x1D15E}$ = 2 counts

$\textstyle\unicode{x1D15E}.$ = 3 counts

$\textstyle\unicode{x1D15E}..$ = 3 1/2 counts

double bar   Two parallel vertical lines (the latter thicker), which signify the end of a section or composition. The double bar preceded by two dots indicates a repeat.

double flat   A symbol ♭♭ indicating a doubly lowered pitch. This is often used in working in keys with many flats. A♭♭ is the same as G.

double sharp   A symbol (x) indicating a doubly raised pitch. This is often used in working in keys with many sharps. Ax is the same as B.

downbeat   1) The first beat of a bar, usually implying an accent. 2) A musician's term that applies to the very first beat of a composition. 3) Musician lingo for "depressing," as in "that story is too downbeat."

echo   A short musical answer. Echoes are of dubious musical taste, but they may be palatable if the echo is more reminiscent than exact and performed on another instrument or in another register.

eighth note   ♪ In 4/4 time an eighth note receives one half beat, in 6/8 time an eighth note receives one beat. The British and Continental term for eighth note is "quaver."

eleventh chord   A chord, often called a suspension, to which the 4th of the scale, the 11th, has been added.

evasion   Avoidance of a final cadence by settling on a suspenseful chord or melody note. This delays the eventual ending, usually by four bars.

fade   A repeated final phrase or section of a song that is repeated over and over with diminishing volume until it disappears. The fade is achieved by the engineer in the recording studio gradually lowering the decibel dial.

feminine rhyme   Rhyme wherein the accent occurs on the next to last syllable. Candy—brandy and laughter—after are examples. The preferred term is two-rhyme.

first ending   The last bar or the last two bars of a section, generally of an A^1, A^2, bridge, A^3 song. This is followed by double dots, double bar, and a repeat of the first theme.

flat   1) Lowering pitch by semitone. 2) The symbol ♭. 3) Pejorative term for anyone who consistently sings under pitch.

folk-rock   A message with a beat. Fusion of a composed folk song with the trappings that comprise rock: an electric guitar rather than an acoustic, and often an allegorical concept that applies to group action.

folk song   A song written anonymously. In recent years some performers have tried to create that effect. The foremost practitioners of folk music have been the Weavers, the Kingston Trio, Woody Guthrie, Joan Baez, Bob Dylan, Judy Collins, and Joni Mitchell.

form   Construction. Form of a song is generally identified alphabetically, such as AABA or ABA.

fox-trot   A dance that spawned many songs popular from 1914 to 1925. The dance, which uses a box-step, is always in 4/4 time, often with a hesitation on the 3rd beat of the bar. This dance developed during a period of animal-named popular dances, such as the turkey-trot, monkey-slide and bunny-hug, and is still a favorite of the older generation.

G clef   Treble clef. The symbol 𝄞, which, when wrapped around the second line of the five-line staff, indicates that the line represents G (above middle C) and that all other pitches are to be determined from that one.

gimmick song   A song built on a tricky, literary idea.

gospel   The precursor of soul. Gospel sounds like soul except that the lyrics are of the church rather than being romantic.

guaracha   A popular Cuban dance in medium tempo.

half note   In common time, 3/4 or 4/4, where the quarter note gets one beat, the half note receives twice that: two beats.

half step   The closest pitch differentiation in our musical system. The twelve intervals into which the octave is divided.

half tone   A synonym for half step.

hard rock   An outgrowth of rhythm and blues that evolved into heavy metal. Hard rock has a hard, driving, shouting sound usually built on the 12-bar classic blues; however, it contains none of the electronic gadgetry of heavy metal. Its early practitioners were Elvis Presley, Jerry Lee Lewis, and Little Richard, and more contemporary aficionados are Eric Clapton, the Rolling Stones, and Cream.

harmonic series   See *overtone series*.

harmony   The art of enhancing a melodic line with desired chords.

headtone   Using the "legit" or soprano register created by resonating air passing over the diaphragm.

heavy metal   Blues and rock generally played stridently, transforming reverb, wah-wah, echo, feedback, and fuzztone into an overwhelming experience. Heavy metal often employs macho singing and deafening decibels. This style reached its zenith in the early seventies. Some early groups were Led Zeppelin, Steppenwolf, Kiss, and Queen. Currently practicing are Metallica, Anthrax, Van Halen, and Korn.

hillbilly music   A derogatory term used until 1927 for country music.

homophonic   Having a single voice carry the melody as opposed to polyphonic or contrapuntal.

hook   The most memorable fragment of the song. A hook may be lyric, melodic, or rhythmic, in the "sound" of the recording, or even a part of the back-up. It is what we come away with after first hearing the song, the "essential" without which no song can achieve hit status.

imperfect intervals   Those that are not "perfect." Seconds, third, sixths, and sevenths.

improvisation   A variation on given material that is created on the spur of the moment.

inspirational song   A musical work intended to give comfort. Its concept usually preaches self-reliance, faith, or patience—as in "I Believe," "Bridge Over Troubled Water," or "You'll Never Walk Alone."

instrumental   A song without lyrics. Many songs that were originally themes ("My Own True Love," "Laura," "Misty," "One-Note Samba") began as instrumentals, but when they became successful, the publisher acceded to the public's desire to have lyrics for them.

interval   The distance between any two pitches.

inversion   In harmony, turning a chord around so that its 3rd, 5th, or 7th—or indeed *any* member other than its root—is its lowest member.

jazz   An ever-evolving art that encompasses rhythm, pulse, syncopation, improvisation, and creation applied to a predetermined melodic and harmonic series.

jazz rock   A movement begun in the late 1960s by the groups Blood, Sweat and Tears and Chicago that added jazz instruments, harmony, and jazz principles to the basic rock concept. More recent exponents of this fusion include Prime Time, Weather Report, Chick Corea, and Herbie Hancock.

leading tone   The 7th note of the scale, so called because it leads smoothly back into the tonic.

lead sheet   The melodic line of a song written on a single staff in treble or G clef, notated on manuscript paper. A lead sheet must have the lyric written below the staff and the letter names of the chords that set off the melody included above the staff. Copyright information should appear at the bottom of the first page.

legit   A shortening of legitimate, meaning proper or operatic singing. Using resonating headtones rather than tight-chest or "belt" singing.

list song   A type of song whose lyric is composed of a rhymed list of items.

Locrian mode   The seventh mode. On the keyboard, the Locrian mode may be created by playing all the white keys from B to B. The mode is almost never used because its tonic triad is a diminished chord.

Lydian mode   The fourth mode. On the keyboard, the Lydian mode may be created by playing all the white keys from F to F. This mode sounds humorous to contemporary ears because its 4th note sounds amusingly "wrong."

lyricist   The creator of the words to a song.

lyrics   The words to a song. It is current practice to have the credits read "music and lyrics by" rather than the formerly used "words and music by."

major   The predominant mode of our Western tonal system.

major seventh   A chord composed of four superimposed thirds whose relationship to each other is major third, minor third, and major third.

mambo   An Afro-Cuban dance form that was in vogue in the 1950s.

march   An optimistic, quick-tempoed piece in 2/4, 4/4, or 6/8.

masculine rhyme   Rhyme occurring on an accented last syllable—see-tree or confess-regress. The currently preferred term is one-rhyme.

measure   1) A musical unit divided by a bar line; 2) a synonym for bar.

mediant   The 3rd degree of a scale, for example, E in the scale of C.

melisma   The use of two or more pitches for setting a single syllable. A trademark of soul.

merengue   A fast dance in 2/4 or 4/4 that originated in the Dominican Republic.

message songs   (social consciousness songs)   A genre of songs propagandizing antiwar sentiments, social justice, civil rights, love, self-respect, unity, etc. Every age has its own issues.

metaphor   A lyric device in which one thing is compared to and becomes a totally different thing. As in "All the world's a stage."

meter   The scheme of regularly returning accents as indicated by a time signature.

metronome   A mechanical device of adjustable speed that sounds or flashes a regular pulse. A metronome set at 60 will emit one tick (or flash) per second. The metronome is useful for recording an unvariable click-track.

minor   The lowering of the 3rd and sometimes the 6th to create a more intense scale.

Mixolydian mode   The fifth mode. The Mixolydian mode can be created on the keyboard by playing the white notes from G through G. The mode is the basis of much jazz and Latin music.

mode   A set of scalelike notes from which melodies may be constructed. Modes may be referred to by their classic Greek names (Aeolian, Dorian, etc.) or by degree of the scale (first mode, sixth mode). Mode can also be a synonym for scale.

modulation   Changing from one key to another. Modulation is not done to accommodate a voice (that is transposition) but to create interest in an arrangement.

motive   The basic germ of a musical idea. A series of notes set in a rhythm that will be used again and again in various ways throughout the song.

natural   1) A note that is neither flat nor sharp. 2) The sign ♮, which indicates such a note. A natural sign is used where this has been made necessary by the presence of a sharp or flat in the key signature or of an accidental earlier in the same bar.

new wave rock   An offshoot of British punk in the 1970s and '80s that was anti-establishment and tended toward the outrageous and noisy. It prized intensity of emotion over technical proficiency. Successful groups included the Sex Pistols, Talking Heads, New Order, and the Jam.

ninth chords   As a seventh chord is a series of 4 superimposed tones each separated by a third, so a ninth chord is a series of 5 superimposed notes, again, each separated by a third.

nonsense song   A song whose lyric exists primarily for the joy of singing primarily nonsense syllables. "Ob-La-Di, Ob-La-Da" and "Marezy Doats" are examples.

notation   The technique of setting a melody on staff paper.

novelty songs   Incorporates kid tunes, nonsense songs, sound effect songs, and the like. Songs in this genre include "Yakety-Yak"; "50 Ways to Leave Your Lover"; "Escape (The Piña Colada Song)."

oblique motion   Describing two melodic lines or a melody and bass line one of which remains fixed while the other one moves.

octave   The interval between the 1st and 8th note of the diatonic scale.

onionskin (skins)   A transparent master sheet from which reproductions of handwritten music manuscripts were made. Today, onionskins have been replaced by high-speed digital photocopiers.

onomatopoeia   The formation of a word by imitating the natural sound associated with the object or action described (*tinkle, buzz, whisper*).

ostinato   A repetitive motive, most often appearing in the bass (basso ostinato). Ostinato is most frequently used in Indian raga or hard rock.

overtone   The supplemental secondary vibrations of a string or air column. These are generally obscured to the ear by the principal vibration.

overtone series   The secondary vibrations as created on every instrument (except a tuning fork) are octave, fifth, fourth, major third, minor third, major second.

paper rhyme   Words that appear on a page as though they ought to rhyme but do not, such as splash-squash and tomb-bomb.

parallel minor   A scale using the same pitches as its major counterpart except for the lowering of its 3rd and 6th tones.

Paso Doble   Literally, "double step." A quick Spanish dance played at bullfights.

pentatonic scale   1) A 5-note scale comprised of tonic, step, step, 1½ step, step, and 1½ step. (It may be performed by playing the black keys of the keyboard in ascending order from F♯.) This scale is useful for spirituals ("Swing Low, Sweet Chariot"), American Indian music, and pseudo-Chinese music. It was a favorite of French Impressionists Debussy and Ravel. 2) The division of the octave into five equal parts, creating the ancient music of Java and Bali.

perfect intervals   The intervals of the prime (unison), the fifth, the fourth, and the octave.

period   A unit of a song, usually eight bars.

phrase   A unit of a song, usually four bars.

Phrygian mode   The third mode. The Phrygian mode may be created by playing the white notes of the piano from E to E. This mode is useful for creating a pre-Bach or medieval sound.

pitch   The placement of a musical sound. Pitch is determined by the number of vibrations per second of a string or air column. The ear is extremely sensitive to deviations from pitch and can easily detect missteps above and below the intended pitch, which we call sharp and flat, respectively.

polka   A moderately quick dance of Bohemian origin in 2/4 or ¢ time. Some successes have been "Beer Barrel Polka," "I Love Louisa," and "Shall We Dance?"

polyphony   A style of music composition in which the composer pays particular attention to the movement of each part; as distinguished from monophony, where melody and its harmonization are paramount.

polyrhythmic   Sounding two or more different rhythmic patterns at the same time. Latin, reggae, and African music all use polyrhythms.

pop rock   An enduring form of rock, usually with a strong hook. Groups as diverse as the Coasters, the Drifters, and the Eagles were involved, as have been artists like Billy Joel, Elton John, Rupert Holmes, and Barbra Streisand.

pop soul   A mixture or crossover sweetening pure gospel sound with the commercialism that is known as Motown sound, often covering the gospel piano and tambourine with strings. Marvin Gaye, Stevie Wonder, the Stylistics, Dionne Warwick, and Diana Ross all might be included in this category.

portamento   A concert term meaning to audibly slide the voice from one pitch to the next, touching all the intervening notes. This is often used by gospel singers, by whom it is called "scoop" or "slur." Ballad singers like Sinatra and Streisand also use it to good effect.

prosody   The blending of words and music. Good prosody coupled with an artist's good diction will make a lyric understandable.

public domain   Usable by the public at large without payment of royalty. Works are in the public domain when their authors are unknown, if their copyright has expired, if there is an invalid copyright notice, or if the notice of copyright is missing entirely.

punch-line song   A song whose lyric contains a surprise at its conclusion, often in the very last syllable.

punk rock   A musical style that developed through the 1970s representing a rebellion against the rock establishment and the upper and middle class. Punk tries to be outrageous enough to provoke anger from respectability. Torn clothes, Nazi regalia, purple hair, spitting, vomiting, foul odor, self-mutilation, abuse of the audience, performing loud, sloppy, formless music devoid of melody—all these are aspects of punk.

quarter note   The basic pulse of most popular music. In 4/4 time, the quarter note is so named because it gets one-fourth the duration of the whole note.

quarter-note triplets   Three notes, each of which looks like a quarter note, which are fitted into two beats. This gives each member of quarter-note triplets 2/3 of a beat. Quarter-note triplets must be marked with a slur.

quarter tone   Half of a semitone, which is the smallest interval in our harmonic system. Quarter tones are sometimes used in concert music and in avant-garde jazz rock.

quaver   British and international term for an eighth note.

R & B   Rhythm and blues, the precursor of rock and roll.

raga   A combination of tones similar to our diatonic scale. A raga (of which there are 72) usually expresses a single mood. Indian sitarists often maintain this mood through variations on their scale for half an hour.

raga rock   A form of rock based on the ragas. This was first introduced by the Beatles after their Indian experiences.

ragtime   A piano style popular between 1890 and 1914 wherein the left hand plays stride or oom-pah while the right hand plays figures most often derived from broken chords with added syncopation.

range   The vocal palette. In popular song pre-1950, this was limited to a tenth. Burt Bacharach, the Beatles, and Billy Joel were instrumental in expanding range to the current twelfth or fourteenth.

rap   A style in which the singer talks in metered rapid verse. Rap often uses inconsequential nonsense rhyme over an unimportant musical background.

refrain   1) The entire 32-bar chorus. 2) A recurring 8- or 16-bar section.

reggae   A style that originated in Jamaica in the mid-1960s, evolving from ska and rock steady. Ska simulated the sound of a guitar. Reggae has been called rock with a calypso beat.

relative   A minor scale starting on the 6th note of its major and related to it by using the same key signature.

release   1) A synonym for the bridge of a song. 2) The issuance by a record company of a new recording.

repeat   1) Double dots that enclose a section that is to be played twice. 2) 𝄎 means to repeat the previous one bar. 3) 𝄎 means to repeat the previous four bars.

reprise   A custom in long-ago musicals of repeating a song often in several parts of the show in order to make it more indelible. In the original *Pal Joey*, "Bewitched, Bothered and Bewildered" had seven reprises.

rhythm   The organization of music with respect to time.

rhythm and blues (R & B)   A style that flourished from 1944 to 1960 and mixed blues with boogie-woogie and shuffle. R & B also introduced the electric guitar and featured the tenor saxophone. Some of its famous artists were Fats Domino, Dinah Washington, B. B. King, Lloyd Price, and Chuck Berry.

riff   A short improvised, usually virtuosic interlude.

rock   A catch-all label for the most prevailing form of popular music after 1950. Rock is built on a 12-bar blues, while popular music from 1920 to 1955 was built on the 32-bar song. Rock stresses an eight-to-the-bar rhythm with a strong backbeat, while most popular music insists on a straight 4/4. Rock is purer and simpler harmonically, using little pull from the circle of chords. Rock emphasizes sensuality and energy, while pop is concerned with the expressivity and beauty of the melodic line.

rockabilly   An early form of rock and roll mixed with country. Some call it blues with a country beat.

rock and roll   A term whose coinage is generally credited to disc jockey Alan Freed, referring to a basic style of jumping blues. Rock and roll ushered in sweeping changes in popular music. Some general differences between rock and roll and popular music are listed below.

POPULAR MUSIC	ROCK AND ROLL
piano as basic instrument	guitar as basic instrument
big band with reeds, sometimes brass and strings	small electrified string combo
32-bar chorus—AABA or ABAC form	verse-chorus form, 12-bar blues
small independent record producers	major record companies
printed sheet copy appeared before recording	printed sheet copy appeared after recording
most hits written by seasoned veterans about mature love	most hits written by new young artists about young feelings

rumba   A Latin dance imported from Cuba in the 1930s.

samba   A native Brazilian dance in fast 2/4 time.

scale   An ascending or descending series dividing the octave. The number of divisions depends on the ethnic origin of the scale. The space—half- or whole step—between each division creates the mode.

scale-tone sevenths   Four-note chords, (3 superimposed thirds) conforming to the scale.

scale-tone triads   Three-note chords, (2 superimposed thirds) conforming to the scale.

scat   Nonsense or wordless vocal improvisations in which the singer uses his or her voice as an instrument.

score   1) Music written down so the parts for different performers appear vertically. 2) As the verb *to score*, to make a fuller arrangement than a lead sheet—anything from a two-hand piano version to a full orchestration.

second ending   Usually after a repeated section, an ending more final than the first one that leads to the next strain or bridge.

segue   Italian for "follow," a musical direction meaning to proceed to the next section without pause or break.

semitone   A half tone, half step. In our musical system the next nearest pitch, since the octave is divided into twelve semitones.

sequence   The repetition of the same melodic pattern on a different pitch.

seventh chord   A chord of four tones; three superimposed intervals of the third.

sextuplet Six notes that are to be performed in the time of four in the prevailing meter. Sextuplets must be so indicated.

sheet music Printed editions of a single song containing the words, melody (either incorporated into the piano part or written alone on its own staff), chord listing, and a piano realization.

show tune A song—generally an ABAC or AABA form—that is intended for a musical comedy. Show tunes generally have drive, but they rarely cross over into the pop charts. A few, like "Send in the Clowns," "I Don't Know How to Love Him," and "What I Did for Love," have become better known.

shuffle A rhythm, similar to boogie-woogie, consisting of a dotted eighth-note followed by sixteenth-note carried 8 to the bar.

sightsinging The technique of singing without preparation or accompaniment from notated music.

simile 1) In music, a direction (abbreviation sim) indicating to continue in a similar pattern. 2) In lyrics, a poetic technique in which one thing is compared to another dissimilar thing by the use of *like* or *as*, as in "I'm as corny as Kansas in August" or "her tears flowed like wine."

sixth chord A triad with an added note which is found a full step above the 5th, (top) of the triad.

ska A component of reggae that emerged from rhythm and blues. Ska has a strong, steady beat.

skiffle An up-tempo style that merged country sound and fast shuffle. This style used homemade instruments—washboards, jugs, and percussion—and was in vogue from 1953 to 1957.

skip A musical interval that is more than a whole step.

slur A curved line over or under a group of notes that indicates to be played or sung smoothly.

soft rock A gentler, more melodious type of rock. Among its practitioners were the Lovin' Spoonful, Captain and Tenille, Carole King, James Taylor, and Sonny and Cher. In the eighties, the Eagles, Christopher Cross, Billy Joel, Barry Manilow, and Barbra Streisand seemed to be pointing in that direction.

soul A movement begun in the sixties to enhance black pride. Soul is the wedding of R & B with gospel. Its originators were Ray Charles, Aretha Franklin, Otis Redding, James Brown, Jimi Hendrix, and Nina Simone.

spirituals Folk songs that grew out of black slaves' contact with Christianity. Most spirituals deal with stories of slavery and suffering based on the Old Testament stories of the Hebrews' plight in Egypt or with the life of Christ.

They frequently use a statement-and-response form suggesting performance by a preacher and congregation.

staff   The five lines enclosing four spaces upon which we indicate pitch.

statutory copyright   The standard legal copyright acquired by a song when it has been registered in the copyright office and then is published with the standard legal copyright notice.

story song   A song whose narrative is its most important feature. Story songs frequently use the verse-chorus form.

stride   A style of piano playing popular in the 1920s in which the left hand strides back and forth bouncing between low roots or tenths and the full chord in middle register.

subdominant   The 4th degree of the diatonic scale (F in the scale of C). The subdominant chord is one of the three principal triads — tonic, dominant, and subdominant — in any key.

submediant   The 6th degree of the scale (A in the scale of C).

suspension   A non-chord member that formerly had to resolve to a chord member. Contemporary popular music uses suspensions more liberally than most harmony books permit and does not oblige them to resolve. The most frequently used suspension is the 4th.

swing   A form of jazz popular from 1935 to 1945, usually performed by a big band. Swing uses four-to-the-bar rhythm with orchestra sections frequently answering each other.

syncopation   Misplacing accents that are normally felt on the 1st and 3rd of the bar.

synthesizer   An electronic instrument that can imitate almost any acoustic instrument or sound. Useful in recording for its clean cut-off effect. Groups experimenting with synthesizers have included the Beatles, Stevie Wonder, The Who, David Bowie, and Vangelis.

tacit   1) A term used to indicate that the melody is to be sung with no harmonic backing. 2) An indication that the voice or instrument does not play certain passages.

tag   An extension to a song, sometimes called a "coda."

tango   An Argentine dance in 4/4 or 2/4 whose accent comes in the middle of the bar.

tempo   The pace of the song.

tenth   1) The interval of an octave plus a third. 2) A component of the left hand in stride piano occurring on the first of the bar.

tessitura   The general range of a composition. Songs that remain largely around the top of their range are said to have a high tessitura, and those around the bottom are said to have a low tessitura.

theory   The study of harmony, counterpoint, canon, fugue, etc.

thirteenth chord   A composed chord in which both the seventh and the sixth appear. In our system of superimposed thirds, the thirteenth chord is as far as we can go. (The thirteenth is actually the sixth; a fifteenth would be the same as the root and is nonexistent.)

three-chord structure   Using only the I, IV, and V chords, a simplistic conception used in naïve folk tunes or early rock and roll.

tie   A slur that connects two or more notes of exactly the same pitch, indicating that the second note is held but not sounded.

time signature   An indication at the start of a piece of the number and type of note values in each bar. The figures are placed one above the other immediately after the clef sign and key signature.

tonality   The scale or key of a composition.

tonic   The first member of the scale (C in the scale of C). The origin of the word *tonality*.

torch song   A song of unrequited love with one person, usually the singer, still submissive in spite of mistreatment. From "My Man" through "If You Go Away" to "Don't Cry Out Loud," the torch song has been ever present. In the mid-eighties it received new impetus from albums by Linda Ronstadt and Frank Sinatra.

track   A portion of a recording that is individually recorded in the studio and later mixed into the total recording. With current digital multitrack recordings, tracks can be added or eliminated at will.

transposition   Changing the key of a song or composition. Music is generally transposed when the vocal range is uncomfortable for the lead artist.

tremolo   Rapid reiteration of a single note or alternation of two or more.

triad   A chord of three notes, two superimposed thirds.

trio   The middle section of a song, originally performed by three instruments. In contemporary language, this is called an interlude.

triplet   Three notes fitted evenly into one count and so indicated.

turnaround (turnabout)   A series of chords leading back to a repeat of any section. Turnarounds usually appear in A^1 A^2 bridge A^3 songs at the end of A^1.

una corda   Literally, "one string." An indication to "soft pedal." Pressing this pedal on an acoustic grand piano will slide over the action, allowing it to miss hitting all the strings, thus reducing the volume.

upbeat   A lead-in or pick-up. The beat before the bar line and downbeat. Upbeat is so named for the position of the conductor's arm

up-tempo   A quick pace. Usually indicated by ¢ .

vamp   A repeated chord pattern usually ad-libbed until the entrance of the solo artist.

verse   1) Since 1960, the section of a song preceding a repeated chorus. 2) Before 1960, the mood setting, expendable introductory section preceding an ABAC or AABA chorus.

vibrato   A much desired tone in concert singing or instrumental music. Not so prevalent in popular music, vibrato is produced by a rapid oscillation of the vocal chords. Billy Eckstein and Sarah Vaughan were famous for their wide vibrato.

waltz   Although generally written in 3/4 time, the waltz is most often performed with one beat to the bar.

whole note   In common time, 4/4, where the quarter note receives one beat, the whole note receives four beats.

whole tone   A full step, two half steps.

whole-tone scale   A scale made up entirely of full steps only two whole-tone scales are possible in our musical system, one beginning on B and the other beginning on C. All others are repetitions of these.

worrying   A blues term for embroidering a single tone in melismatic fashion.

BIBLIOGRAPHY

Anderson, Marian. *My Lord, What A Morning.* New York: Viking Press, 1957.

Atkinson, Brooks. *Broadway.* New York: Macmillan Company, 1971.

Belz, Carl. *The Story of Rock.* New York: Oxford University Press, 1969.

Boardman, Gerald. *American Musical Theatre.* New York: Oxford University Press, 1978.

Brown, Peter and Gaines, Steven. *The Love You Make.* New York: McGraw Hill, 1983.

Cahn, Sammy. *I Should Care.* New York: Arbor House, 1974.

Cahn, Sammy. *A Songwriter's Dictionary.* New York: New American Library, 1983.

Cohn, Nick. *Rock.* New York: Stein and Day, 1969.

Davis, Stephen and Simon, Peter. *Reggae International.* New York: Rogner & Bernhard, 1982.

Engel, Lehman. *The American Musical Theater.* New York: Macmillan Company, 1975.

Engel, Lehman. *Their Words are Music: The Great Theatre Lyricists and Their Lyrics.* New York: Crown Publishers, 1975.

Engel, Lehman. *Words With Music.* New York: Macmillan Company, 1972.

Ewen, David. *Complete Book of the American Musical Theatre.* New York: Holt, Rinhart & Winston, 1970.

Gershwin, Ira. *Lyrics on Several Occasions.* New York: Alfred A. Knopf, 1959.

Gilbert, Bob and Theroux, Gary. *The Top Ten: 1956 to the Present.* New York: Simon & Schuster, 1982.

Gillet, Charlie. *The Sound of the City: The Rise of Rock 'n Roll.* New York: Dell Publishing Company, 1972.

Gray, Michael. *The Art of Bob Dylan.* New York: St. Martin's Press, 1981.

Green, Stanley. *The World of Musical Comedy.* New York: Ziff-Davis, 1960.

Gridley, Mark. *Jazz Styles.* Englewood Cliffs, N.J.: Prentice-Hall, Inc., 1978.

Grove's Dictionary of Music and Musicians. New York: Macmillan Company, 1935.

Handy, W. C. *Blues, An Anthology.* London: Collier Macmillan Publishers, 1926, 1949, 1972.

Heath, Edward. *Music: A Joy for Life.* London: Sidgwick & Jackson, 1976.

Jablonski, Edward, ed. *The Gershwin Years in Song.* New York: Quadrangle Books, 1973.

Joplin, Scott. *Collected Piano Works.* New York: New York Public Library, 1971.

Johnson, Burges. *New Rhyming Dictionary and Poet's Handbook.* New York: Harper & Row, 1957.

Kasha, Al and Hirshhorn, Joel. *If They Ask You, You Can Write a Song*. New York: Simon & Schuster, 1979.

Kimball, Robert, ed. *Cole*. New York: Holt Rinehart & Winston, 1971.

Kimball, Robert, ed. *The Complete Lyrics of Cole Porter*. New York: Alfred A. Knopf, 1983.

Kimball, Robert, ed. *The Unpublished Cole Porter*. New York: Simon & Schuster, 1975.

Kimball, Robert and Simon, Alfred. *The Gershwins*. New York: Atheneum, 1973.

Kolb, Sylvia and John. *A Treasury of Folk Songs*. New York: Bantam Books, 1948.

Lees, Gene. *The Modern Rhyming Dictionary*. Greenwich Ct.: Cherry Lane Books, 1981.

Lewis, Emory. *Stages: The Fifty-Year Childhood of the American Theatre*. Englewood Cliffs, N.J.: Prentice-Hall, 1969.

Lindsay, Cynthia, ed. *The Frank Loesser Songbook*. New York: Simon & Schuster, 1971.

Marsh, David. *Born To Run: The Bruce Springsteen Story*. New York: Dell Publishing Company, 1979.

Martin, George. *Making Music*. London: Pan Books, 1983.

McNeel, Karl and Luter, Mark. *How to Be a Successful Songwriter*. New York: St. Martin's Press, 1978.

Miller, Jim. *Illustrated History of Rock & Roll*. New York: Random House, 1980.

Morley, Sheridan. *The Stephen Sondheim Songbook*. London: Chappell & Company, 1979.

Okun, Milton, ed. *The Great Songs of Lennon & McCartney*. New York: Quadrangle Books, 1974.

Oliver, Paul. *The Story of the Blues*. Radnor, Pa.: Chilton Book Co., 1969.

Pascal, Jeremy. *The Illustrated History of Rock Music*. New York: Galahad Books, 1978.

Price, Steven. *Take Me Home: The Rise of Country & Western Music*. New York: Provenger Publishers, 1974.

Rachlin, Harvey. *The Songwriter's Handbook*. New York: Funk and Wagnalls, 1977.

Rappoport, Victor. *Making It in Music*. Englewood Cliffs, N.J.: Prentice-Hall, 1974.

Richards, Stanley. *Great Musicals of the American Theatre, Volume 1*. Radnor, Pa.: Chilton Book Company, 1973.

Richards, Stanley. *Great Musicals of the American Theatre, Volume 2*. Radnor, Pa.: Chilton Book Company, 1976.

Rodgers, Richard. *Musical Stages*. New York: Random House, 1975.

Sanders, Ronald. *The Days Grow Short: The Life and Music of Kurt Weill*. New York: Holt Rinehart and Winston, 1980.

Schafer, William and Reidel, Johannes. *The Art of Ragtime*. Baton Rouge, La.: Louisiana State University Press, 1973.

Shaw, Arnold. *Dictionary of Pop/Rock*. New York: Macmillan Publishing Company, 1982.

Shemel, Sidney and Kraslovsky, M. William. *This Business of Music*. New York: Billboard Publications, 1977.

Uslan, Michael and Solomon, Bruce. *Dick Clark's The First 25 Years of Rock and Roll*. New York: Crown Publishers, 1983.

Westrup, J. A. and Harrison, F. L. *The New College Encyclopedia of Music*. New York: W. W. Norton, 1976.

Whitburn, Joel, ed. *#1 Hits of the '70's: The Billboard Song Book*. New York: Big Three Music Corporation, 1981.

Wilder, Alec. *American Popular Song: The Great Innovators, 1900-1950*. New York: Oxford University Press, 1972.

Wilk, Max. *They're Playing Our Song*. New York: Atheneum, 1973.

Wood, Clement. *Complete Rhyming Dictionary: The Essential Handbook for Poets and Songwriters*. New York: Doubleday, 1936.

Young, Jean and Young, Jim. *Succeeding in the Big World of Music*. Boston: Little, Brown, 1977.

Zadan, Craig. *Sondheim & Company*. New York: Macmillan, 1974.

COLLECTIONS AND FAKEBOOKS

These are some solid collections and fakebooks past and present that may be useful to the reader.

Morris 555 Song Book of Show Music
Hits of the 50's, 60's and 70's—The Big Red Fakebook
1001 Jumbo Fakebook
100 Best Songs of the 20's and 30's. New York: Crown Publishers, 1973.
Great Songs of Broadway. New York: Quadrangle Books, 1973.
The Ultimate Fake Book. Milwaukee: Hal Leonard, 2003.
Your First Fake Book. Milwaukee: Hal Leonard, 2005.

PERMISSIONS

Pages xvii–xviii: "Getting to Know You" (Lyric by Oscar Hammerstein II, Music by Richard Rodgers). Copyright 1951 by Richard Rodgers and Oscar Hammerstein II. Williamson Music, Inc., owner of allied rights of the Western Hemisphere. All Rights Reserved. Used By Permission.

Page 17: "My Funny Valentine" (Music by Richard Rodgers, Lyric by Lorenz Hart). Copyright 1937 by Chappell & Co. Inc. All Rights Reserved. Used By Permission.

Pages 17–18, 98, and 160: "The Man I Love" (Music by George Gershwin, Lyric by Ira Gershwin). Copyright 1924 by New World Music Corporation. Renewed by Warner Bros. Music, Inc. All Rights Reserved. Used By Permission.

Pages 18, 35, and 175: "Bewitched" (Music by Richard Rodgers, Lyric by Lorenz Hart). Copyright 1941 by Chappell & Co. Inc. Copyright renewed. International Copyright Secured. All Rights Reserved. Used By Permission.

Pages 18–19: "Night and Day" (Music and Lyrics by Cole Porter). Copyright 1932 Harms & Co. Inc. Copyright renewed. All Rights Reserved. Used By Permission.

Page 19: "Someone to Watch Over Me" (Music by George Gershwin, Lyric by Ira Gershwin). Copyright 1926 New World Music Corporation. Copyright renewed by Warner Bros. Music, Inc. All Rights Reserved. Used By Permission.

Pages 19–20 and 106: "It Never Entered My Mind" (Music by Richard Rodgers, Lyric by Lorenz Hart). Copyright 1940 by Chappell & Co. Inc. Copyright renewed. International Copyright Secured. Used By Permission.

Page 21: "I Got Rhythm" (Music by George Gershwin, Lyric by Ira Gershwin). 1930 New World Music Corporation. Copyright renewed by Warner Bros. Music, Inc. All Rights Reserved. Used By Permission.

Page 21: "The Coward of the County" (by Roger Bowling and B. E. Wheeler). Copyright © 1979 by Roger Bowling Music Co. and Sleepy Hollow Music Co. All Rights Reserved. Used By Permission.

Page 28: "Dallas Blues" (Words by Lloyd Garrett, Music by Hart A. Wand). Copyright 1912 by Mayfair Music Corp. Copyright Assigned to Edwin H. Morris & Co., Inc. Copyright 1925 by Edwin H. Morris & Co., Inc., New York. Copyright renewed. All Rights Reserved. Used By Permission.

Page 29: "St. Louis Blues" (Words and Music by W. C. Handy). Copyright 1914 by W. C. Handy. Copyright renewed. All Rights Reserved. Used By Permission.

Pages 30 and 149: "Can't Help Lovin' Dat Man" (Lyric by Oscar Hammerstein II, Music by Jerome Kern). Copyright 1927 T. B. Harms & Co. Copyright Renewed. All Rights Reserved. Used By Permission.

Pages 31–33: "Kiss Me Again" (Lyric by Henry Blossom, Music by Victor Herbert). Copyright 1905 by Victor Herbert and Henry Blossom.

Pages 85–86: "Eleanor Rigby" (Words and Music by John Lennon and Paul McCartney). Copyright © 1966 by Northern Songs Limited. All Rights for the United States of America, Canada, Mexico, and the Philippines controlled by Maclen Music Inc. International Copyright Secured. All Rights Reserved. Used By Permission.

Page 87: "My Blue Heaven" (Words and Music by Walter Donaldson). Copyright 1927 by Walter Donaldson and CBS UNART. Copyright renewed by CBS UNART and CBS Feist. All Rights Reserved. International Copyright Secured. Used By Permission.

Pages 87–88: "The Hive" (Words and Music by Jim Webb). Copyright © 1968 by Canopy Music Inc. All Rights Reserved. International Copyright Secured. Used By Permission.

Pages 89–90: "Ten Cents a Dance" (Music by Richard Rodgers, Lyric by Lorenz Hart). Copyright 1930 Harms Inc. Copyright renewed by Warner Bros. Music, Inc. All Rights Reserved. International Copyright Secured. Used By Permission.

Page 92: "Gee, Officer Krupke" (Lyric by Stephen Sondheim, Music by Leonard Bernstein). Copyright © 1956 by Chappell Inc. All Rights Reserved. International Copyright Secured. Used By Permission.

Pages 92–94: "The Physician" (Words and Music by Cole Porter). Copyright 1933 by Cole Porter. Renewed by Warner Bros. Inc. International Copyright Secured. All Rights Reserved. Used By Permission.

Page 95: "Little Lamb" (Lyric by Stephen Sondheim, Music by Jule Styne). Copyright © 1958 Chappell & Co. Inc. International Copyright Secured. All Rights Reserved. Used By Permission.

Page 96: "Darling, Je Vous Aime Beaucoup" (Words and Music by Anna Sosenko). Copyright 1932 Chappell & Co. Inc. International Copyright Secured. All Rights Reserved. Used By Permission.

Pages 96–97: "Only in America" (by Jerry Leiber, Cynthia Weil, Mike Stoller, and Barry Mann). Copyright © 1963 by Screen Gems-EMI Music Inc. All Rights Reserved. International Copyright Secured. Used By Permission.

Pages 98, 113, and 158: "(All of a Sudden) My Heart Sings" ("En écoutant mon coeur chanter"). English Lyric by Harold Rome, Jamblin, and Herpin. French Lyric by Jamblin. Copyright 1941, 1943 by France Music, New York, N.Y. Copyright renewed. Sole Selling Agent MCA Music, a Division of MCA Inc., New York, N.Y. All Rights Reserved. Used By Permission.

Pages 100–101: "All in Fun" (Lyric by Oscar Hammerstein II, Music by Jerome Kern). Copyright 1942 by Williamson Music Corp. All Rights Reserved. Used By Permission.

Pages 101–102: "Confession" (By Howard Dietz and Arthur Schwartz). Copyright 1931 Harms Inc. Copyright renewed by Warner Bros. Music, Inc. All Rights Reserved. Used By Permission.

Page 104: "The First Time Ever I Saw Your Face" (Words and Music by Ewan MacColl). Copyright © 1962, 1966, 1972 by Stormking Music Inc. All Rights Reserved. Used By Permission.

Pages 108, 157, 172, and 178: "Over the Rainbow" (Lyric by E. Y. Harburg, Music by Harold Arlen). Copyright 1938 (Renewed 1966, 1967) Metro-Goldwyn-Mayer Inc. All Rights Controlled and Administered by Leo Feist, Inc. All Rights of Leo Feist, Inc., Assigned to CBS Catalogue Partnership. All Rights Controlled by CBS Feist Catalogue. International Copyright Secured. All Rights Reserved. Used By Permission.

Pages 111 and 234: "Gonna Fly Now" (Words by Carol Connors and Ayn Rolkins, Music by Bill Conti). Copyright © 1976, 1977 by United Artists Corporation. Rights Throughout the World Controlled by United Artists Music Co. Inc., and UNART Music Corporation, Catalogues of CBS Songs Division of CBS Inc. International Copyright Secured. All Rights Reserved. Used By Permission.

Page 113: "Ace in the Hole" (Words and Music by Cole Porter). Copyright 1941 by Chappell & Co. Inc. Copyright renewed. Assigned to John F. Wharton, Trustee of the Cole Porter Musical and Literary Property Trusts. Chappell & Company, Publishers. International Copyright Secured. All Rights Reserved. Used By Permission.

Page 114: "I Get a Kick Out of You" (Music and Lyrics by Cole Porter). Copyright 1934 (Renewed) Warner Bros., Inc. Used by Permission of Warner Bros., Inc., and Robert H. Montgomery. Jr., as Trustee of the Cole Porter Literary and Property Trusts. All Rights Reserved. Used By Permission.

Page 114: "It's De-lovely" (Words and Music by Cole Porter). Copyright 1936 by Chappell & Co. Inc. Copyright renewed. All Rights Reserved. Used By Permission

Page 115: "Moonlight in Vermont" (Words by John Blackborn, Music by Karl Suessdorf). Copyright 1944 by Michael H. Goldsen, Inc. Copyright © renewed 1972 by Michael H. Goldsen. All Rights Reserved. Used By Permission.

Page 116: "Love Will Keep Us Together" (Words and Music by Neil Sedaka and Howard Greenfield). Copyright © 1973 by Entco Music Co. Used By Permission.

Page 116: "Love for Sale" (Music and Lyrics by Cole Porter). Copyright 1934 (Renewed) Warner Bros., Inc. Used by permission of Warner Bros., Inc., and Robert H. Montgomery, Jr., as Trustee of the Cole Porter Literary and Property Trusts. All Rights Reserved. Used By Permission.

Page 116: "The Night Chicago Died" (Lyric by Pete Callander). Copyright © 1974 Intune Ltd. Copyright assigned 1981 to Dick James Music, Ltd., James House, 5 Theobalds Road, London WC1X 8SE, England. All Rights for the United States and Canada Controlled by Dejamus Inc., 24 Music Square East, Nashville, Tenn. 37203.

Page 117: "Some People" (Lyric by Stephen Sondheim, Music by Jule Styne). Copyright © 1958 Chappell & Co. Inc. International Copyright Secured. Used By Permission.

Page 117: "What Are You Doing the Rest of Your Life" (Lyric by Alan & Marilyn Bergman, Music by Michel Legrand). Copyright © 1969 by United Artists Music Co., Inc., 729 Seventh Avenue, New York, N.Y. 10019. International Copyright Secured. All Rights Reserved.

Page 118: "Joey" (Words and Music by Stephen Citron). Copyright © 1982 by Orpheus Music Inc. All Rights Reserved. Used By Permission.

Page 120: "Put on a Happy Face" (Music by Charles Strouse, Lyric by Lee Adams). Copyright © 1960 by Lee Adams and Charles Strouse. All Rights Controlled by Edwin H. Morris, a Division of MPL Communications, Inc. All Rights Reserved. Used By Permission.

Page 124: "All the Things You Are" (Lyric by Oscar Hammerstein II, Music by Jerome Kern). Copyright 1940 by Harms Inc. Copyright renewed by Chappell. All Rights Reserved. Used By Permission.

Page 125: "What's the Use of Wond'rin'" (Lyric by Oscar Hammerstein II, Music by Richard Rodgers). Copyright 1945 by Williamson Music. All Rights Reserved. International Copyright Secured. Used By Permission.

INDEX